The Customering Methoa

Despite the promise of enhanced customer engagement through new technology, consumer trust has suffered widespread collapse and annual corporate losses are in the trillions. This book exposes the faulty foundation of the populist Customer Experience (CX) movement, upturns long-held beliefs in its effectiveness, and details an alternative – industrial – approach to the customer asset base.

Aarron Spinley is recognized as a foremost mind in the realm of customer science and strategy. His work helps us to understand – and extract – customer value based on evidence, and in so doing, influences our relationship with technology for better results. *The Customering Method* marries the sciences and managerial precedent with contemporary capability: optimizing the intersection with marketing, mitigating risk and attrition rates, increasing sales propensity, and restoring profitability. Throughout, Spinley provides practical examples that are relatable, actionable, and defensible.

These concepts have already influenced senior leaders, CEOs, chief marketing officers, and directors of customer experience across many organizations. Now in published form, this is perhaps the most important book in the field for decades.

Aarron Spinley is a Fellow at the Field Bell Institute (www.fieldbell.org). He is recognized as a foremost mind in the realm of customer science, noted for his signature approach: measuring the intersection of established management method, complex economics, and scientific precedent to confirm and systemize, or disrupt, for effect. As a writer or commentator, Aarron has featured in leading publications including *Forbes, ZDNet, MyCustomer, CMO, Mumbrella*, and *Mi3 Media*, and has appeared on five continents as a sought-after keynote speaker.

"*The Customering Method* fits the knowledge needs of marketing professionals, consultants, and anyone associated with CRM and the technology sector. It also suits the classroom, especially graduate studies at the MBA level and beyond. I recommend it as a supplement in traditional MBA marketing management classes, and it may suit some academics as a core text."

Dr Stephen A. LeMay, *Professor of Marketing and Logistics at the University of West Florida*

"If you work in marketing, customer management, or technology and consulting – this should be the new number 1 book on your shelf. Better yet, keep it open, with a highlighter close by, at the very center of your desk!"

Jason Hemingway, *CMO and Fellow of the Chartered Institute of Marketing*

"What makes this book exceptional is its concentration on the economics… He matures the field in a way that finally we can say it is truly a science of business."

Paul Greenberg, *Managing Principal, The 56 Group LLC*

"Despite claims to the contrary, plummeting satisfaction statistics suggests management has forgotten customer-centricity basics. Spinley's timely book is just what companies need to put customers back at the centre of profitable business. Take my advice: buy it, read it, and apply it. Your customers will thank you. And so will your shareholders."

Dr Graham Hill, *Optima Partners*

"Aarron Spinley's book proves that he truly gets what it's like to be a customer, and what it's like to be an organisation designing for them. In a world of mass generalisation, of forced chatbots, badly timed surveys, and mediocre customer service, *Customering* makes it clear that Context is King."

Alex Mead, *Global Customer Service Experience Chief, Alvarez & Marsal*

"For too long, customer management has been plagued by populist practices. Without a systems view, managers have failed to create beautiful music by obsessing over one instrument at a time. In *The Customering Method*, Spinley equips you with the sheets to Beethoven and the conductor's wand to rouse the symphony you've always known is possible."

John Rizzo, *Chair of the Monash University Marketing Department Industry Advisory Board and Former Act. Chief Strategy Officer at BUPA*

"In *The Customering Method*, Spinley helps readers rediscover business with service and experience at the center."

Brian Solis, *Author of* Mindshift, X, *and Head of Global Innovation, ServiceNow*

"In an era of dogma, Aarron Spinley takes us back to First Principles: customization, budget allocation, customer loyalty, and revenue [and profit]."

R "Ray" Wang, *CEO Constellation Research and Best-Selling Author*

The Customering Method

From CX Dogma to Customer Science

Aarron Spinley

Routledge
Taylor & Francis Group

LONDON AND NEW YORK

Designed cover image: Getty Images

First published 2025
by Routledge
4 Park Square, Milton Park, Abingdon, Oxon OX14 4RN

and by Routledge
605 Third Avenue, New York, NY 10158

Routledge is an imprint of the Taylor & Francis Group, an informa business

British Library Cataloguing-in-Publication Data
A catalogue record for this book is available from the British Library

ISBN: 978-1-032-84542-5 (hbk)
ISBN: 978-1-032-82308-9 (pbk)
ISBN: 978-1-003-51372-8 (ebk)

DOI: 10.4324/9781003513728

Typeset in Garamond
by Deanta Global Publishing Services, Chennai, India

This book is dedicated to the finest man I've ever known, the late Barry Spinley, who rests with my Danica – until I see you again, Dad; to my Mother, Jan, who I admire so deeply; to my rock and my rhythm, my peace, my love, and my inspiration, Tarryn; and finally, to Isaak, Jacob, Rocco, and Luca – my one true legacy.

Dogma

The literal meaning in ancient Greek, "something that seems true", and a set of beliefs that people are expected to accept without any doubts.

--

Science

The pursuit and application of knowledge and understanding of the natural and social world following a systematic methodology based on evidence.

Contents

Figures

Tables

Abbreviations

ACSI	American Customer Satisfaction Index
AEP	Adaptive Engagement Profile
AI	Artificial Intelligence
API	Application Programming Interfaces
ATL	Above the Line
B2B	Business to Business
BAU	Business as Usual
BRV	Business Referral Value
BTL	Below the Line
CAC	Customer Acquisition Cost
CBCV	Customer-based Corporate Valuation
CCO	Chief Customer Officer
CCPA	California Consumer Privacy Act
CDP	Customer Data Platform
CEE	Customer Experience Excellence
CES	Customer Effort Score
CFO	Chief Financial Officer
CGAMC	Customer-governed Application of Marketing Communications
CIAM	Customer Identity and Access Management
CJO	Customer Journey Orchestrating
CLA	Causal Layered Analysis
CLV	Customer Lifetime Value
CM	Conversion Model
CMO	Chief Marketing Officer
CMS	Content Management System
COGS	Cost of Goods Sold
CPA	Customer Profitability Analysis
CRM	Customer Relationship Management
CRV	Customer Referral Value
CSAT	Customer Satisfaction
CX	Customer Experience

CXO	Customer Experience Officer
D2C	Direct to Customer
DXP	Digital Experience Platform
EBI	Ehrenberg Bass Institute
EBIT	Earnings before Interest and Taxes
ESG	Environmental, Social, and Governance
ESOV	Excess Share of Voice
EX	Employee Experience
FTE	Full-time Equivalent
GAAP	Generally Accepted Accounting Principles
GDP	Gross Domestic Product
GDPR	General Data Protection Regulation
IMC	Integrated Marketing Communications
IVR	Interactive Voice Response
JTBD	Jobs To Be Done
KPI	Key Performance Indicator
MATES	Maturity, Access, Transactional, Execution, Sanity
NBC	Next Best Conversation
NIH	National Institutes of Health
NLP	Natural Language Processing
NPS	Net Promoter Score
NPS	Score and Customer Satisfaction
OLM	On-line Messages
POS	Point of Sale
PV	Present Value
ROAS	Return on Advertising Spend
ROI	Return on Investment
ROI	Return on Investment
RPS	Routinized Problem Solving
RTIM	Real-time Interaction Management
SDK	Software Development Kit
SDL	Service-dominant Logic
SG&A	Selling, General, and Administrative Expense
SMART	Specific, Measurable, Ambitious, Realistic, Time-related
STP	Segment, Target, Position
UI	User Interface
USP	Unique Selling Proposition
UTM	Urchin Tracking Module
UVP	Unique Value Proposition
UX	User Experience
VES	Value Enhancement Score
WACC	Weighted Average Cost of Sales
XM	Experience Management

Foreword

I've known Aarron Spinley for quite some time. And I've been in the world of customer facing technology, strategy, and practice for even longer. And one thing I know for sure – as certain as anything is these days – is that Aarron is one of the more important contributors to the thinking in this domain because he has not only done it in real life, but he is thoughtful and insightful about it – and knows how to extract the key practices, lessons, and frameworks from that experience, and from his research.

For a long time, the discussion in the business world has focused on a company's ability to communicate and engage its customers in a way that is ultimately both satisfying and profitable to the company.

On the one hand the company's fundamental purpose if we are being honest about it, is to make money selling products or services and, some say it also has a responsibility to give back to the world that it makes money in. The customer gets involved with that company because he or she as a consumer or a representative of a business, needs some version of the product and/or services that the company provides to do whatever job, and achieve whatever outcome, that they seek.

The customer "loves the company" is pretty much either exaggeration, fluff, or misinterpretation of something.

Back when I got involved in customer relationship management, which in its earliest promising days was defined around things that "customer experience" folk now claim to be the arbiters of, I put a well-accepted series of definitions out there as to what I thought CRM was. The one I want to dwell on for a moment is: "It's the only science of business that attempts to reproduce an art of life – how humans behave". I would put forth here that what Aarron is doing around customer engagement in this book is that with one modification – "It's the only science of business that attempts to model an art of life – how humans behave" – and to industrialize its management.

While CRM to some degree, sadly to this old heart of mine, settled to a system and technology that is customer-facing and operational, Aarron's book promises to achieve what we didn't around CRM – create the framework, the model, the measurement, the practices and the context for the contemporary REQUIREMENT of modern business, which is, to understand its customer groups and individual customers, well enough to not merely personalize outward communication, but to individualize all-of-engagement for sustained economic effect. What Aarron calls "customering".

What makes this unique, and why my nearly three decades in this business screams "Yeah dude, you get it!" is that Aarron is doing something for customer management that will make it less mysterious and haphazard then it has been, and actually create what I call "an applied vision" to something that makes it valuable and usable for any business.

Look, I think we all know that we live in an era where we have an enormous amount of noise coming from all the forms of media and communication that we deal with every day. Everyone from wannabe brand influencers to mega enterprises trying to get the attention of you as a consumer, or you as a buyer, or influencer of a business deal. But that noise is complex, not uniform, nor simple. There are economic and political influences, there are social influences, and there is constant cultural impact.

Thus, the noise is often unreliable. It requires some knowledge of the truth to make sense of it or, more importantly, to separate signal from noise. To make that even more difficult, for both company and customer, is that there is a lot of good stuff out there that is meaningful. So, you don't only have to separate signal from noise, but signal from signal. As a business, that requires a focus on context or you will never be able to foster engagement, protect custom, or increase the desire of the customer to continue to do business with you beyond initial brand preference.

And that's only the beginning. If you are an enterprise – and let's say you have three million customers – there are three million individuals – some of which have things in common, yet with different lived realities that shape their behavior. Their uniform expectation is that whatever they are looking to obtain or acquire from you they can get, and at minimum it is convenient (which is by far the most important) and at optimum, engaging enough to perhaps inspire more value.

My mantra for years since my early CRM days expressed that simply as:

> "If a customer likes you and continues to like you, they will continue to do business with you. If they don't, they won't".

But now, thanks to digital communications and their ubiquitous use, we also have enormous volumes of individual customer information – from transactional data, to records of interactions in relevant locations, to sociographic data et al, ad infinitum.

And, at least in theory we have the tools to figure out what to do with that data, organize it, gain insight at scale – and to capture, analyze, and interpret it in real time. With the advent of AI, especially GenAI, we now have the means to query that data with more timely and useable outcomes, such that it becomes actionable through knowing what a customer needs, and maybe at times even things that they might want.

Ah, but there is one more thing. And that comes when interpretation of the data is involved.

For example, one of the most popular benchmarks over the past couple of decades has been the Net Promoter Score which purports to be a good measure of customer loyalty – beyond satisfaction. At its base level, it asks a single question which is "Would you recommend this company to someone you know?" The higher the score, it is proposed, the more committed the customer base. It has been widely used and heads roll sometimes if the score is low, and millions are spent to "fix" whatever problems caused it.

But there is an inherent problem.

Years ago, Dr V. Kumar, an academician at the time, did a study where he asked 15,000 telco and banking respondents four questions. They were:

1. Would you recommend this company to someone you know? (The same as the NPS question but not an NPS survey)
2. Did you recommend this company to someone you know?
3. Did they become a customer?
4. Are they a loyal customer?

The relevant questions for our purposes are one and two. Question two was asked of those who answered question one with a yes. Around 67% reported that indeed, they did actually recommend the company (though later research has found that the reality is much, much lower than this).

Question one goes to general sentiment: a respondent basically lazily answers the question without an intent to follow through. Even an intention (to promote) isn't good enough, nor a reflection on their subsequent behaviors. In truth, loyal customers are only those whose sentiment or intention results in actions that benefit the company – and in return or more accurately, precedingly, and conjointly, the company must offer interactions that protect – and then foster – that loyalty.

So, you can see how hard all of this is. Very large numbers of customers comprise nuanced and complicated individual human beings and, as a business, you must provide ongoing interactions that resolve the needs of those complicated people such that they to continue buying things from you – maintaining if not enhancing brand perception.

Enter Aarron Spinley.

All of the old folks like me have been talking about this field and some of us have managed to be at least wily enough to roll with the times, adjust, and try to help develop effective approaches and models. But honestly, we haven't been that good at it (though I know some who would tell me on hearing that "speak for yourself, Paul").

Aarron is that good at it.

What he is able to do in this book, is to systematize the necessary component disciplines – including a simple frame for all that data out there – to affect the management of customers as an enterprise "asset", and to measure the success of target customer engagement and that of the model itself.

He also blows away the fluff that you literally must both tune out and completely eliminate from your strategies. I love the simple way he puts this; you have to eliminate "the delusions of customer delight and brand love". A big amen to that.

But what makes this even more exceptional is his concentration on the economics and value that a successful framework with the right model of engagement will deliver. The best way I can say it: he matures the field in a way that finally we can say that engagement of customers is truly a science of business.

But enough from me. I just wanted to introduce you to Aarron. He'll take it from here.

Paul Greenberg
aka The Godfather of CRM
Managing Director and Principal Analyst, The 56 Group, LLC
Author of CRM at the Speed of Light (Four Editions: 2001–2010), and The
Commonwealth of Self-Interest (2019)

Acknowledgments

A debt of gratitude is owed to the men and women of science and professional rigor, on whose shoulders this work stands. They lead us out of myths and dogma.

Special thanks to two great friends and luminaries: The Godfather of (aka the Mickey Mantle of) CRM, Paul Greenberg – for his long and generous mentorship, support, and virtual hugs; and the world-leading martech and architectural thought leader in advanced engagement fabric, Henry Hernandez-Reveron – for his friendship and collaboration.

Glossary of Reference Models and Operating Principles

M 1. **The Marketing to Customering Bowtie**
Marketing and customering are counterparts of one another requiring complimentary but distinct operating models and measurements.

M 2. **The Four Pillars of Customer Management Model**
Orienting all disciplines and functions within the correct pillar – identity, intent, interactions, and measurement – enables a coherent, evidence-based, and sustainable management model.

M 3. **Customer Governed Application of Marketing Communications**
The optimal messaging construct at the intersection of marketing communication to existing customer cohorts.

M 4. **The Optimal Growth Model**
Growth is optimized by an acquisition rate above the average (marketing) and an attrition rate below the average (customering). The former is prime, the latter supportive.

***

OP 1. **The Barrier to Churn Principle**
Removing the obstructions to our customer's natural bias to loyalty.

OP 2. **The Complexity Barrier**
The increase in complexity owing to consumer attitudes, technology, channel, touchpoint, and journey proliferation, challenges the delivery of baseline customer service standards.

OP 3. The Service Imperative

Fulfilling a customer's job (meeting their intent) is the quintessential essence of service, and the ongoing foundation of customering.

OP 4. The Services to Experience Ratio

It is estimated that services (99%< in some categories) are the dominant layer that interfaces with customers, far outweighing experiences.

OP 5. The Service Recovery Paradox

The visibility of empathetic and proactive resolution to a customer's acute problem, can improve that customer's retention and if applicable, their advocacy.

OP 6. The Segmentation Error

The damaging practice of segmenting a customer base, a concept borrowed imprecisely from marketing practice.

OP 7. Channel-less Trumps Omnichannel

Companies may think in terms of its channels and channel strategy, but customers themselves are, channel-less.

Glossary of Laws and Principles

The application of existing bodies of work, scientifically and or empirically established, to the field of customer management is termed "the customer sciences". The following originate from marketing science,[1] consumer psychology, or design principles.

AS 1. Laws of Double Jeopardy and Retention Double Jeopardy
The customers of brands with less market share (and fewer buyers) exhibit less loyalty, resulting in a higher proportionality of customer churn.

AS 2. Attitudes and Brand Beliefs Reflect Behavioral Loyalty
Customers are more aware, and say more, about brands that they use compared to those that they don't, and so larger brands score higher on surveys that assess attitudes toward them due to a higher market share, and a more loyal customer base.

AS 3. Duplication of Purchase Law
A brand's customer base will overlap with that of its competitors in line with its market share.

AS 4. Pareto Law 60:20
Circa 60% of a brands purchases come from 20% of its customers (heavy buyers), while the remaining come from the bottom 80% (light buyers).

AS 5. Hick-Hyman Law
The time it takes to make a decision, increases with the number and complexity of choices.

AS 6. The Choice Paradox
Allied to the Hick-Hyman Law, too many consumer choices can cause decision paralysis or abandonment.

AS 7. **Millers Law**
The average person can only keep seven (plus or minus two) items in their working memory.

AS 8. **Occam's Razor**
When presented with competing hypothetical answers to a problem, one should select the one that makes the fewest assumptions (also Ockham's razor; Latin: *lex parsimoniae*, "law of parsimony").

AS 9. **The Peak End Rule**
People recall an event largely based on how they felt at its peak moment (memorability) and at its ending.

AS 10. **The Von Restorff Effect**
Predicts that when multiple but similar objects are present, people will notice and most likely remember the one that differs the most from the rest. (also known as The Isolation Effect).

AS 11. **The Observer Effect**
The disturbance of, and change caused to, an observed system, party, or individual resulting from the act of observation. Most problematic in customer surveys.

AS 12. **The Doherty Threshold**
Psychological engagement soars when a system and its users interact in 400ms or less, which ensures that neither must wait on the other.

AS 13. **Loss Aversion**
A cognitive bias that suggests that for individuals the pain of losing is psychologically twice as powerful as the pleasure of gaining.

AS 14. **Law of Least Effort**
Even in its resting state, the human brain uses over 20% of the body's energy and so displays a tendency to take the path of least resistance in pursuit of an objective.

AS 15. **The Solow Paradox**
As more investment is applied to information technology, the productivity of workers may go down instead of up (also known as the productivity paradox)

Note

1. Referenced marketing laws and definitions cited are from the Ehrenberg-Bass Institute

Introduction

There is no better example of a core strategic and fiscally critical function that is nonetheless characterized by widespread illiteracy than customer management. It is an arena of misadventure with consequences that extend beyond individual companies, to entire industries and the international economy.

Case in point, the global digital transformation market, of which customer programs are a considerable proportion, is projected to grow from US $2.71 trillion in 2024 to US $12.3 trillion by 2032 at a compound annual growth rate of 20.9%.[1] Yet, the forecast failure rate of 87.5%[2] underscores that deficiencies in customer management literacy and its governance are not solved by technology. Beyond the investment waste, the fiscal implications are manifold.

Both upstream and downstream of these transformation projects, the compounding effects of failed customer management are eye-watering. Accenture reported that customer switching between companies correlated to poor service "triggers" costs a whopping US $1.6 trillion per annum in the USA alone.[3] Another study in 2021 went further, calculating that the annual global risk to sales from "bad experiences" is US $4.7 trillion,[4] and there is significant corroboration as to both the pattern and proportions. For instance, 2018 research by NewVoiceMedia estimated that US $75 billion is lost to American businesses due to the failings of contact centers, which is but a single channel.[5] In 2020, Statistica calculated that new spending on operational customer management amounted to US $323 billion, with over US $75 billion of that spent on customer loyalty programs[6] despite scant evidence of correlated value. Meanwhile, the Institute of Customer Service estimates that poor service results in additional needless customer interactions and costs UK businesses £11.4 billion *per month*.[7]

In the cold light of these staggering losses, the lack of an industrialized customer management model, reminiscent of established professions, is a cavernous gap in global commerce and it raises the question: *how did we get here?*

The Profession that Wasn't

The earliest detectable customer-based traditions date back to 3,000 BC, but it is the 1950s that historians and economists credit for the Services Revolution.[8] The first progression of macro-economic value since the Industrial Revolution, it was based on the primacy of the customer rather than purely on production efficiency. And so, in the shadow of World War Two, as society and its consumers sought easier lives, the foundations of what we now recognize as customer proximity first occurred.

Yet the critical imperative for a true customer management profession, and a quality management system for the customer asset, did not emerge until the digital communications era began more than a half century later. As channel and device proliferation swelled, accelerating the effects of consumerism, the value drivers – and risks – of the customer franchise were unprecedented. Just as the arrival of market-based economies at the start of the twentieth century had necessitated the development of *the marketing method*, this time, it was a method for the customer asset that become paramount.

And yet a strange thing happened – or didn't happen, as it turns out.

Historically, when a field becomes material to both industrial success and to the apparent best interests of consumers, market and regulatory forces conspire to ensure its standardization, for both control and repeat effectiveness. This has been true of legal services, architecture, the fields of medicine and engineering, aviation, accounting, construction, design, plumbing and electrical trades, maritime professions, nursing, teaching, and many more. Each is now characterized by recognizable industrial management practices, discipline-specific language, aligned educational infrastructure, and well-enforced barriers to entry. Yet this did not occur in customer management.

And so, when the digital era arrived, the field was not prepared as other vocations were. There was simply no large scale procedural integrity resembling that of established professions that could allow the field to properly leverage the new capability. After such a long period of analog customer interaction, the world changed fundamentally and far too quickly for the customer management vocation to handle.

By 2007, there were one billion internet users, delivering critical mass for internet-based business models. The internet itself would go onto become the most powerful source of commoditization in history, significantly impacting brands and the behavioral loyalty of consumers. By 2012, cloud computing had become mainstream and bled into the rise of application development and mobile devices, which in turn spawned social media and extreme device proliferation. The evolution continues, more latterly shifting to Web3.0, the Metaverse, and all manner of generative AI-based technologies. And so, in less than two decades, the world evolved from one or two, perhaps three, customer "channels" to manifold channels. In fact, by 2018 a study at Google found that a customer journey ranged between 20 and 500+ touchpoints.[9]

It was this combination – the absence of mature management practice together with the rapid increase of complexity owing to technology, channel, touchpoint, journey, device proliferation, and associated consumer behaviors – that has proven to be a perfect storm for customer management (Figure 0.1).

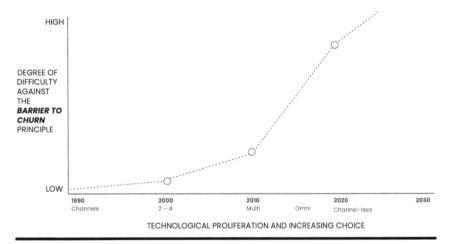

Figure 0.1 The Complexity Barrier (Spinley, 2024)

The Cost of CX Populism

As the bubble-like valuations of service-as-a-software companies erupted throughout the 2010s, product marketing teams were let loose with massive budgets. This saw novel technologies, with catchy sales slogans, flooding a market teeming with newly cashed-up but ill-informed clients. All were swept along by the hype, and without a north star governing model in sight, the customer experience (CX) movement was born.

Of course, there are many legitimate customer management leaders who, in the absence of an alternative, fall under the "CX" banner – myself included on occasion. While a diminutive minority, they are serious people who apply intellectual rigor to their work. These aside, however, the vast majority of the field is best characterized as populist.

Populism has become a central theme – and threat – to western societies and has been increasingly studied in economics, sociology and, of course, in political science. It is a phenomenon that is always detrimental to performance[10] and that marginalizes expertise and knowledge (or facts) in general.[11] Specifically, populism:

- Holds simplistic views of both problems and solutions.
- Proposes simplistic policies which do not match the complexity of reality.
- Seeks to align with or secure the fealty of counterparts and sources of influence.

- Prefers loyalty (groupism) over expertise.
- Is serial in nature (prone to re-generate).
- Stimulates institutional and vocational decay.
- Presents as negative to economic and other measures of performance.

In a similar, if more entertaining, vein, American philosopher Harry Frankfurt's 2005 book *On Bullshit* defines the concept in societal terms and analyzes its applications in the context of communication, determining that

> bullshit is speech intended to persuade without regard for truth. The liar cares about the truth and attempts to hide it; the bull-shitter doesn't care if what they say is true or false.[12]

Frankfurt notes that "bullshit" is not always deliberate, can be well intentioned and even driven by conviction, offering a strong connection to populism when present in groups. He draws the same directional conclusions as the Center for Economic Policy Research did, arguing that the rise of populism is dangerous because it accepts and enables a growing disregard of the truth, fact, or knowledge.

Undoubtedly confrontational for many, the paradigm of populism is nevertheless critical to understand in any examination of the CX movement. The fledgling vocation, absent an industrialized method, was caught in a groundswell of trendy, post-modern business ideals (e.g., brands seeking to be more "human"), conditions in which the fever of populism was to flourish. The second paradigm to understand is the Solow Paradox.

The Solow Paradox

It is not unusual for technology companies developing capabilities in the advancement of existing management disciplines to lead the way in pioneering new approaches. Their business model often allows for well-funded research and development, both for their products and for industry-level expansion of knowledge. But many confuse the two. Product development and positioning is ultimately a function of marketing. The clear commercial agenda is one of sales growth, which is of course entirely legitimate but is not a reliable basis for management theory.

Distinguishing between pure commercial posturing and legitimate critical theory falls to the market, which in customering is a fraught task given the absence of industrial standards. Thus, we encounter a version of Solow's Paradox:[13] as more technology investment is applied, the effective productivity of workers goes down instead of up.

Of course, there are plenty of examples where technology vendors have made meaningful contributions. One is the (now defunct) research department of Thunderhead, which from 2011 undertook useful work spanning behavioral and data sciences within the frame of company to customer interactions. Among other work, it explored the psychological difference between customer engagement and mere involvement, and the operational implications for companies and their customer programs.

ServiceNow is another striking example of robust scientific endeavor. Renowned industry analyst Brian Solis is its head of global innovation and, as I write this, its impressive research team comprises around 65 members, each hailing from leading academic institutions. "ServiceNow Research" works on seven emergent fields of study:

- Human–Machine Interaction Through Language.
- Human decision support.
- Low data learning.
- Large language models lab.
- AI trust and governance lab.
- Emerging technologies lab.
- Research management.

Salesforce, too, is heavily invested in the field. Its "Salesforce AI Research" team is staffed by academic experts and is regarded as a world leader. Both companies explore fields such as dialogue, large language models, human–machine interaction, natural language processing, intent classification, symbolic reasoning, trustworthiness, tech transfer, and more. Add in companies on the cutting edge of synthetic data in areas such as market diagnostics such as Evidenza, and in neuroeconomics – for example, Dr. Paul Zak's digital platform *Immersion* – and there is ample evidence of genuine leadership in the vendor community.

At the other end of the paradox, however, much vendor research is agenda-based, with the promotion of "findings" simply product marketing in disguise. Examples include the survey software category's wildly successful scheme to create a vocation in its likeness, and similar parallels from the marketing technology (martech) sector, albeit from a more fragmented base. There are over 11,000 offerings as of the time of writing.[14]

To generate unnatural demand for the inherently constrained utility of surveys, this category deploys a range of clever positioning concepts. While all are easily debunked, they have proven highly successful in an industry with populist traits. Chief among its many fables are the irrational claims that feedback – not expertise – is foundational to industrial practice, and that self-reported data is reliable as behavioral insight. The creative injections of statistical analysis to invoke a false sense of scientific validation, the half-misappropriated idea of the "voice of the customer"[15] and even the re-branding of survey use as "experience management" – a concept entirely at odds with the available science – are other examples. While survey superstitions remain strong, category participants have begun adding more robust offerings, perhaps recognizing these limitations; nonetheless, the promotional hyperbole remains prevalent.

Lost within this rabbit warren, legitimate and contemporary customer management theory failed to form, and absent this guardrail customer interactions have been overtaken by a near-total focus on campaigns, offers, promotions, and wholesale or triggered sales activation. Due the influence of martech within digital teams, common use cases are invariably aimed at customers instead of the market, and in default sales mode. But customering is not marketing: the purpose, and methods, are distinct, and those who are blind to this division use digital tools imprecisely, becoming toxic to the customer mission.

Procter & Gamble is among the companies most admired by marketing commentators and scholars, so it is no surprise that it was at the forefront of "digital marketing" as it took hold in the 2010s. However, it was also among the first to recognize much of its folly. In 2016, its chief brand officer, Marc Pritchard, said:

> In this digital age we're producing thousands of new ads, posts, tweets, every week, every month, every year. We eventually concluded all we were doing was adding to the noise.[16]

A pity that the wider market did not prove so discerning. Instead, rampant sales activation and customer targeting has been responsible for the collapse of service, and customer trust with it. In fact, the dystopian business model of social media, first rationalized by advertising executives, has leached into daily commerce and is now so pernicious that law makers around the world are taking steps to protect our own customers – from us! Built on populism and digital superstition, the conflation of marketing activation and customering is arguably among the greatest strategic errors of our time.

The CX Movement Has Failed

Considering the financial consequences of survey addiction as proxy for domain expertise, and of marketing-creep in place of service, the unavoidable conclusion is that the populist CX movement has been a calamity. Yet, while there may be suspicions at the executive table, this failure is not widely recognized in the movement itself – consistent with the sociology of populism.

Aside from foisting survey disruptions and high-repeat sales activation (lessening propensity to buy), the acute reductivity of important issues like customer loyalty has been matched by erroneous claims as to the effect on brand differentiation. The CX movement clumsily dismantles the serious meaning of well-established terminologies (experience, brand, growth, etc.) while disseminating debunked methodology (NPS, traditional journey mapping, etc.). Meanwhile, the companies they work for manifest what can only be described as corporate dementia – routinely forgetting who customers are (if they could identify them to begin with) – and yet with no sense of irony the movement espouses doctrines such as "customer obsession".

If all this sounds familiar, that is because you will find it at corporate headquarters, on stage at CX conferences or giving Ted-X presentations, in lists of top influencers, and among authors of innumerable quasi-non-fiction books on the subject. Many are otherwise effective executives or polished speakers, their assuredness stemming from genuine faith in the narrative and met by the enthusiasm of an audience already deep in the echo chamber. But the movement's almost total unfamiliarity with the customer management mission, the proper economics of the field, and relevant critical theory and measures, have made it easy prey for agenda-based "research" and sales jargon, which it parrots with regularity – and inanity. Ironically, prematurely, and extraneously, it is marked by a near-constant call for "innovation".

To compound matters, we have witnessed the rise of an educational machinery distributing the dogmas of the movement, with "certifications" providing sham validation and mimicking the language of traditional institutions. In each instance explored during my research, the same patterns quickly emerged. Each presents surveys as foundational and offers qualifications in "feedback" or "customer insights", which read as if drafted by product marketing departments. These are almost always the primary offering, followed by the usual range of debunked or non-critical concepts as modules attracting credits or "specialisms". And so, while attendees become "certified" in one form or another, they are never educated. The fundamentals of legitimate customer management, the science, and economic underpinnings of its proper administration, remain foreign to them. I hope that, for some, this book will change that (Figure 0.2).

Enter Industrial Customering

The prevailing economics of customering at scale, attained through the nuanced and yet programmatic engagement of the individual as first envisioned in the 1950s and in later concepts like "mass customization",[17] remain largely – and inexcusably – unfulfilled.

Instead, as leaders stare down a progressively volatile world economy, they face needless uncertainty about how best to prioritize investment across the people, operations, and technology of their customer programs. The subsequent losses, in their trillions, mount up annually through avoidable customer attrition,

Figure 0.2 A Timeline to Populist CX (Spinley, 2024)

cost of operations, realized risk, and failed digital transformation projects, all diminishing profit and shareholder value. There is no question that the absence of industrialized customer management standards continues to have growing consequences.

An inflection point beckons.

Accordingly, this book is intentionally forthright in outlining the transformation needed – a move toward professionalism and away from populism and pseudo-leadership. When we embed a mature industrial process and allow the power of modern-day capability to enrich it, rather than overtake it, we will enter the next stage – one that historians, economists, CFOs and shareholders, and customers alike, will appreciate significantly more.

A Shortcut Guide to this Book

ACT 1 – The Imperative of Professions and Distinguishing from Marketing

Chapter 1 reviews the historical rise of professional industries and the hallmarks of industrialized management models that underlie them all, before a short introduction to the Four Pillars Customer Management Model itself, applying those same principles.

Chapter 2 looks at the closest cousin of customer management, the marketing vocation, explaining the component parts of the management model.

It helps the reader understand the clear delineation between marketing and customering, and to avoid the common confusions that plague the field, while offering a case study in evidence-based, linear management construction.

ACT 2 – The Chief Customer Officer's Handbook

Chapter 3 introduces the economic imperatives of customer management, before **Chapters 4 to 7** detail the Four Pillars of the Customer Management Model.

Chapter 8 takes a practical look at the specific areas in which marketing and customering legitimately collide, and how to manage that collision. Given the huge toll that the mismanagement of this area takes on the customer franchise, this is essential reading.

Finally, **Chapter 9** will address some of the big myths of the populist CX movement that have both distracted companies from the core mission and crippled their ability to execute world-class customer management. It is sure to ruffle some feathers, but also to educate.

***

Note: If you are a formally trained marketer, you may want to skip Chapter 2, although it could prove an enjoyable refresher. If you are not, but operate in or around marketing, you should read this and pay attention! On the other hand, if you are a customer management practitioner, I strongly recommend that you read it closely, because it is sure to give you clarity on what your marketing colleagues are doing – or are supposed to be doing – and on the differences between the two functions, which will prove useful later. Either way, it provides an important industrial management reference before we deep dive into formal customer management.

No matter your background, the fact that you are here indicates a desire to understand the proper management of the customer asset. Or perhaps you have recognized the folly of populism and aspire to more robust, mature approaches upon which to stage your career. I am grateful that you are here at all. We'll get along just fine.

Welcome.

Notes

1. Fortune Business Insight, *Digital Transformation Market Size, Share, Growth, Trends* (2032), https://www.fortunebusinessinsights.com/digital-transformation-market-104878.

2. Didier Bonnet, "3 Stages of a Successful Digital Transformation," *Harvard Business Review*, September 20, 2022. https://hbr.org/2022/09/3-stages-of-a-successful-digital-transformation.

3. NewVoiceMedia, "Research Reveals Bad Customer Experiences Cost U.S. Businesses $75 Billion a Year," *Business Wire*, May 17, 2018. https://www.businesswire.com/news/home/20180517005043/en/NewVoiceMedia-Research-Reveals-Bad-Customer-Experiences-Cost-U.S.-Businesses-75-Billion-a-Year.

4. Bruce Temkin and Moira Dorsey, "Bad CX Puts $4.7 Trillion in Global Consumer Sales at Risk," *XM Institute*, February 8, 2022. https://www.xminstitute.com/blog/bad-experiences-risk-sales/.

5. NewVoiceMedia, "Research Reveals Bad Customer Experiences Cost U.S. Businesses $75 Billion a Year."

6. Julia Faria, "Business Spending on Customer Loyalty Worldwide 2019, by Type," *Statista*, March 15, 2023. https://www.statista.com/statistics/1239203/business-spending-on-customer-loyalty-world/.

7. Anna Tims, "Poor Customer Service Costs UK firms Billions – So Why Can't They Get It Right?," *The Guardian*, January 30, 2023. https://www.theguardian.com/money/2023/jan/30/poor-customer-service-costs-uk-firms-billions-so-why-cant-they-get-it-right.

8. William J. Regan, "The Service Revolution," *Journal of Marketing* 27, no. 3 (1963): 57–62.

9. Google, "Consumer Journey," *Consumer Insights*, no date. https://www.thinkwithgoogle.com/intl/en-apac/consumer-insights/consumer-journey/.

10. Manuel Funke, Moritz Schularick, and Christoph Trebesch, *DP15405 – Populist Leaders and the Economy* (Centre for Economic Policy Research, 2022).

11. Gabriele Gratton, Luigi Guiso, Claudio Michelacci, and Massimo Morelli, "From Weber to Kafka: Political Activism and the Emergence of an Inefficient Bureaucracy," Working Paper 560 (Innocenzo Gasparini Institute for Economic Research, Bocconi University, 2015).

12. Harry G. Frankfurt, *On Bullshit* (Princeton University Press, 2005).

13. Jack E. Triplett, "The Solow Productivity Paradox: What do Computers do to Productivity?," *The Canadian Journal of Economics/Revue Canadienne D'Economique* 32, no. 2 (1999): 309–334.

14. Scott Brinker, *2023 Marketing Technology Landscape Supergraphic: 11,038 Solutions Searchable on martechmap.com*. https://chiefmartec.com/2023/05/2023-marketing-technology-landscape-supergraphic-11038-solutions-searchable-on-martechmap-com/.

15. Abbie Griffin and John R. Hauser, "The Voice of the Customer," *Marketing Science* 12, no. 1 (1993): 1–27.

16. Patty Odell, "Don't Fall for the Content Crap Trap: P&G's Marc Pritchard," *Chief Marketer*, October 21, 2016. https://www.chiefmarketer.com/dont-fall-for-the-content-crap-trap-pgs-marc-pritchard./

17. B. Joseph Pine II, *Mass Customization: The New Frontier in Business Competition* (Harvard Business School Press, 1993).

Chapter 1

Professions and Industrial Management

The Rise and Value of Professions

Modern western professions are believed to have emerged from the traditional functions of pre-modern European society, such as healing and education, and have since developed through a range of social, scientific, technological, governmental, and entrepreneurial factors.

But while these ancient vocations may have provided a historical starting point, modern expressions of industrial professionalism are far more recent inventions, occurring over the last two centuries in the period that historians refer to as "the modern era". Scholars point to the period of Jacksonian America (1830s–1850s),[1] where debate over the merit of professions gained wide traction. The themes of this debate included cultural responses (and class-based ones) to the issue of governmental monopolies and were set against a climate of anti-education views and skepticism about science. Regulation and emerging economic drivers also affected the development of modern professions.

On one hand, proponents of professions claimed that they offered a moral good and were socially important. On the other hand, critics recognized the pattern of professions monopolizing entire domains on the premise of exclusive scientific expertise and perceived an evil. Perhaps most famously, Adam Smith wrote in 1778[2] that professions act as a "conspiracy against the public, or some contrivance to raise prices".

But the advancement of professions, the standards that enable their consistent delivery, and therefore the confidence of the public and its market(s), eventually overcame these tribulations. The second half of the twentieth century saw

DOI: 10.4324/9781003513728-2

11

an explosion in the range of occupations, and the population of individuals that occupied them, which in turn drove a surge in demand for tertiary education. Perkin[3] suggests that the arrival of true professions signified the third major societal evolutionary step, following the transition from hunter-gatherers to farming, and thence to industrialization. Similarly, Martin[4] describes the arrival of corporate managers and professionals as the twentieth century's two success stories for the middle classes in western societies. This may be going too far; the evidence did not support wholesale wealth creation by its constituents, and far too many vocations became regarded as professions, irrespective of scientific expertise, simply because they were deemed "white collar".

Eventually, however, the issue of professional quality was settled – firstly, by more consistently recognized controls (performance measures, error rates, quality control, internal audit, etc.) and, secondly, via the implied relegation of vocations that didn't meet such standards through the explicit, commonly accepted, elevations of those that did. Think: legal and accounting, aviation and medicine, architecture and design, teaching, blue collar professions (the trades), and others.

Many scholars have delved into the development of the professions, from the role of labor markets[5] to the various influences in the provider-consumer relationship, such as the concept of "heteronomy"[6] whereby the two parties co-create the defined service relationship, through to the dynamics introduced by intermediaries. In the end, though, the unifying themes of all legitimate professions are their scientific knowledge and rules of governance, without which they have no prospect of mastering the third tranche, so critical today: emergent technological opportunity.

The Modern Day

Since the turn of the current century, the rise of abstract digital knowledge has unsettled vocations that lacked foundational structural knowledge. Many enthuse over this dynamic as "disruption", but their enthusiasm is not well placed. This type of disruption was never value-creating. In fact, it has proven to be quite the opposite. In contrast, vocations resting on a well-established industrial foundation have been relatively sheltered from the winds of populism and able to leverage emerging digital innovation intelligently and selectively for their own advancement. These are the true professions of the modern era, and they exhibit four key elements:

- An industrial management model.
- Disciplinary language.
- An aligned educational infrastructure.
- A barrier to entry.

Technology enhances their operations, but it doesn't redefine their mission, nor their model.

If your niece approached you and said, "How do I become a lawyer?", you would advise her to get her grades to the minimum law school entry requirements out of high school, to complete her degree, perhaps do an internship, and eventually pass the bar exam to be admitted to the profession. Likewise, if she instead nominated teaching, engineering, architecture, a field of science, accounting, software development, company management, medicine, psychology, the building, plumbing, electrical trades or any other number of fields, you would offer similar advice: it all starts with education, you would tell her, and it requires traversing a barrier. An education starts with the core tenets of the field and its disciplinary language. No matter what professor a student of medicine attends, and no matter the university, they will find that the field applies standardized, clinical language. Disciplinary language is one of the foundations of every profession.

Industrial Management Process

With scientific knowledge informing both the management model and its disciplinary language, the education system can impart standardized, essential knowledge on a reliable basis. For instance, someone studying the law will learn about the case law approach: legal principles, the application of precedent and analytical methods; and about legal research and writing standards. From there they move onto civil procedures: the process of adjudication, motions and pleadings, pretrial procedure, the structure of a lawsuit, and subsequent appeals process. Similarly, they will study contract law, criminal law and procedure, property law, torts, and of course, underpinning it all, the overall workings of the legal system and its processes.

Other fields are just as exacting. There is no room for those that are not qualified, cannot speak the clinical language of the field, and are unable to understand or exercise the requisite processes to a professional standard. Professionals are licensed, monitored, carry the necessary insurance, and if they fail to meet professional or ethical standards, may be struck off or simply fired, if not sued. Barriers to entry do not only operate at the beginning, but throughout the professional lifecycle, to protect the practitioner themselves, the customer, and the market.

So, to recap, the hallmarks of genuine professions are an industrial management model, associated disciplinary language, an aligned educational infrastructure, and a barrier to entry. What should strike you is that professions don't just teach areas of knowledge in isolation: each capability sits atop a key pillar, is usually interconnected with other capabilities from the same pillar, is informed by the preceding pillar, and is informative of the next (Table 1.1).

Table 1.1 The Legal Profession

Practice	Legal System	Civil & Criminal Procedure	General Law
Governance Engagement Work People Risk Mmanagement	Legal principle Precedent Analytical methods Research and writing Legal system Evidentiary standards Professional responsibility Conflict of laws	Adjudication motions and pleadings Pretrial procedure Lawsuit structure Appeals Criminal responsibility Enforceability of sanctions Offenses against public order and well-being The rights guaranteed to those charged	Contract law Property law Torts Administrative law Civil litigation Commercial law Corporations Family law Taxation Wills and trusts International law Environmental law Labor law (etc.)

Law School Admission Council, Discover Law, no date. https://www.lsac.org/dis cover-law/what-you-can-expect-your-law-school-experience

Of course, doing quality legal work, for example, involves a lot more than just knowing the law. There are many practice management requirements necessary to provide both a quality service, and a compliant one, and differing jurisdictional bodies erect standards for their members. Let's consider others (Tables 1.2 and 1.3).

Table 1.2 The Accounting Profession

Financial Accounting	Managerial Accounting	Tax Accounting
Generally Accepted Accounting Principles (GAAP) and International Financial Reporting Standards (IFRS) Balance sheet, income statement, statement of cash flows, and statement of retained earnings	Information for internal decision-making Planning, and control processes Business needs analysis Budgeting and forecasting	Tax laws and jurisdictional regulations Tax planning and compliance Credits, deductions, incentives, and risk

Rizwan Ahmed CPA Scholarship, Unveiling the 3 Pillars of Accounting, February 29, 2024. https://rizwanahmedcpascholarship.com/unveiling-the-3-pillars-of -accounting/

Table 1.3 The Teaching Profession

Planning	Revision	Assessment	Implementation
Goal setting: entire semester (syllabus) Goal setting: single class (lesson plan) Goal setting: critical understanding of core concepts	Revising pedagogy Orient to richer meaning in lecture/ discussion/test/ grade process Ensure the scholarship of teaching as a culminating activity of the research Revise discovery, integration, and application	Regular self-assessment Regular student assessment Process effectiveness Feedback solicitation (end of semester and periodically) Teaching strategy assessment	Apply planning, revision and assessment outcomes to change process Maintain the courage for, and bias for, change Experimentation: teaching execution Experimentation: advancing teaching skills

Georgetown University, Teaching as a Process, no date. https://cndls.george-town.edu/atprogram/twl/teaching-as-process/

As always, you will note two levels:

■ *Management model* is the governing and linear model of the vocation.
■ *Disciplines or functions* are those capabilities that reside in each pillar of the management model.

The evidence for structured management models is overwhelming. Each recognized profession applies a codified management process within which different functions or disciplines exist.

Yet, none of this is true of customer management. Instead, wrapped in populism, "CX" comprises a series of isolated functions which have created their own terms, tools, networks, methods, and metrics. To compound matters, it has misappropriated "agile", a software development methodology, as if it were a customer management one. It infers that we must "fail fast", in direct contrast to the premise of industrial processes which are designed to limit failure and ensure consistency of execution for target and repeat outcomes. It also infers, erroneously, that we don't possess core knowledge and so must experiment.

As we discussed in the premise, another consequence of the absence of codified practice is the propensity to confuse customering with marketing. So then, let's consider that model (Table 1.4).

Table 1.4 The Marketing Vocation

Diagnostic	*Strategy*	*Tactics*
Market orientation Market research Market segmentation	Branding Targeting Positioning Objective setting Budgeting	Product Pricing Distribution Integrated communications

As you can see, marketing too, has a range of separate functions and disciplines, and each is applied in context of their pillar. The disciplines that operate in the diagnostics pillar cumulatively inform the strategy pillar and the execution of its disciplines, and this in turn informs the decisions made on the four areas of the tactical pillar.

Each function is important, and a marketing department that is run by formally trained marketing leadership will not have any aspect of the operation that does not understand its role. They certainly don't have independent functions, assuming that they are marketing unto itself (although advertising agencies have history of attempting that at times), nor do they import irrelevant methods from other fields that do not make critical contribution to the overall mission.

Note that I did not call marketing a profession. While it satisfies the first three tests (industrial management model, disciplinary language, and educational infrastructure), it does not impose a barrier to entry, which undermines the first three and diminishes its consistency of quality, and therefore its trustworthiness to wider corporate leadership.

Customer Management Is not Marketing

You might notice that nowhere in marketing's management model above does it contemplate customer management. Despite this, a presumptive takeover by elements of the marketing fraternity is a major structural blunder that can have serious consequences without proper know-how.

As a case in point, several of the world's member-based marketing institutes prescribe competency models which include "customer experience". One even classifies it as a "core marketing competence". However, as you will see, customering is not material to marketing's core mission, and, even if it was, none of these institutions exhibit critical knowledge of the field. As is the layman's error, they assert their own extraneous context over the precision of the customer mission. Moreover, they fail to serve the correct strategic agenda, and gravely diminish the corporate value of the customer franchise.

So, let's be clear. Although they are related, customering is not marketing. To start with, it is important to understand that marketing resides at the market level, while customering resides at the individual level, and the management implications are all defining.

Marketing is geared to dealing with very large groups of people, the mass market or segments therein, which are themselves large groups out in the wild of society. There might be tens or hundreds of millions (even billions) of people in a company's market, and hundreds of thousands, millions, tens of millions or more in each of that market's heterogeneous segments. In contrast, proper customering deals with each *individual* – no matter how many of them there may be – one by one by one.

You have shifted gear, from literally many millions of people to a single person. Thus, as just one example of common misdirection, customering does not require market diagnostics or its "segmentation" process, because we are not engaging groups. The customer management industry must stop thinking about customers as marketing segments or campaign targets, and equally must dismiss misplaced marketers who propose doing so. There is some nuance to this and variation in execution by category, which I'll get into in later chapters, but generally, such practices are terminal to the value derived from customers.

The other major difference between the two is that while marketing goes *out to* the market, it is customers (or prospects) who come *into* the company. Members of a segment are targeted to receive a communication, and the company chooses the form that takes. In contrast, customers always have the power – they choose whether to engage and how, not the other way around. One is hunting, the other is hosting. One is shooting, the other is serving (Table 1.5).

Table 1.5 Operational Distinctions

Marketing	*Customering*
Is concerned with *populations*.	Interacts with *individuals*.
Targets the market.	*Engages* with people.
Profiles the *anonymous*	Relates to the *known*.
Is primarily *outbound*.	Is primarily *inbound*.
Is a *messaging* (one-way) model.	Is a *conversational* (two-way) model.

My Bowtie model below illustrates the respective work of both by way of the management process (Figure 1.1).

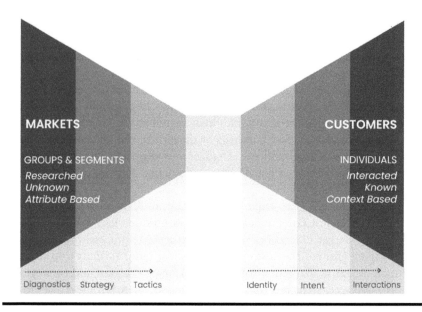

Figure 1.1 The Marketing to Customering Bowtie Model (Spinley, 2022)

You will recognize the marketing management model on the left-hand side: Diagnostics, Strategy, and Tactics. Note its characteristics.

- It requires research to understand those large groups.
- Even with the best research, these are never known people.
- Therefore, we operate based on attributes: psychographic, demographic, socio-economic,etc.
- We then strategize (targeting and positioning) and employ outbound tactics.

Moving your gaze to the right-hand side, note that the characteristics of customering are quite different. Specifically:

- These are individuals who have personally interacted, or are personally interacting, with us.
- They are recognized as actual people with characteristics (individualization).
- We comprehend, firsthand, their specific needs and personal context.
- We can engage individually and bi-directionally.

Introducing the Customer Management Process Model

Despite their very profound differences, you will note the linear process of both fields, and that customering comprises its own three management pillars:

- Identity.
- Intent.
- Interactions.

Along with Measurement, these make up the four pillars of the customer management model. Stated simply, within the context of engaging with individuals we must first have a sound process of identifying who it is that seek to engage with us. Make no mistake: it is them to us, not the other way around. Identification is naturally foundational to interactions with each customer in their context, which means we must be able to discern their personal intent. Just as in everyday life, it is only when we realize who we are talking to, and what they are saying to us, that we can retrieve appropriate data from our memory banks to interact with them appropriately (Table 1.6).

Table 1.6 The Four Pillars Customer Management Model

Identity	Intent	Interactions	Measurement and Reporting
Capture Stitching Systems Privacy	Jobs to be done Discernment • Behavioral. • Conversational. • Unsolicited. • Self-reporting.	Engagement stack Touchpoint assets Messaging assets Ecosystems and channels Orchestration	System tests Business tests Corporate reporting

Relative complexity only arrives in the actual functions and disciplines that reside within each pillar and in their inter-dependencies, which is why the absence of a governing management model has been so problematic, and why so many chief customer officers (or equivalent) are ineffective. Most hail from an isolated function and have populist-level knowledge, or they are generalist managers on rotation through the business. Self-evidently, any leader operating absent the requisite expertise will fail, and so it is here.

Notes

1. Sean Wilentz, *The Rise of American Democracy* (W. W. Norton & Co., 2005).
2. Adam Smith, *An Inquiry into the Nature and Causes of the Wealth of Nations* (1776).
3. Harold Perkin, *The Third Revolution: Professional Elites in the Modern World* (Routledge, 1996).
4. Bill Martin, "Knowledge, Identity and the Middle Class: From Collective to Individualised Class Formation?," *The Sociological Review* 46, no. 4 (1998): 653–686.
5. Andrew Abbott and D. Randall Smith, "Governmental Constraints and Labor Market Mobility," *Work and Occupations* 11, no. 1 (1984): 29–53.
6. T. J. Johnson, "Work and Power," in *The Politics of Work and Occupation*, ed. Geoff Esland and Graeme Salaman (Open University Press, 1980), ch. 11.

Chapter 2

The Marketing Method

Some may ask why I am devoting a chapter to marketing in a book about the formal management of customering. It's a fair question. The answer is that, as we already touched on, the two fields are very commonly confused, and sometimes the fastest way to explain what something is (customering), is start by explaining what it is *not* (marketing) – and that begins with exploring the latter with enough detail to make the case.

This is an important objective of the book, because the conflation of the two is responsible for very significant losses of company profits the world over.

The CX movement routinely borrows from marketing concepts, absent any understanding of them or their implications. Equally, many marketing folks stumble, clumsily, into the customer domain and quickly damage their business. This chapter exposes the marketing process, while the next does the same for customer management model; in Chapter 8 we will look at the legitimate, but limited, intersections of the two.

I hasten to note that there is significant, world-class educational infrastructure surrounding marketing, some of which you will find referenced in the following pages. This chapter does not presume to replace it – not even remotely! Indeed, the management model is described at about a million-foot view. We will soar above the diagnostics, strategy, and tactical pillars of marketing, their linear and interconnected nature, and we'll take a pinch or two from some leading executives and scholars in the field. And throughout the book, we will refer to this chapter periodically, re-iterating and re-emphasizing the critical differences between the marketing and customering regimes.

And, finally, a bonus. If you're at all interested in learning about actual marketing management, reading this section will place you, perhaps, in the top half or so of all "marketers", at least in understanding what the process is supposed to look like. A 2018 study by the UK's *Marketing Week*[1] found that:

DOI: 10.4324/9781003513728-3

More than half of marketers (53.8%) say they have not studied a marketing-related academic or professional qualification of any kind.

There is a suspicion that this figure is actually higher, but if we accept the number and then consider that what you are about to read is the basis of what is taught in management schools around the world,[2] you should feel confident that you are attaining some useful knowledge. If you enjoy this section and want to take your career down this path, you can pursue formal training to learn more, in depth, and properly.

Diagnostics

Marketing is inherently an inside-out function. It is about achieving company goals – primarily increased market penetration, and therefore improved sales revenue. In the 1970s the great Phillip Kotler wrote one of the classic marketing management textbooks, *Marketing Management*, in which he stated that:

> Marketing management seeks to determine the settings of the company's marketing decision variables that will maximize the company's objective(s) in the light of the expected behavior of noncontrollable demand variables.[3]

These are internal objectives that, when realized, come about by deploying processes designed to extract as much value as possible from the market. Marketing wages campaigns aimed *at* prospective buyers, and to be at its most effective marketing must at least understand the market so that its strategies and tactics have the greatest chance of success.

Market is after all, the root word of *marketing*.

Ever heard of the "the humility of marketing"? In four words, it reminds all marketers and company leaders that no matter who they are – their seniority, their tenure in their business or the category in which they operate – they are not, and never will be, the market. Consequently, they should never make decisions about that market, or how to approach it, based on internal thinking or opinion.

Many people struggle with this. They see part of their value as being to know such things, irrespective of the fact that the actual market shifts and changes and does what it chooses, without any regard for your own sense of value. To be successful in addressing their market(s), companies must therefore become "market-oriented". This is the foundation of market diagnostics, which, as you will see, generates the critical understanding necessary for effective strategy. It underpins the effectiveness of marketing in its entirety.

Market Orientation

Perhaps the most notable literature associated with the concept of market orientation is the famous 1993 *Harvard Business Review* article "Spend a Day in the Life of Your Customers", which proposes that:

> At industrial companies, there is no substitute for senior managers' personal sense of the market.[4]

This widely celebrated paper reinforces the value of market research and segmentation. John Narver, Professor Emeritus of Marketing at the University of Washington, states:

> A market orientation is a business culture in which all employees are committed to the continuous creation of superior value for buyers … Recent research has shown what intuition suggests: that businesses that are more market-oriented enjoy higher profitability as well as superior sales growth, customer retention, and new product success.[5]

Yet I believe that the historical conflation of market orientation with customer-centricity, on display in the above citations, has not translated to the modern age of omni-consumerism. I happily concede that both come from the same philosophical lineage, but the management model and operational distinctions are now profound – as we'll discover soon.

Nevertheless, the data is clear that market orientation is important to marketing effectiveness – yet many companies have trouble embedding the concept at management level. This is largely because of other forms of orientation which you might recognize.

Product Orientation

Product orientation is one of the hallmarks of the digital era, with start-ups spruiking their disruptive new technology or app and many corporates trying to mirror the start-up community with the "garage", or internal design agency model. For a period, "agile" was so in vogue that it was all anyone in business and design seemed to talk about. The compound effect was an unnatural preoccupation with products instead of markets, something that prompted popular marketing and business author Seth Godwin to call for a return to the premise of market orientation:

> Don't find customers for your products. Find products for your customers.

Yet today, many companies start and end their management discussions with their product (or service). Build it and they will come ... In 1992, Phil Knight, the founder of Nike, made his now often-referenced comments to the *Harvard Business Review*.

> For years, we thought of ourselves as a production-oriented company, meaning we put all our emphasis on designing and manufacturing the product. But now ... we've come around to saying that Nike is a marketing-oriented company ... We used to think that everything started in the lab. Now we realize that everything spins off the consumer ... We have to innovate for a specific reason, and that reason comes from the market. Otherwise, we'll end up making museum pieces.[6]

Sales Orientation

Similarly, many companies are heavily oriented toward sales. At first glance you might be forgiven for thinking, "Well, duh! Aren't we all?", and you'd be right – but ironically, sales-oriented organizations typically sell less, are less profitable, or both.

We've seen quite of a lot of this at corporate level in recent times. As investment markets were awash with capital, huge positions were taken particularly in technology, with founders and their equity partners seeking company valuations derived from extreme multipliers of earnings before interest and taxes (EBIT). In another example, this time more US-specific – where corporations law typically requires company directors to act in favor of shareholders instead of a duty to the company entity itself – the rise of activist shareholder groups has had significant impacts. Demanding cost cuts such as layoffs to drive an improved short-term balance sheet, and therefore more favorable stock performance, it inherently creates major sales pressure. Strategy goes out the window, as does culture, and rampant short-termism takes hold.

This is one of the hallmarks a sales orientation. Whatever the reasons for this bias, companies that find themselves here tend to live month to month, or quarter to quarter, or at least it will feel that way for its people. They'll find themselves in sales forecast meetings, sometimes on multiple occasions every week, and playing make-believe in their customer relationship management (CRM) system.

The second major hallmark of sales orientation is an internally focused business. Companies see themselves as the only variable in any equation. They are rarely well-targeted because, in their minds, all customers are good customers. They never truly understand their markets and are heavily focused on revenue in ways that are not healthy, nor reliable. As you can imagine, product and sales orientations are quite often bedfellows.

Advertising Orientation

Lastly, an advertising orientation is often a marketing-centered problem. This is when marketers, or those who claim the title (remembering that there is no barrier to entry), confuse one part of the communications function with the entire field of marketing management. Their belief is that great content, or great creative, or great placement, etc., is the answer to all of marketing's questions. Creative, social, campaigns, the Metaverse, etc. – all are tactics in need of strategy.

Without a strong market diagnostic, advertising – and all other forms of brand communication – is simply a solution looking for a problem. Market orientation identifies and frames the problem.

Measuring Market Orientation

There are a number of ways to measure market orientation, the most famous of which is the MORTN scale,[7] a managerially inclined approach to aid senior leaders that has been found to be effective by an independent assessment by scholars at the Louisiana Tech University[8] (Figure 2.1).

The key takeaway from all of this is that if you accept that a company should be oriented to its market – and you should – then you should be concerned with you how we do that. Enter: market research.

Market Research

First, let's distinguish between legitimate market research and the misplaced practices of the CX movement that assume a role via the idea of "customer research", which really has nothing to do with customer management. Well-intentioned but ultimately ignorant of its proper function, they have taken upon themselves market level activity, and in doing so they impose inappropriate interactions on their customers.

Higher score = more market oriented.

Market Orientation Question:	1 Strongly Disagree	2 Disagree	3 Neither	4 Agree	5 Strongly Agree
1 Our business objectives are driven primarily by customer satisfaction.					
2 We constantly monitor our level of commitment and orientation to serving customer needs.					
3 We freely communicate information about our successful and unsuccessful customer experiences across all business functions.					
4 Our strategy for competitive advantage is based on our understanding of customers needs.					
5 We measure customer satisfaction systematically and frequently.					
6 We have routine or regular measures of customer service.					
7 We are more customer focused than our competitors.					
8 I believe this business exists primarily to serve customers.					
9 We poll end users at least once a year to assess the quality of our products and services.					
10 Data on customer satisfaction is disseminated at all levels this business					

Figure 2.1 The MORTN Scale in Excel

Can you imagine a lawyer, an accountant, architect, pilot, etc. asking their customers how to do their job? No, because they are trained; they understand the management process together with the functions and disciplines that reside within them. Customer feedback is one thing. Asking what to do next, or how to do it, is quite another. We'll cover appropriate forms of customer insight in Chapter 5, but for now, the takeaway is that market research is not a customer function – it's a marketing one, and it works like this.

Once a business understands that it needs to orient itself to the market, it follows that to do so, it needs to understand that market. For the marketers who are reading this, you should note that this is true whether your company applies a traditional STP approach – segment, target, position (STP) – as explained in these pages, or a mass market model, as advanced by the likes of the Ehrenberg Bass Institute, or, as many others advocate, both. To be clear, however, the importance to the field of market orientation, research and segmentation is not debated by marketing scholars.

So, what does market research involve?

There are two broad types of research, qualitative and quantitative, and both are required as part of your research architecture. Indeed, the generally accepted best practice is to start with qualitative methods to best understand the market-perceived variables, and then move into quantitative methods to measure them. I'll follow that order.

Qualitative Research

The two main forms of qualitative research are focus groups and ethnographic research.

A focus group is exactly as it sounds. A group of people drawn from the market are, for instance, set up in a room and deal with a range of questions through a group discussion. It is good practice to video the sessions, which are then observed and analyzed by managers; if you have a two-way mirror like in a TV detective show, you could use that too. In order to inform the content of a focus group, market researchers also use a range of external information sources – for example:

■ Search engines.
■ Social media.
■ Earlier research.
■ Academic and industry reports.
■ Media coverage.

In contrast, ethnographic research works by turning the tables. Instead of asking customers into an alien setting like a meeting room, companies observe them in the wild – in other words, in all the places where the brand and or its offerings are discussed, purchased and consumed. In today's world, with multiple digital and physical alternatives for these activities – some within the company's control and many in external ecosystems – it can be hard to achieve full coverage. However, it remains a source of powerful insight. Ethnography was probably first used to better understand the "natives" of new lands by exploring cultural phenomena from the point of view of "the subject", or, in this case, the market. Famously, Alan Lafley, the former CEO of Procter & Gamble, remarked (Table 2.1).

> If you want to understand how a lion hunts, don't go to the zoo.
> Go to the jungle.

Table 2.1 Summary of Qualitative Methods

Type	Strength	Weakness
Focus Groups	Fast results. Relatively cost effective. Good for profiling your target and testing existing positioning. Great tool for attaining management buy-in.	Lacks context. Is not representative. Hinges on the skills of the moderator. No sizing / scaling of the expressed opinions (small samples).
Ethnographic Research	Operates in context. Offers behavioral insight (unspoken). Very rich in learnings.	Time intensive. Small samples.

Quantitative Research

Given its inherent weaknesses, qualitative research is of course never adequate by itself. Making strategic decisions without first testing the insight for magnitude across larger samples is a serious error. The most common form of quantitative research is the survey.

Typical market surveys operate in three parts:

- **Demographics**: e.g., age, income, years of experience.
- **Attitudinal**: e.g., ease of use.
- **Behavioral**:[9] e.g., preference, usage, satisfaction.

A popular survey method is the Likert scale (named after social scientist Rensis Likert) because they are one of the more reliable ways to measure opinions, perceptions and behaviors, and to capture more granular feedback. Rather than yes/no or other binary questioning, Likert scales use a 5- or 7-point scale with extreme positions at either end and moderate or neutral options in the middle. You will no doubt have seen these before.

Regardless of the type of survey employed, it is critical to ensure an adequate sample size so that its primary purpose – to test for magnitude – is not lost. Of course, just as qualitative research is inadequate by itself, so too for quantitative data. Companies that do little other than send surveys – of which there are many – make equally poor decisions as those that might only use focus groups.

There is much more to this extensive subject, but again, if you want to learn more, I suggest that you study marketing. In the meantime, you can deduce that research is a tricky business, because it is.

Market Segmentation

Market segmentation is the beginning of the traditional STP management model. Each step informs the next and must be executed in a walled manner, not conflating one with another.

The importance of the segmentation process, at a high level, is to remove from the organizational thinking any hypothetical and imaginary market ideology. It provides both the detail and the rigor to undercut internal myths about the market and its component parts, and it stops the business from thinking that there is a standard, or average, buyer. After all, any strategy built on fairy tales is destined for failure.

The segmentation discipline allows a company to trade off on generic go-to-market activities which might cost less due to volume, and activities that home in on specific groups to drive better outcomes but which may cost more to achieve. As we will see as we advance through this chapter, it also provides the critical foundation for making informed "market-fit" decisions about the company's offering, be it products, services, experiences, or a combination thereof. At the same time, it is important to note that market segmentation is not about stereotyping, the lazy, sweeping generalizations you might hear people talk about. For instance, "millennials", "boomers", "soccer moms", and "college kids" are not segments.

It should also be noted that if you have three companies operating in the same market, and each conducts a robust segmentation process, they should all arrive at the same conclusions. Remember, all you are doing here is mapping the market – it is not about you or your brand. Think about it this way: if you and two friends decide to take road trips, in separate cars and a week apart from each other, to a place none of you have been before, each driver will follow the map. That map is the same for everyone; the terrain does not change just because the driver does, or the vehicle does, or based on how many people are in each car, what they are wearing and so on. How you respond to that map – where you might take a break along the way or the best kind of vehicles for the trip – is what we will deal with in Strategy, but for now we are just talking about the map itself.

Lastly, a key principle that ultimately drives the rigor used to segment a market is that each segment must be both internally homogeneous and heterogeneous to other segments. Simply put, that means a person should not fit into more than one market segment. If they do, the segment parameters are not sufficiently defined. The data drawn on to establish segments comes from the market research phase of the Diagnostics pillar, as previously described.

Segmentation Methods

There are four common variables of segmentation – demography, firmography, psychography, and behavioral – which can be plotted to establish the various distinct segments (Table 2.2).

Table 2.2 Segmentation Variables

Variable	Meaning
Demographics	Age, gender, income, location.
Firmographics	For B2B marketers: number of employees, industry, revenue etc.
Psychographics	Beliefs and attitudes.
Behavioral	Observable distinct behavioral differences.

For example, a popular cloud service provider for socio-economic segmentation is called "geoTribes".[10] It looks at different societal segments and can apply geographical context as well. For our million-foot view, however, let's leave demographics and firmographics here because they are somewhat self-explanatory, and while they provide key data for the segment it is the beliefs and attitudes, and behavioral nuances, that tell us how to use that data to form the most accurate segments. So let's look briefly at psychographics and behavioral variables.

Psychographics

Using a series of questions such as "agree/disagree", we can group people with particular traits into distinct cohorts. For instance, Starbucks found two such groups dominated its research:

- "I'm a non-coffee drinker but I still want to socialize".
- "I'm a serious coffee drinker."

Of course, there are usually more than two, and each group is defined in a little more detail than just a headline statement, including the proportion that they represent. For instance, a healthcare provider found it had five different groups (Table 2.3):

Table 2.3 Example of Segments

Category	Proportion	Description
Compliant leaders	35%	I rely heavily upon the recommendations and opinions of my healthcare professional.
Martyrs	9%	I tend to worry about the health and well-being of others over my own.
Life-stylers	31%	I'm super proactive in seeking information and guidance to promote my health and wellness!
Worryers	12%	I'm always on the lookout for ailments before they get me
Old Schoolers	13%	I reject the validity of naturopathic or holistic medicine. Give me the white coats any-day.

Behavioral

The behavioral segment builds on the attitudinal insight gained from the psychographic variables by adding the observable action (behavior) in relation to the market options; when we couple attitudes with behaviors, we start to get a picture. For example, a newspaper brand might find cohorts that see digital subscription as the future and hate being interrupted by adverts (attitudes), and that exhibit one of two relative behaviors: they currently read its newspaper, or they currently do not. It decides to call those that do not read its paper "Digital Lopers", and can now compare that group to the balance of its demographic data. Using the sample size, it is able to estimate the proportion of the market that they represent. Thus (Table 2.4):

Table 2.4 Segment Valuation

Digital Lopers	34% of market	1,700,000 consumers US $714 million value

Naturally, because we have estimated this segment as 34% of the market – a percentage that we will no doubt track year on year in our diagnostics program

– then we must also have other segments that represent the other 66%. When we capture each of these in the same way, they we begin to fill out our market map.

From there, many marketers use tools such as the "Meaningful/Actionable Grid", which plots each of the variables into segments. This provides clear market segments, each with a name that a sales team will easily recognize and understand, and it exposes how each segment influences or is influenced by others.

The Whole Map, and Nothing but the Map, Your Honor

Segmentation is difficult, and it has exacting standards that must be met if it is to be its most effective:

- It must capture the market in its entirety (not simply those we think are our targets).
- Each segment must be named for its primary behavior.
- However, all segment dynamics must be established and recorded.
- Each segment must be homogeneous unto itself, and heterogeneous to others.
- A person (potential customer) must only belong (fit) to one segment.

The marketing professor under whom I studied suggested another test. "If", he said, "Joe from the sales team reviewed your segmentation, what would be their response?" The concept here is that if the people who spend their time on the front lines don't recognize any of your segments, you probably have it wrong!

Artificial Intelligence and the Future of Market Diagnostics

Before we leave this section, it is worth touching on the emergent application of AI to this work. While not prevalent at the time of writing (in early 2024), a term that may be by the time you are reading this is "synthetic data".

Synthetic data is derived from AI and replicates primary consumer research. It has been found to mirror, with about 95% accuracy (which will only improve), solid market diagnostic data. In practical terms, marketers spend US $40 to 60 thousand over a few weeks on a primary research project, yet with synthetic data they can obtain the same results almost instantaneously. This is expected to automate the generation of reliable market segmentation and other useful data points that marketers care about, such as excess share of voice (ESOV), funnels, pricing analysis, category entry points, and more.[11]

This is another example where the injection of advanced technological capability into *established* professional practice can deliver massive efficiency and cost upsides; in the case of market diagnostics it will be truly transformative.

So, we have established a company that seeks to be market-oriented and has invested in research and in robust segmentation. We know exactly how the market, in all its native glory, is constructed. Now, we are in a position to devise our strategy.

Strategy

Many people talk about strategy. It is probably one of the most overused words in business, and in marketing at least, one of the most misunderstood. Many think that marketing strategy is the beginning of the process, although, as we have established, trained marketers know better and conduct the necessary diagnostics work first so that their strategy is not guesswork.

Others, possibly the majority, don't, and therefore guess. It is little wonder that marketing leadership struggles for credibility in the boardroom compared to more robust professional leadership, such as the CFO. No doubt, if conducted properly and consistently, that would change. Once you are in possession of strong diagnostics, your marketing strategy will be made up of brand development interconnected with four key components:

Table 2.5 Four Elements of Strategy

Targeting	Who in our market should we target?
Positioning	Given the characteristics of our target/s, how should we position ourselves?
Objectives	Based on the market composition and valuation of those targets et al, what are our business objectives?
Budgeting	What budget do we need to achieve them?

As you can see, it is not just the pillars themselves that are linear in nature (a characteristic that marketing shares with customering, as you will soon read); even the disciplines in the marketing pillars inform the next in the process.

Again, I remind readers that this is million-foot view ... let's begin.

Targeting

The first thing to understand about strategy is that we are shifting our focus to ourselves. Diagnostics is all about the market. It is a map, a critical map, but nothing more. Strategy, however, is about our company, or our brand(s).

Who – which segment or segments – is it that we will focus our investments and our tactics on? We will need to consider our resource constraints, the posture of our competitors, the dynamics of the segments that we have identified and, of course, their relative values. One of my all-time favorite quotes applies perfectly to this work. In his legendary book on strategy, *The Art of War*, Sun Tzu wrote:

> There are roads which must not be followed, armies which must be not attacked, towns which must not be besieged, positions which must not be contested, commands of the sovereign which must not be obeyed.

Targeting is about making choices. Where do we focus our finite resources for the greatest effect? Is it the most valuable segment? Is it the one that we have the least penetration in? Is it the segment that represents the most likely future buyers?

One of the big questions is whether one segment might be influential upon another. Often this is called "spillover". For instance, because people in their mid- and late teens tend to follow the trends set by people in their early twenties, targeting the older group might be effective in attracting the younger.

Influence can work in other ways too. Consider this (from researchers, Amir Fazli and Jeffrey D. Shulman):[12]

> In September 2014, all CVS pharmacy locations stopped selling tobacco. While the move was estimated to cost CVS $2 billion from lost cigarette sales, CEO Larry Merlo stated that removing tobacco products could benefit CVS's overall business. In 2 January 2016, Aldi announced plans to stop selling unhealthy snacks such as candy bars in their checkout lines, while Target started testing the same policy in select stores in September 2015. Managers of these retailers and industry analysts have speculated that this move can increase profits; Senior Vice President of Merchandising for Target, Christina Hennington, viewed the move as "a huge business opportunity." [citations omitted]

In short, these companies sacrificed one major segment – cigarette buyers in the case of CVS and unhealthy foods in the case of Aldi – to appeal to the attitudes and beliefs of those in other segments. In both cases, they were choiceful, deliberate, and calculated. This is strategy, only made possible because of the data that is obtained through sound diagnostics.

In their renowned book *The Long and the Short of It*,[13] Les Binet and Peter Field propose a ratio of how much to spend on brand building to how much to spend on sales activation within target segments. Based on analysis of the Institute of Practitioners in Advertising (IPA)'s Databank, they suggest that the two main marketing mechanisms – brand building and sales activation– work in very different ways.

In very short, brand building is about building salience – which is to say, distinctive memorability – over time, optionally differentiated against the alternatives among potential buyers, which means that they are more likely to respond favorably in buying situations. Activation, on the other hand, is about rationally, consciously processing offers or promotions.

The former relies in what the late Nobel laureate and behavioral psychologist Daniel Kahneman called "System 1", a fast-thinking mode that operates largely in the unconscious mind and requires little or no effort, while the latter relies on "System 2" slow-thinking, described as "effortful" cognitive load which demands significant attention.[14] Binet and Field propose that we need both. Where they found some resistance in recent years was their proposed ratio, widely reported as 60:40 in favor of brand building, although they are on record as saying that there are many different contexts – such as start-up versus established company, market penetration, and others – that impact on the ratio (Figure 2.2).

SECTOR ASSESSED	PROPOSED RATIO BRAND : ACTIVATION
FNANCIAL SERVICES	80 : 20
RETAIL	64 : 36
PACKAGED GOODS	60 : 40
DURABLES	58 : 42
OTHER SERVICES	51 : 49
THE AGGREGATE	**62 : 38**

Figure 2.2 Findings From "Effectiveness in Context" by Binet and Field (2018)

Targeting versus Mass Marketing

More recent years have seen a push back toward mass marketing in place of targeting. This has been largely advocated by Professor Byron Sharp, director of the renowned Ehrenberg Bass Institute and author of ground-breaking 2013 book *How Brands Grow*.[15]

Sharp and the team at EBI made a case for focusing on the mass market in brand building, rather than targeting, arguing with some hefty evidence in support that it is overall brand performance that is fundamental to market penetration. He describes "catching customers as they fall", which is to say that activation only works if you have established salience and works better if that has already translated into increased market penetration.

Speaking to WARC in 2020, Sharp said:

> When we see rival brands of toilet cleaner or cleaning products, they all sell to pretty much the same sort of households, and in most countries that's everyone. So, you might do some segmentation to work out that, you know, some places have bigger houses than others. Some have more people in the house than others. Some households do speak Spanish. That's useful. But the idea that your brand is only for [certain] households – that's just crazy.

So, to mass market, or to target?

Well, as Binet and Field suggest, and as Sharp recognizes to some degree in his advocacy of sales activations, there must be a mix. Today, some companies do exactly that. They maintain a sound, ongoing and always on-brand building campaign, and they support this with heavily targeted campaigns that rely on the targeting process. Branding speaks to the top of the marketing funnel, while targeting represents the bottom.

Market diagnostics are necessary to inform both.

Positioning

Thus far we have mapped the market and used that to make deliberate decisions about what parts – or all – of the market we will target. Now we start to shape exactly who it is that we want to be in the minds of those specific people and the market at large. To do this, we use positioning, a term coined by marketing legends Al Ries and Jack Trout and expanded on in their first book, *Positioning: The Battle for Your Mind*.[16]

So, what exactly is positioning? Well, it's pretty much all the buzzwords that you have probably come across, wrapped up in one: brand values, brand DNA, brand promise, brand personality, brand essence, etc. More scientifically described, it is the pursuit of "salience" – the establishment of memory structures – in the minds of the people we want to attract. As Ries and Trout put it, brands are in "a battle for your mind".

The other significant term in this arena is "mental availability", which, again, refers to the memory structure a brand manager is trying to create in the minds of their market. This is one half of an equation that also includes "physical availability" – which simply means that when someone comes to buy, that there is easy access to the product or service. But physical availability alone is inadequate if we haven't established mental availability or positioning.

There are some ground rules to get this right. Most importantly, keep it tight. Convoluted messaging – trying to take too many positions – just gets lost and fails to create memory. If you're Coca-Cola, you're "Great Times, Great Taste"; if you're Nike, you're "Just Do It". Ideally, a brand uses one primary attribute, such as "great times" or "great taste", which has emotional connectors. As we will discover in Chapter 6, when we talk about experiences versus services, memory is predicated on emotion, and separately, *feelings*. This is an extremely important aspect of positioning and branding in general.

The Three Cs

A central tool marketers use to derive their positioning is the Three Cs. Devised by Kenichi Ohmae, this is a triangle model with a variable at each corner: Customer, Company, and Competition. Specifically, it asks: does our positioning satisfy the following tests?

- ▪ *Company*: Is this something our company (organization) can create, develop, or deliver successfully?
- ▪ *Customer*: What does the customer need, and how can we meet that need whether expressed or latent?
- ▪ *Competition*: What is the competition doing in this area, and how can we differentiate ourselves?

Satisfying only one won't work. If a company makes a blatant claim that the market knows is spurious, it will backfire, even if that positioning is well considered to outflank or neutralize a competitive threat and seems to be in the interest of customers. For instance, in 2018 VW ran a new advert that seriously raised some eyebrows. The ad itself wasn't that memorable, other than for the fact that it came soon after its diesel emissions scandal, in which the company deliberately lied about its data. One independent estimate claimed that this directly resulted in 59 deaths in the USA.[17] Despite this, no executives had been fired or resigned, and no vehicles were recalled. Yet the advertisement, depicting the life of an apparent VW customer from a toddler to early middle age, used the strapline:

"It's more than just a car. It's keeping your promises".

No one was buying the idea that VW, at that point in its history, was keeping any promises at all. It was terrible positioning that was always going to provoke the ire of an already angry public. Anyone in VW's marketing team applying the Three Cs principle would have yanked it from production, but instead it prolonged the scandal – and the damage to VW's brand.

Even if your positioning promise is valid (unlike VW's ad), and it supports a market need, it still won't work if doesn't differentiate your company. Equally, if it differentiates the company and is a deliverable promise but doesn't meet a market need, that won't work either. In short, good positioning must do all three.

Other Common Tools in Positioning

Again, I am not attempting to address all available marketing concepts in this chapter, nor am I deep-diving those I have chosen to cover, but there are a couple that require a quick overview as part of the positioning processes in the strategy pillar.

The Benefits Ladder

This is a derivative of a long-standing technique used in sociology and psychology called "laddering", which is designed to reveal why people really do the things that they do, beyond obvious – and often wrong – surface-level assumptions. Broadly following on from Maslow's theory, with origins in the 1970s,[18] in the marketing context it is essentially a structure of cause and effect, and captures the escalation of value that goes beyond the immediacy of the product. It is useful to *tighten* the positioning, albeit always using data from the diagnostics phase (Figure 2.3 and Table 2.6).

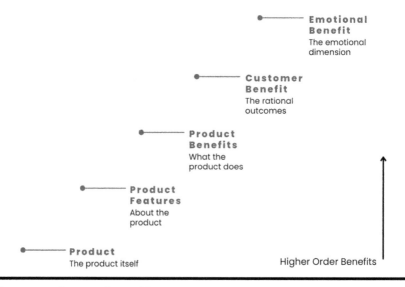

Figure 2.3 The Benefits Ladder

Table 2.6 The Ladder Explained

Product	Making people understand what the offering is and how they can get it,
Product Features	The physical characteristics of the offering,
Product Benefits	What the offering does,
Customer Benefits	The promise you make to the customers and the value (rational benefits),
Emotional Benefits	Linking to values or emotional dimensions,

Remember the "humility of marketing"? Well, one of the things I like about the benefits ladder is that it forces the marketer to consider how the offering benefits those who might consume it, and, when it comes to the actual brand, how they feel about it. For instance, Coca-Cola's positioning is as much about the amazing social experience one can enjoy by drinking Coke with your friends as it is about quenching your thirst. This triggers a higher emotional reaction from recipients of that messaging – and, as we have covered and will cover again in Chapter 6, that is essential for memory creation.

Another key tool is "Perceptual Maps", which speaks especially to the notion of differentiation.

Differentiation is about the relativity of the product in relation to the alternatives. There is a lot to this, but we'll keep to our million-foot view and so, in shorthand: If the market loves yellow things, I don't have to be totally yellow, I just have to be more yellow than my competitors. A perceptual map helps marketers understand where they might sit in the market's estimation, and how to respond – or to defend – when it comes to positioning. Many use a comparable, such as price and quality, though there is more granularity when using a two-dimensional map. A good example is offered by Anthony Murphy, who assessed the learning industry (Figure 2.4).

Of course, this process must be based on market research, not internal opinions, or perceptions inside the four walls, and your early diagnostics together with your intended positioning will also inform you on the dimension variables you will want to assess.

Distinctiveness versus Differentiation

Before I close this oh-so-short summary of the positioning discipline, it is important to clear up the confusion that often occurs between differentiation – the relative perception of your brand compared the alternatives – and distinctiveness.

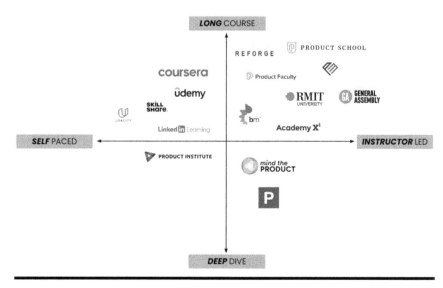

Figure 2.4 A Perceptual Map by Anthony Murphy.[19]

For a long time the marketing vocation has focused heavily on differentiation, a folly that was called out by the Ehrenberg Bass Institute (EBI) as part of its advocacy of mass market over targeting that we discussed earlier. Instead, the EBI has argued that it is distinctiveness, not differentiation that companies should focus on. In essence, this is predicated on the idea – an accurate one on the evidence – that participants in many categories find it almost impossible to differentiate themselves from alternatives, For example, a law firm, aside from emphasizing specialty areas of practice or geographical location etc., is going to be perceived by most as much the same as all the other law firms. In this context, distinctiveness is argued to be more important than differentiation.

At the time of writing, most academics and industry leaders seem to have assessed that an overly pronounced swing in the direction of distinctiveness is likely to be problematic as well, and that, in fact, we need both operating hand in hand. I have covered differentiation very briefly on the previous page, and it is a topic we will return to later in the book, so let me add a touch of color to distinctiveness and why it is important (Table 2.7).

Table 2.7 Distinctiveness versus Differentiation

Distinctiveness	Connecting and creating memory structures: non-rational
Differentiation	Contrasting a brand or offering with the alternatives

In essence, brand distinctiveness is key to creating memorability. It is the emotional, less rational working of the human mind. To do that, brands seek to create distinct elements or associations, such as the following examples from Sharp's *How Brands Grow*:

- Colors – such as the Coca-Cola and Vodafone red.
- Logos – such as McDonald's golden arches.
- Taglines – such as Nike's "Just do it".
- Symbols/characters – such as Tiger Woods for Nike.
- Adverting styles – such as MasterCard's "priceless" campaign.

One of the greatest sporting brands in the world is New Zealand's national rugby team, the All Blacks.[20] The All Blacks are one of the most successful sporting teams of all time, sustaining a near 80% win record over more than 130 years. Even their closest rival, the famous Springboks of South Africa, muster only a 37% win rate against them. The global growth of rugby audiences and media has enshrined them as an iconic brand that has transcended the sport itself. Not surprisingly, it has been a central part of the Adidas sporting stable for many years, and their distinctive all-black playing kit, the silver fern on the left chest (a national symbol), and the famous "haka", a cultural mark of respect originating from the country's indigenous Māori people, are all central to its history, its legacy, and now its commercial brand codes.

But this kind of salience could not be achieved by differentiation alone, such as the All Blacks' winning record. It required the ongoing distinctive elements that provide the personality and respect (for example) that mark the brand's emotional memorability and marketability. It is even reinforced by the way that the team plays the game, which is regarded as part of its brand identity. For example, at the 2023 Rugby World Cup it scored more than 100 points more than the next best team, scored 49 tries while the next best was 35, etc. In other words, the team plays exciting, attacking, attractive rugby, dominating the sponsor's highlight reels, and here's where the rubber hits the road: they attract audiences. The All Blacks have fans all over the world, many of whom aren't general rugby followers, and many of whom have a national rugby team that plays against the All Blacks.

Establishing brand distinctiveness relies on this kind of persistency and consistency, and it allows a company to refresh the way that it reminds consumers of core messages, instead of laboring for new points of difference, which are invariably inconsequential from the consumer's perspective.[21]

Let's look at another example. The multi-billion-dollar brand M&Ms, manufactured and marketed by Mars Incorporated, is, at a product level, identical to the Nestlé Smarties product, a seriously delicious candy-coated chocolate pebble. And yet M&Ms is many orders of magnitude more successful – with an acquisition rate well above the average – than Smarties. The reason? The M&Ms

characters. As I write this, and as you read it, I don't even have to explain what they are because most likely you are already picturing them in your mind. In comparison, you are probably unable to recall anything about Smarties. That is the power of brand. It is the seeding of memories, which is powered in the main, by distinctiveness.

It does seem strange that marketers struggle with the distinction between the two, because the courts don't. The legal system protects the interests of the consumers first and foremost, and so, even if Smarties had tried to claim that Mars had stolen the idea of the product, the court would cite benefit to the consumer and allow Mars to continue. The only caveat to this, of course, is when a company has a patent – but even then, patents are not typically granted in perpetuity and eventually retire. On the other hand, if, for argument's sake, Nestlé copied the M&Ms characters, the courts would say that these are protected symbols of Mars Incorporated, that they communicate to consumers where the product is coming from, and would protect Mars from the theft of those characters.

Thus, in general, the law does not protect differentiation but it does protect distinctiveness.

As a closing note, in very interesting findings by the Ehrenberg Bass Institute, it turns out that loyalty is also underpinned by salience. Again, we won't deep dive that here, but the takeaway is that distinctiveness plays a role throughout the entire marketing funnel, as well as the long-term profitability of the ongoing customer base.

***

That completes the positioning section, which means that we have now covered the famous STP of marketing: Segment, Target, and Positioning. Now let's complete the strategy pillar with a look at objectives and budgeting.

Objectives and Budgeting

This is the last component of strategy. It comprises the business level objectives that fall out of the process so far, the value of achieving them, and the investment that the company needs to consider in their pursuit. Let's start with objectives.

Objectives

As with any field of management, clearly stated objectives are very important because they provide the basis on which we measure success. It is also important to componentize the objectives so that we can deal with areas that need attention and leave alone those that do not, and in marketing terms, the "marketing funnel" is the primary tool supporting these management functions.

To inform the way that we think about the funnel, we first must make sure that we have defined the "big 3" of the strategy equations (Table 2.8):

Table 2.8 The Big 3

Who	... are we going after in our segmentation / mass market?
What	... are our objectives for our target segments?
How	... are we positioning to effect those goals?

As you can see, the linear theme continues. To set objectives properly, we must have done the work in the previous disciplines, so that we can get specific enough to be both actionable and measurable. This means allocating objectives by the stage of the marketing funnel. Equally, to construct our marketing funnel we will need to draw on the relevant data from our diagnostics work. You will note that I said, "construct". It is important that we don't just blindly adopt a popular funnel model – just Google the term and you will come across many – that may not be fit for purpose in our market and the way that it operates.

To do that, we need to understand the actual process the market goes through in making its decisions in the category. This process uses qualitative data to customize the marketing funnel, and the quantitative data to populate the overall percentages that are representative, as per the example below (Figure 2.5):

Figure 2.5 A Basic Marketing Funnel

From there, you want to calculate the conversion rate from one stage to the next. In this example, your data is telling you that 80% of your market is aware of your brand, and that 66% actively consider you. Instantly, this may tell you that you want to get to 100% (category and market depending). There is a potential first objective. You also know you have a conversion rate between Aware and Consider of 72.5%. Hence, you might set a specific objective to increase this. Notice as well, at least in this example, that there is only a 50% conversion rate between Consideration and Preference, and so many firms will have ambitions to increase this. There is your third objective. And so forth.

Given the financial data we obtained during our research, we can also estimate the increases in revenue associated to such improvements, and this gives us clear financial objectives to work with. Now, when it comes to funnels, I will repeat a fantastic piece of advice that my marketing professor gave to me, or at least, to our class. He asked us to imagine the funnel as a leaky pipe, where potential customers were "leaking out", and that our job was to be plumbers. He said:

- Look for the biggest hole.
- Look for the easiest one to fix.
- Look for further holes down the pipe.
- Don't try to fix too many at once.

This last part is key. You must address the market in the context of your resources. We might be able to increase these resources when it comes to budgeting, or we may not. Either way, this is another area in which to make prioritized choices, and some advocate restricting strategic objectives to between three and five in any given period. This plays into the final point I want to make about objectives: be smart about them. Management theory junkies will instantly know what I'm about to say, but for the rest of us, let me introduce you to SMART:

- **S**pecific.
- **M**easurable.
- **A**mbitious.
- **R**ealistic.
- **T**ime-related.

The term was first proposed by George T. Doran in the November 1981 issue of *Management Review*[22] and can be applied to any field of management. For example (Table 2.9):

Table 2.9 Poor versus SMART Objectives

A Poor Objective Statement	SMART Objective Statement
To increase our sales of shoes through increasing affinity and our marketing automation program.	To increase awareness in the "Digital Lopers" segment from 43% to 70% by the end of Q3, 2026.

See how all that work in the diagnostics pillar, and our resulting considered approach to targeting and positioning, is now informing our key objectives? This is the beauty of all industrial management processes.

Finally, you may have noticed that my funnel only consists of four stages. Most funnels do include later stages such as "re-purchase" or "loyalty". I will deal with this when we discuss the collision of marketing and customering in Chapter 8, so put a pin in this for now.

***

If we have done our job well, we have balanced our ambition with the reality of our circumstances and now we have:

- Specific funnel conversion objectives.
- Specific financial goals as a result.
- A timeline for the execution.

And that means we can now talk about budgeting.

Old School Budgeting

Historically, many companies treat marketing budgets as a maths exercise in the accounting department. Sitting in their silo, a million miles away from the realities of the market or any of the data of the diagnostics phase, and the careful decision making in the strategy disciplines, a simple formula is applied. There are different versions of this nonsense, but by and large they look something like this:

1. Finance looks at the current year's sales data.
2. They apply a basic compound annual growth rate.
3. They imagine next year's sales revenue.
4. They apply an advertising-to-sales ratio.

In this scenario, a marketing budget is magicked out of thin air and one of business's most strategic functions is reduced to standing in line like an orphan with their hand out, begging for their dinner.

> "Please sir, I want some more".

Of course, this dynamic is not the fault of finance teams. It is a direct result of the more general failure of marketing to become a bona fide profession and to behave like one, conditioning its colleagues to proper management practice. So, then, if that's not how to do it, how should companies be approaching this?

Welcome to Zero Sum Budgeting

First, we remove all assumptions about total spend. This is harder than it sounds, especially for fellow executives and even more so for those with finance backgrounds who, for very good reasons, must baseline company expenses and reduce them where appropriate. Second, unlike the finance department example above that simply assumed an advertising spend, there must be absolutely no assumptions about the value of spend on any particular tactic.

Instead, it requires a CMO or equivalent to sit down with the CFO or equivalent and work through the strategic marketing process, explaining to them how we need to arrive at an informed investment decision. Specifically, the marketing leader must convey that:

1. We complete market research annually.
2. We update STP (segmentation, targeting, and positioning).
3. We build a proper purchase funnel calibrated to our actual market.
4. We decide on a limited number of SMART objectives.
5. We calculate the value (e.g., revenue) of achieving them.

Then, and only then, is the company able to make an informed decision on the investment it is prepared to make in pursuit of that value. Again, linear management process in action.

Tactics

Tactics are the peaks of the marketing iceberg that are visible above the waves. They really are all that anyone unfamiliar with the significant bodies of work in both diagnostics and strategy, will ever see. Most only notice a campaign, perhaps an advertisement, a sponsorship, or other forms of communication, but, in truth, this represents roughly 7–10% of the marketing management process throughout any given year.

Now, you may have heard people talk about the "4 Ps of Marketing" – Product, -Price, Place, -Promotion. This is the idea that we execute our go-to-market program via the combination of four elements. In fact, many think that this is the entirety of the marketing process. They are wrong. The four are the components of the tactical pillar alone.

The origin of the 4 Ps is attributed to James Culliton, a Professor of Marketing at Harvard University.[23] In 1948, Culliton published an article[24] in which he likened marketers to "mixers" of ingredients and the term "marketing mix" was born. It is a clear and concise execution model advanced by marketing scholars and the industry alike, and provides the framework for applying diagnostics, strategy, and marketing science. Despite this, there have been the usual tinkerers who have proffered alternatives, such as 7 Ps, the 8 Ps, etc., which Professor Mark Ritson has expertly debunked – I recommend you read this article.[25]

Of course, as marketing has evolved to keep pace with wider business model evolution, and to cope with the proliferation of channels in the digital era, the 4 Ps have undergone some minor renaming, to Product, Pricing, Distribution, and the quite wordy "Integrated Marketing Communications", which many shorten to simply Integrated Communications, or further still to simply "Comms". Whatever you choose to call them though, they remain the four disciplines of this pillar (Table 2.10):

Table 2.10 The Four Ps

Original Term	Meaning	Contemporary Term
Product	What the business offers for sale and may include products or services, e.g., quality, features, benefits, style, design, packaging, warranties, guarantees, etc.	Product
Price	The price for each offering including variations by distribution (wholesale margin etc.), and its rules (payment terms etc.).	Price
Place	The direct or indirect channels to market, geographical distribution, catalogs, inventory, logistics, and order fulfillment; and may refer to alternative direct channels such self-service website versus a store or call center etc.	Distribution
Promotion	The communication to market. This may include advertising, public relations, sponsorship, and sales promotions etc.	Integrated Communications

Product

Phillip Kotler, known as the "father of modern marketing", is something of a legend in the field and for over 50 years has taught at the Kellogg School of Management. His book *Marketing Management* is reportedly the most widely used textbook in marketing around the world. On product he has this to say:

> A product is anything that can be offered to a market for attention, acquisition, use or consumption. It includes physical objects, services, personalities, places, organizations and ideas.[26]

Companies will sell commodities, products, services, experiences, either individually or in combination. This is their offering, and in many companies today, the decision making as it relates to that offering is not handled by marketing at all. Marketing is simply handed the offering and told to "market it". Others ensure, through the advocacy of a strong CMO who runs a robust diagnostics program, that marketing is a major voice in the process. In more mature organizations, product strategy resides in the marketing department, noting that this is a critical component of how the company is presented to the market. In other words, product decisions must be market-oriented. However, I acknowledge that all these scenarios exist.

Most Products Fail

It is telling that, depending on the citations you dig up, that there is between a 75% and 95%[27] failure rate for new products launched to market. Whatever the real number, which likely varies by category, there is little doubt that this is due to a lack of due diligence, misalignment to the market, and a failure to support the product adequately whether in pricing, distribution, or communications. Equally, many failures occur when companies branch into new categories without adequate understanding of them, or the product itself is just too revolutionary, or too early to market (i.e., ahead of its time). All this supports the argument for returning product decision making to the marketing department, or at least ensuring they are central in the work.

It's not just new products that fail, however. Sometimes the performance of long-standing products wanes. Companies must always be engaged in the process of:

- Considering new offerings.
- Modifying existing offerings.
- Killing established offerings.

Needs Over Features

This is where we introduce the Jobs To Be Done (JTBD) framework. It is one of the few management theories that has legitimacy in both marketing and customer management, albeit for different reasons. In Chapter 6 we will look at the critical role of JTBD – used in a dynamic state – in informing the Interaction pillar, but here in the marketing context JTBD provides an approach to expose the deeper consumer need required to deliver well aligned and successful offerings. Originally conceived in the pursuit of corporate innovation by Tony Ulrick,[28] marketing professors teach it in MBA-level curriculum for use in the strategy function. Clayton Christensen co-wrote the book *Competing Against Luck*,[29] in which he said:

> When we buy a product we essentially "hire" something to get a job done. If it does the job well, when we are confronted with the same job, we hire that same product again. And if the product does a crummy job, we "fire" it and look around for something else we might hire to solve the problem.

In other words, companies need to hone in on the job the prospective customer wishes to get done. For example, one of the examples Christensen writes about was a condo developer that was targeting retirees who wanted to downsize their homes. Sales were weak until the developers realized their business was not construction but transitioning lives. Instead of adding more features to the condos, they created services assisting buyers with the move and with their decisions about what to keep and to discard. Sales took off.

In Chapter 6 I will cover the workings of the Customer Engagement Stack (delivering existing customers a layered construct of services and experiences) which will reference this example as well, but in the context of *shaping* a company's offering, note that the condo developer altered its offering to meet the actual need – or the job – of the customer, and as a result the core product became successful. Thus, building a clear understanding of need is far more powerful in product development than other methods. In short:

1. Understand the job.
2. Deliver an offering that does that job.
3. Make sure your communications address the job, not the product.

Just to state the obvious, the data needed to take this approach all comes from the diagnostics pillar. Specifically, it relies on market orientation, behavioral segmentation, and ethnography, and, I should add, must be aligned to the strategy, in particular our SMART objectives. Again, the linear flow of an industrial management model in action.

Extensions

Assuming of course, that a company has followed the above methods in aligning its offering to the market, there are a range of options. One of those is to extend a line, or indeed, a brand.

Brand Extensions

A brand extension seeks to trade on the established trust and salience of an existing company or offering. It relies on consumers feeling safe in buying a new offering from a company because that company is a known entity, and it leverages the long tail of brand investment that has been happening over a long period of time. It may even allow for that company to sell a new line at a premium price, should that be the location of its inherent brand position.

For example, Audi is able to sell branded ancillary products – such as car seat covers, floor mats, mobile phone accessories, roof racks, and sunglass holders – to people who already have that brand affinity. These people know that they could buy the same products elsewhere, and probably at equivalent quality with a lower price, but choose the Audi-branded products instead. We see the same approach from luxury watch brands and clothing brands who start to sell sunglasses, such as Tag Heuer and Versace.

In a totally different setting, such as personal services, the value is not in the premium nature of a brand but in the utility value, or convenience qualities. We have seen telecommunications companies begin to offer subscriptions to Netflix, sports coverage, and energy bundles. We have seen energy retailers do the same in reverse. In fact, almost all industries that are diversifying are often relying on brand extensions to do so. There is often more risk associated with a brand extension. What if the new product isn't perceived as in keeping with the key brand positioning of the company? Do people want to associate coffee cup holders with Audi? And what if that new product failed in some way? Could the rapidly increasing costs of supplying energy impact negatively on how consumers see our telecommunications brand? Could we incur brand damage? Are we best to stick tightly to our knitting?

But where there is higher risk, there is often higher return. Finding success in a whole new offering creates entirely separate lines of revenue that may be immune to the economic headwinds of core offerings. Again, only quality market diagnostics can help to answer those questions. Never forget the humility of marketing.

Line Extensions

Often considered a safer bet than a brand extension, albeit with potentially less reward, a line extension stays within the core offering. Many premium brands now offer a value (cheaper) offering. Sometimes a brand has several options in the one category – watches, for example – to cater to several needs. It may be simply to frame the preferred offering: we'll talk about framing in the next section on pricing. Or, as the extension proposition suggests, it may be to cater to a different segment of the market. For example, a brand may have a range of dress watches and extend into sports watches, or smart watches, and so on. Some brands will also cater to a new segment simply to protect their most important one. A retail bank may offer generous – and loss-making – saving accounts for school children together with fee-free debit cards as part of a longer-term strategy to gain their loyalty and move them into higher yield products as they move into adulthood, and eventually the holy grail, a mortgage. This is not extending the brand into whole new offerings. Rather, it is merely extending the existing offering.

Co-branding

Another product tactic companies use is partnering with another brand to provide co-branded offerings. This can serve to increase your brand's reach, affecting both salience and attitudes toward it, by aligning an offering with another brand. Each company enriches the other, advancing their respective position in important segments that share similarities. Additionally, or centrally, the partnership may provide reach into new geographies. A usually lesser, but nevertheless potentially valuable consideration is the ability to share the cost of the program.

Many have said that co-branding is also a chance for a less established brand to leverage the trust or brand affinity of their partner, advancing their own brand. Of course, in theory this is true for a lesser player, but in practice any partnership must deliver mutual value and an established company is unlikely to risk its brand on one that doesn't. Case in point, consider the prominent examples of co-branding below.[30]

- GoPro and Red Bull.
- The ill-fated Kanye and Adidas (or Kanye and anyone, to be fair to Adidas).
- BMW and Louis Vuitton.
- Starbucks and Spotify.
- Apple and MasterCard.
- Levi's and Pinterest.
- Amazon and American Express.
- UNICEF and Target.
- Bonne Belle and Dr. Pepper.
- Taco Bell and Doritos.

While each brand has different positioning and target segments, it will be important that they have at least strategic synergies in both elements, pre-existing standing in their own categories, and a stark difference from the other.

Pricing

As I keep saying, I am touching on all the pillars of marketing at about a million-foot view. None of these sections are remotely exhaustive, but it could be argued that this section in particular is more like a trillion-foot view! Pricing is a *big* subject.

Of course, pricing is the rubber hitting the road. It is the point at which the value exchange occurs. Get it wrong and you may not attract your market at all. Get it wrong and you may lose entire segments. Get it wrong and you may compromise, if not destroy, the profitability of the company. It is simply so important that major and diverse names across the business world have all felt the need to comment.

The single most important decision in evaluating a business is pricing power.

— Warren Buffett

Pricing is by far the biggest tool for earnings improvement.

— McKinsey & Co

You know you're priced right when your customers complain – but buy anyway.

— John Harrison

Lowering prices is easy. Being able to afford to lower prices is hard.

— Jeff Bezos

The moment you make a mistake in pricing, you're eating into your reputation or your profits.

— Katharine Paine

Basic Theory

Two simple words, "pricing theory", headline a subject that would take a book, or three, to begin to cover. And you wouldn't read it anyway, because there is already a lot out there written by experts in the field, which I am not. Nevertheless, this section will give you an introduction to the topic and, as always, show how the linear management model informs this critical discipline.

Sadly, a common form of pricing is "cost-plus", in which the company calculates the cost to produce an offering, decides upon the margin that it wishes to make, and sets its price. Whether or not the market accepts that price is entirely down to luck. What about the ratio of volume to value, and the impact the price has on the company's brand? Of course, cost can be hard to define once you combine all fixed and variable costs, and try to distill that into a unit cost, so often this is wrong to start with, and obviously it is not remotely market-oriented.

The other big problem is that companies that don't know how to price almost always default to under-pricing and discounting and thus erode their profits, sometimes critically. Under-pricing is a bit of disease; it eats away at the health of a business by reducing revenues and profit, undermines brand perception, diminishes equity, traps a business at a low price point, and makes it more vulnerable to price wars. In short, the net result of under-pricing, over time, can be terminal.

Discounting has very similar effects. Like under-pricing, it is very difficult to get out of, because once a company has trained its market to wait for the discount it is almost impossible to reverse. This happens to big companies as well. Most of the global enterprise software businesses – some of the largest companies in the world – have trained their corporate customers to buy from them in the final quarter of the financial year, and even to wait until the very end of the quarter when the internal pressure to close the year strongly is at its highest.

It also leaves the business open to being commoditized, unable to trade on value. It diminishes the brand and thus potential customer loyalty, and it can signal weakness to the market. One facet of this that stood out to me when I was studying this subject was that discounting is ultimately using a negative tactic to resolve inadequacies of strategy.

The Impact on Profitability

There are four levers for company profitability – sales, price, fixed costs, and variable costs – and they are all interrelated. However, many companies seek to lower their costs as much as possible and discount in the market.

Yet a common benchmark is that if a company reduces fixed costs by 1% it can increase profit by 2.5%, while increasing sales by 1% serves to increases profit by 3%. Equally, when a company reduces its variables by 1% it will increase profit by 6.5%, compared to increasing price by 1%, which will increase profit by 10%. So, while there is no doubt that reducing costs is good for profit, the more powerful levers to pull are sales and price. Just think about that for a moment. Now, consider the impact of routine discounts …

So, then, if cost-plus pricing doesn't work, and if under-pricing and discounting are toxic to overall business performance, what to do?

Value Pricing Thermometer

The "Value Pricing Thermometer" (Figure 2.6) was developed in 2009.[31]

In this model, which you can interact with here,[32] product price represents the internal drivers of pricing (e.g., "cost-plus"); perceived value represents the perception of the customer as to the value of the offering; and objective value represents the value of the product to consumers relative to alternatives, irrespective of whether customers recognize that value.

Objective value is also referred to as the so-called "true economic value", which I resile from. Ultimately, it is always the market that defines true economic value, not a mathematical model devoid of the human beings central to the outcome. This is the classic case for "complex" economics. To give Dolan

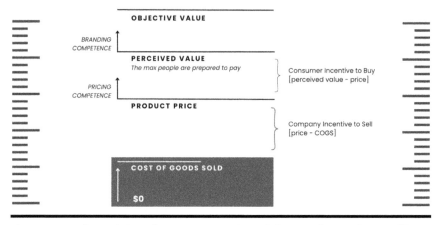

Figure 2.6 Value Pricing Thermometer (adapted from Dolan and Gourville 2009)

and Gourville their due, they acknowledge that it is the perceived value that is representative of the maximum price consumers are willing to pay.

The trick for all companies, then, is to find the point at which the price is optimized for the market so that penetration is not compromised while profit is not diminished. In short, they need to price their offerings at or as close to perceived value as possible. Of course, the perception of a company's or a brand's value is affected by the position and status of the brand, and this is not a rational, not mathematical, equation. This is why complex economics – the economic value derived from the non-rational human behavior – has such an important role to play in all aspects of both marketing and customering. In the case of pricing, this gives rise to a range of tactics – namely, framing, bundling, and rundling.

Price Framing

When you think about it, you will probably recognize that this is a very common practice of online subscription businesses. In essence, the tactic is to present (for example) three options. The first is the low-value option: cheap, but without the key features your market research has told you is most desired, or with some other material limitation. The other end of the extreme is quite expensive with lots of extra features, usually one the market research has identified as "nice to haves" without being essential. Finally, the middle option, which is the offering the business wants you to buy – and is usually the most profitable – is based on the core needs of the market. The first two options, while available, are primarily there to frame the price of the middle option.

In many cases, companies will even prompt potential buyers by promoting the middle option as "most popular".

Price Anchoring

Anchoring is like framing, but the reference is usually used in support of an offer. For example:

■ "Usually $120. Today only $95".

The anchor is, of course, the $120 price, against which the recipient of the message will base their decision on whether they want to take advantage of the lower price. A common tactic within anchoring is to make the offer time-bound, to create more urgency and make the value exchange explicit. Essentially, if you buy now, you get to save money; if you don't, you don't. But it only works with an anchor.

Price Bundling

You've also seen this plenty. Instead of a company using framing to incentivize customers to a particular offering, it uses bundling to incentivize the purchase of more than one offering. For example:

■ Snorkel set:	$300
■ Wetsuit:	$700
■ Snorkel set and wetsuit bundle:	$850

Price Rundling

This one is little less obvious; a rundle is a "recurring revenue bundle" and is very common, again, in businesses that want to drive an ongoing subscription or services. Apple do this a lot. A customer can subscribe to Music, or to Music and Arcade, or to Music, Arcade, and News, or to Music, Arcade, News, and iCloud, and that's all before they rundle in products – like an iPhone.

Price Researching

To really get your price points and tactics right, pricing research will use qualitative methods to test pricing positions and surveys to scale the directional findings. The van Westendorp Sensitivity Meter was introduced in 1976 by Dutch economist Peter van Westendorp. The question formats can vary but generally follow a similar format to the below:

■ At what price would you consider the product to be so expensive that you would not consider buying it? (Too expensive).

- At what price would you consider the product to be priced so low that you would feel the quality couldn't be very good? (Too cheap).
- At what price would you consider the product starting to get expensive, so that it is not out of the question, but you would have to give some thought to buying it? (Expensive/High Side).
- At what price would you consider the product to be a bargain – a great buy for the money? (Cheap/Good Value).

The cumulative frequencies are then plotted, and their intersection is regarded as informative for price optimization[33] (Figure 2.7):

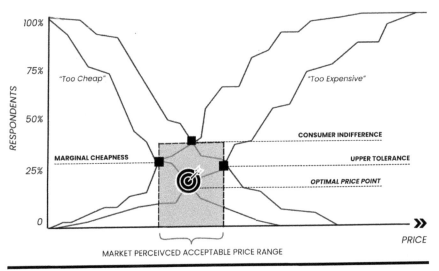

Figure 2.7 Example of The Van Westendorp Price Sensitivity Meter (Based on Van Westendorp 1976)

Finally, many companies also engage in live experimentation with their pricing. Perhaps most famous, or infamous, is the case of Amazon. In 2020 the giant e-commerce retailer was forced to issue an apology, and refunds, for its price testing program, which charged some customers more than others for the same products. But the company denied claims that the different prices charged were based on demographic information collected from customers, which is what many accused them of. In fact, they were experimenting to try to find the right price point for specific offerings, by testing on live customers. The company's price levels were varied "on a totally random basis" in an attempt to determine how sales would be affected by lower prices, with CEO Jeff Bezos commenting:

We've never tested, and we never will test prices based on customer demographics.[34]

I am sure that the experiment did yield very useful data, and I suspect that, demographics aside, those learnings will have been applied in the context of market segments. Amazon is one of the most forward-thinking companies in the world and so an advanced approach to researching price is no surprise. And yet its 2020 experience is an example of the potential perils of the practice, particularly reputationally.

Despite this, there are many who advocate the practice of "dynamic pricing"[35] – which has been further enabled by technology and is now a product feature of major e-commerce platform vendors. Aside from the wider reputational issues, which only really stem from the media coverage, the main risk of these types of experimentation is creating potential friction for existing customers, as distinct from the market, which has an impact on relative value assessment by each impacted individual. To quote Bezos again:

> What we did was a random price test, and even that was a mistake because it created uncertainty for customers rather than simplifying their lives …

So, experimentation can be powerful, but even in its most advanced and seemingly covert digital form, extremely risky.

That concludes our whistle-stop tour of the complex subject of pricing. Again, you'll see the value of the prior pillars and disciplines informing this one.

Distribution

Distribution is simply the modes by which a company delivers its offerings to market. Some have a direct relationship with their customers, others a disaggregated one – meaning they sell through third parties – while some use both modes. For instance, Dulux is a major paint manufacturer in Australia and New Zealand. In each country they have appointed retailers, who carry the Dulux range. They have also appointed independent trade centers that serve the commercial market. Both of these operate their own independent businesses.

At the same time, Dulux owns and operates its own "Dulux Centers", serving both retail and commercial markets. For businesses trading internationally, there may be more than one vertical partner in the distribution model, because there is often the company's own local office, then distributors and wholesalers involved, before the product lands at the retailer (Table 2.11):

Table 2.11 Distribution Channels

Vertical Model	Horizontal Models			
Brand	Brand	Brand	Brand	Brand
Direct to Consumer	⇓	⇓	⇓	Local Subsidiary
			Distributor	Distributor
		Wholesaler	Wholesaler	Wholesaler
	Retailer	Retailer	Retailer	Retailer

In a further layer of complexity, a relationship with a large retailer may bypass the wholesaler layer entirely (Table 2.12):

Table 2.12 Wholesaler Bypass

Brand
⇓
Distributor
⇓
Retailer

All of this creates channel-management requirements – how to avoid or minimize conflicts and streamline logistics – as well as pricing considerations. There must be adequate margin for each of the businesses to be viable, and price consistency – in alignment with the manufacturer's brand position and objectives (in this case, Dulux itself) – must be maintained.

In contemporary terms, the word "channel" has also taken on the meaning of customer engagement points. As technology has evolved these have proliferated, a source of the common confusion between marketing and customer management with which I deal in this book. "Channel management" now also incorporates web versus store, versus mobile, versus contact center, and so on. We had a mono-channel for so long, which became dual channel, and eventually – for some – omni-channel. As you will see in the discussion of customer management, we aspire to be channel-less. More on that later.

In this context, a marketing channel is anywhere that a potential customer can interact with, or purchase, your brand (Table 2.13):

Table 2.13 Mono to Omni

Historical mono-channel	Multi-channel	Omni-channel
Store/s	Store/s Web Contact center	Store/s Partner store Web(s) Contact center Partner contact center Service agents Sales reps Mobile app(s) Chatbots Interactive voice response (IVR) etc.

In addition, channels can become even more convoluted. If we stay with the Dulux example, it is not just the company's website but also those of its different retailing partners that must be considered. Finally, the contractual controls between the parties can ensure appropriate governance and protections, while maintaining the independence of each entity. And so, when you peel back the layers, distribution is a more complex discipline than a cursory glance might first suggest.

Advantages and Disadvantages of Separated Distribution

For companies like Dulux and many others, there are huge benefits that stem from such a structure. Separate capital structures mean that the cost of stored inventory, as one example, is spread across the players. Equally, there is a natural mitigation of risk against one part of the supply chain failing. Knowledge of the local market and economic conditions is usually more prevalent in each local supplier. Generally, the closer you are to the customer, the better you understand them, although it is very important that master brands do not abdicate their responsibility for diagnostics, central as it is to their entire strategy and objectives.

Many brands that focus on manufacturing or distributing simply do not have a strong retail competence, which is a complex business model in and of itself, and therefore appoint retail partners to add real strength to the quality of not only the access to market, but the perceptions of the brand as well. We have seen the significant rise of retail brands in recent years, which means that a product brand can leverage the pulling power of its partner. Lastly, because retailers stock lines that are most likely to generate cross- and up-sell opportunities for their customer base, there is in an intrinsic likelihood that each stocked brand will benefit from other products in the same store, and often in the most delicious way possible: sales.

And yet, there are also real advantages to a direct model.

The first is obvious. It is much cheaper. The fewer layers of distribution involved, the fewer mouths to feed, means that there is a significantly higher margin between the production cost and the recommended retail price.

Secondly, you are closer to your market and eventual customers, which means above all else you have first-party data – a subject we'll talk about in the next chapter – enabling richer insights that are most relevant to your activation initiatives. Customer proximity is never a bad thing unless, as is unfortunately the trap many brands fall into, their poor treatment of customers is more damaging to them because it is up close and personal. I'll return to that in several parts of this book.

Of course, the absence of third parties selling your products makes life a lot simpler too. There is no competition within your own go-to-market apparatus, no politics, and in many cases, at least in perception, it can be a much faster model simply because there are fewer moving parts. Nor do you have to consider the ripple effects of a strategic objective, or an unplanned initiative, on the workings of the downstream supply chain.

Consider, as well, that the rise of retailers also has potential negative consequences. What if their brand is more powerful than yours, and they are able to wield market power to your detriment? What about the risk of private labels? In Australia, there is duopoly in the fast-moving consumer goods arena, and both of the giant supermarket companies have been accused of using brands to establish a segment, only to then undercut them with their own "home" brands, thereby taking up a competitive manufacturing position vis-à-vis their original partners. In particular, this has hurt local food growers (farmers) who are losing the family farm as the grocery behemoths decimate their margins.

But there are other less obvious abuses of market power. What if a large retailer refuses to sell your product at the price that is set and, in doing so, creates channel conflict with other participants, or runs discount offers on your product that undermine your pricing strategy and impact negatively on the brand?

No such issues are found in the direct model, which is part of the attraction.

D2C

In the decade ending 2019, we saw the significant rise of a model called direct-to-customer, routinely shorted to "D2C". This emerged from three primary sources:

1. Traditional consumer products companies who sought the benefits of a simplified distribution model as described above.

2. Break-away executives of a traditional business seeking to create a new business model in the industry they had significant experience within.
3. The arrival of young new entrants seeking to "disrupt" established industries.

Each party was fueled by the arrival of digital capability and, quite often, by the idea of applying subscription models.

The last group (young new entrants) is typically a fervent one. While they lack some of the inherent knowledge and infrastructure, they have been spurred along by the almost cult-like energy that surrounds the digital era. As outsiders, they often make a lot of assumptions that can come back to haunt them, although they have also furnished several success stories. They were, and are, easy to spot.

■ Everything is digital-first. Bricks and mortar are swear-words or regarded as the language of dinosaurs.
■ They love the word "disruption", and their founders will take any opportunity to speak at start-up events at which they will utter the term on high-repeat, as though they were being paid per utterance.
■ They often use the word "experience" on a similar loop, although, like most in the populist CX movement, they have no critical understanding of it.
■ Speaking of start-ups, they also revel in that ecosystem, which is fueled by the same digital-socio-philosophies.
■ They often have brand names that rely on shortened wordplay (e.g. Netflix).

This group often lacks the business gravitas to really chase success. Almost of them are heavily dependent on external funding, to the extent that original founders eventually had their equity position so drastically diminished that they were no longer working for themselves, and most lack the marketing expertise to properly validate their proposition, establish brand, or price with discipline, as just a few examples. It was trendy for a time for these businesses to be unprofitable as they "built community", which was lucky because very few of them were. Naturally, that could not be sustain, especially when the capital markets tightened due to recessionary fears and inflationary pressures which they are prone to do cyclically.

In contrast, companies seeking to disrupt their own distribution model are usually operating from a place of financial strength and have advantages in the form of industry experience and brand penetration etc., albeit they are making a gigantic strategic change that comes with serious risk (as all serious strategy does). And as for the industry-experienced executives leaving the incumbents to establish a new business model, perhaps a middle ground between the two other groups, they lack have an established brand to leverage which makes them similar to the younger start-up brigade, but they do have a depth of business experience, industry knowledge, and a better lens on the real gaps.

The question for all of them, however, as we apply the humility of marketing once more, is whether their perceptions of the gaps are *market* gaps, and whether such perceptions are indeed, material realities.

Bringing It Together

As you can tell, distribution decisions must be made on the basis of the strategic market objectives of the company. The management model requires a range of inputs to be considered (Table 2.14):

Table 2.14 Model Considerations

Where does the market want most to buy?	Are customs established, or are they movable?
Do we have access to the market ourselves?	And if not, how can we obtain that access?
How many players does the pricing research indicate can be sustained with acceptable margins?	How many specifically? Irrespective of the pricing capacity, what is the optimal profit model, over time?
What is the core competency of the business?	And if we are to venture into new areas, how will we ensure capability and success?
Is lower margin at higher volume, or higher margin at lower margin optimal?	For our brand (and or our business)? For our profit?
Are we a category that can sustain market orientation despite a separation from day-to-day customers?	Category and strategy specific
Who will "own" the customer relationship?	And what of the data outcomes?
Do we have the infrastructure to manage channel volume?	And is it feasible to alter our model?

Getting this right is important. As the great Philip Kotler remarked:

> Too much of today's marketing is 1P marketing. Companies mainly concentrate on promotion and sales and disregard product, price and place (distribution). This results in ineffective marketing.[36]

Integrated Marketing Communications

Here it is, the final – yet, ironically, by far the highest profile – discipline within the tactical pillar of marketing. This is all most people see, but by now you will know that every advertisement or promotion or sponsorship exists, if the company paying for them knows what it is doing, because of well-defined strategy informed by sound market diagnostics. In fact, one could argue – and many do – that integrated marketing communications (IMC) represents only about 8% of marketing, being that it is one quarter of the 4 Ps, which are themselves only one of the three pillars.

The reason we have moved on from the initial label, "promotion", to IMC speaks to the evolution of the field and, again, the arrival of technology that has increased the ways in which a brand can communicate. Historically, the marketing industry would talk about "above the line" (ATL) and "below the line" (BTL), which really just meant running an advertising campaign (ATL) and complementing it with a range of promotions (BTL). The latter was limited to instore activities and B2B sales teams. In the 1990s, BTL activities evolved to include public relations and direct marketing, which referred to messaging not conducted through the intermediary of newspapers, radio, television, etc. Instead, it included mail, email, and then, eventually, social media and texting.

Sponsorship, interestingly, also took off in the 1990s. It had its origins way back in 330 BCE, when rich Roman elites sponsored the gladiator games to garner public affection,[37] starting a relationship with sport and other events that continues to this day. Most of the artwork of the Renaissance was sponsored[38] by private families, banks, or academic bodies, and the famous Medici dynasty used sponsorship as a vehicle to increase the family's strength via its banks in Italy and elsewhere in Europe. Sponsorship really began to take hold in the modern era, after the invention of the television in 1927.[39] Both TV and radio were central to the family experience and brands sought to harness their influence by sponsoring programs. But it was in the late 1980s and 90s that corporate sponsorships really took off.[40] As broadcast capabilities improved, major sports events, stadiums, and even the players became sponsorship properties.

All in all, the communications options available to marketers were rapidly multiplying, and then something even bigger happened. The internet arrived, and everyone lost their minds.

Suddenly there was a populist groundswell of people claiming that the classic model of ATL and BTL was redundant. The answer, no matter the question, was the internet. Advertising should be via the internet. Promotions should be via the internet. Direct marketing should by via the internet. Even public relations, some believed, should be via the internet. Inevitably, as critical thinking found its voice again, there came the pushback, and thus began a long debate – in which many are still mired today – as to whether we should focus on digital go-to-market means or "traditional" avenues.

This was, and remains, one of the silliest and most ignorant debates in business. Firstly, the most obvious principle applies: your tactics should be dictated by your strategy, and that must be dictated by the market itself. We should never, ever, start a conversation from the point of a tactic.

Aside from the impact on genuine strategy and effectiveness, there are two day-to-day problems that afflict such a mindset.

1. If we start with a tool, we predefine the problem to fit (hammer/nail).
2. The premise of the divide is false to begin with.

This second point is fundamental. The way we do things changes all the time, in keeping with the level of technology capability of any given era. We used to use horse and cart, but then along came the motor car. The *thing* we did – going from point A to point B – didn't change, but how we did so changed dramatically. So why do those who are determined to debate digital versus traditional not realize that most "traditional" forms of media are now absolutely *digital*?

■ What the industry still calls "print media" (e.g., newspapers) is now all online.
■ Roadside billboards are often digital or at the least use modern rapid digital printing capability.
■ Over 80% of direct marketing is digital.
■ Radio is now delivered digitally.
■ Television is delivered using digital streaming (e.g., Netflix) and satellite.

The truth is that there really is no such divide; it is an imaginary dichotomy, made popular by the cult-like obsession with the word "digital". As Nicholas Negroponte once said:

> Like air and drinking water, being digital will be noticed only by its absence, not its presence.[41]

It is easy to see why the word "integrated" is so important to the term integrated marketing communications. We no longer talk about ATL and BTL in their historical context. Some do take ATL to mean paid media and BTL to mean earned media, but most academics do not. Equally, at least in educated circles, we do not talk about digital versus traditional media. Instead, we talk about IMC, and how to wield it for the greatest effect. Don Edward Schultz (1934–2020), Professor Emeritus of Service at Northwestern University's Medill School and noted for his research and writing on IMC, once said:

> Integrated Marketing Communications … ensures that all forms of communications and messages are carefully linked together … At its most basic level … it means integrating all the promotional tools so that they work together in harmony.[42]

What to Integrate?

Having made the points as plain as possible above, there remains a valid discussion about what parts of the communications buffet we should eat from, and indeed, as the late great Professor Shultz said, how we integrate them. Of course, by now you should expect me to tell you that this depends on your strategy. Who is that you are targeting, what is your positioning, and what are your objectives? Beyond this most core principle though, there is good evidence about the performance of different media types most notably in the report *Media in Focus: Marketing Effectiveness in the Digital Era*, by Binet and Field,[43] which exposes the difference in effects between brand and activation, depending on media type. When one returns to their objectives, this kind of information is very helpful.

But remember, the word "integrated" implies the application of different media, not just selecting one based on effectiveness data. Analytic Partners specializes in marketing measurement, and their recent studies[44] shows the compound effect of applying media together (Figure 2.8):

There is a lot of data from various sources to back this up. In just one example, the Institute of Practitioners in Advertising found that by adding old school newspaper advertising to social media campaigns, it increased performance by 118%. Listen carefully, and you can probably hear the digirati cry.

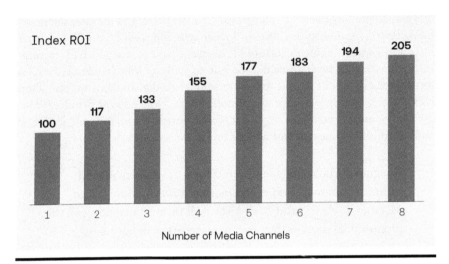

Figure 2.8 Layering and Stacking Marketing Activities by Analytic Partners

Again, there's a lot more to this subject, including specific models for investment and the need to both select and brief agencies well, etc. Equally, I have not remotely discussed brand management in detail, or ventured into the world of creative. For now, the major management takeaways of this section are:

- Don't assume the media (ever!).
- Start with the strategy: Targeting, Positioning, Objectives (or mass market) and Budgeting.
- Then, and only then, pick the tools to get the job done.
- Integrate. Integrate. Integrate! (use them in combination for the best effect).

Notes

1. Charlotte Rogers, "Salary Survey 2019: The Majority of Marketers Don't Have a Marketing Qualification," *Marketing Week*, July 31, 2019. https://www.marketingweek.com/salary-survey-2019-routes-into-marketing/.
2. "Mini MBA in Marketing With Mark Ritson."
3. Philip Kotler, *Marketing Management: Analysis, Planning, and Control* (Prentice Hall, 1972), p. 42.
4. Francis Gouillart and Frederick D. Sturdivant, "Spend a Day in the Life of Your Customers," *Harvard Business Review*, January–May 1994. https://hbr.org/1994/01/spend-a-day-in-the-life-of-your-customers.
5. John C. Narver and Stanley F. Slater, "The Effect of a Market Orientation on Business Profitability," *Journal of Marketing* 54, no. 4 (1990): 20–35.

6. Geraldine E. Willigan, "High-Performance Marketing: An Interview with Nike's Phil Knight," *Harvard Business Review*, July–August 1992. https://hbr.org/1992/07/high-performance-marketing-an-interview-with-nikes-phil-knight.

7. Rohit Deshpandé and John U. Farley, *Understanding Market Orientation: A Prospectively Designed Meta-Analysis of Three Market Orientation Scales* (Working Paper No. 96-125, Marketing Science Institute, 1996). https://ci.nii.ac.jp/ncid/BA34211816.

8. Kenneth W. Green Jr. and R. Anthony Inman, "Measuring Market Orientation in the Manufacturing Sector Using the MORTN Scale," *International Journal of Innovation and Learning* 4, no. 3 (2007): 209.

9. The term "behavioral" is used very narrowly here.

10. https://www.geotribes.com.

11. ESOV is a planning framework used to determine the right marketing spend linked to the overall growth objective. CEPs are the cues that category buyers use to access their memories when faced with a buying situation.

12. Amir Fazli and Jeffrey D. Shulman, "Implications of Market Spillovers," *Management Science* 64, no. 11 (2018): 4996–5013.

13. Les Binet and Peter Field, *The Long and the Short of It: Balancing Short and Long-Term Marketing Strategies* (Institute of Practitioners in Advertising, 2013).

14. Daniel Kahneman, "Of 2 Minds: How Fast and Slow Thinking Shape Perception and Choice" [Excerpt], *Scientific American*, June 15, 2015. https://www.scientificamerican.com/article/kahneman-excerpt-thinking-fast-and-slow/.

15. Byron Sharp, *How Brands Grow: What Marketers Don't Know* (Oxford University Press, 2010).

16. Al Ries and Jack Trout, *Positioning: The Battle for Your Mind* (McGraw Hill Professional, 2001).

17. Steven R. H. Barrett et al., "Impact of the Volkswagen Emissions Control Defeat Device on US Public Health," *Environmental Research Letters* 10, no. 11 (2015), 114005.

18. Simply Psychology, *Maslow's Hierarchy of Needs*, 2024, January 24. https://www.simplypsychology.org/maslow.html.

19. https://www.antmurphy.m

20. https://www.allblacks.com.

21. Kevin Lane Keller, "Reflections on Customer-Based Brand Equity: Perspectives, Progress, and Priorities," *AMS Review* 6, no. 1–2 (2016): 1–16.

22. George T. Doran, "There's a S.M.A.R.T. Way to Write Management's Goals and Objectives," *Management Review* 70, no. 11 (1981): 35–36.

23. Jon Groucutt, Peter Leadley, and Patrick Forsyth, *Marketing: Essential Principles, New Realities* (Kogan Page, 2004).

24. Donald F. Mulvihill, "James W. Culliton: The Management of Marketing Costs" [Review], *Southern Economic Journal* 15, no. 4 (1949): 488-489, p. 488.

25. Mark Ritson, "Attempts to Update the Four Ps Are Embarrassing – They've Endured for a Reason," *Marketing Week*, March 3, 2021. https://www.marketingweek.com/mark-ritson-stop-reinventing-four-ps/.

26. Kotler, *Marketing Management*.

27. Geraldo Diego, "Product Innovation: 95% of New Products Miss the Mark" [Blog post], *MIT Professional Education*, October 2, 2023. https://professionalprograms.mit.edu/blog/design/why-95-of-new-products-miss-the-mark-and-how-yours-can-avoid-the-same-fate/.

28. Strategyn LLC, "Tony Ulwick | Innovation Expert," *Strategyn*, July 19, 2023. https://strategyn.com/tony-ulwick/.

29. Clayton M. Christensen, Taddy Hall, Karen Dillon, and David S. Duncan, *Competing Against Luck: The Story of Innovation and Customer Choice* (Harvard Business School, 2016).

30. Sophia Bernazzani Barron, "21 Examples of Successful Co-Branding Partnerships" [Blog post], *HubSpot*, June 15, 2023. https://blog.hubspot.com/marketing/best-cobranding-partnerships.

31. Robert J. Dolan and John T. Gourville, *Principles of Pricing* (Harvard Business School, 2009).

32. "The Value-Pricing Thermometer," no date, https://s3.amazonaws.com/he-assets-prod/interactives/069_value_pricing_thermometer/Launch.html.

33. https://themaykin.com/blog/a-complete-guide-to-van-westendorp-how-to-graph-it-in-excel

34. ABC News, "Amazon Error May End 'Dynamic Pricing'," *ABC News*, January 7, 2006. https://abcnews.go.com/Technology/story?id=119399&page=1.

35. Dynamic pricing, also called real-time pricing, is an approach to setting the cost for a product or service that is highly flexible, and can change in the moment, based on data that indicates higher or lower demand in general or by groups. This can occur at the market level, or customer level, though not without risk. "Surge" pricing by Uber is one obvious market-level example, although this is scheduled as opposed to truly dynamic.

36. Kotler, *Marketing Management.*

37. Elevent, "Sponsorship History Part 1" [Blog post], *Elevent*, 2022. https://elevent.co/sponsorship-history-part-1/.

38. Aline Cohen, "How Italian Renaissance Art Was Used for Political and Religious Power," *Artsy*, August 21, 2018. https://www.artsy.net/article/artsy-editorial-italian-renaissance-wealthy-patrons-art-power.

39. Cornell Computer Science Department, "The History of Television (Or, How Did This Get So Big?)," *Cornell University*, no date. https://www.cs.cornell.edu/~pjs54/Teaching/AutomaticLifestyle-S02/Projects/Vlku/history.html.

40. Elsie Bernaiche, "Brief History of Sponsorship" [Blog post], *Thought Leaders*, April 7, 2022. https://www.thoughtleaders.io/blog/brief-history-of-sponsorship.

41. WIRED Staff, "Negroponte," *WIRED*, December 1, 1998. https://www.wired.com/1998/12/negroponte-55/.

42. Don E. Schultz, Robert F. Lauterborn, and Stanley Tannenbaum, *Integrated Marketing Communications: Putting It Together and Making It Work* (McGraw-Hill Education, 1993).

43. Les Binet and Peter Field, *Media in Focus: Marketing Effectiveness in the Digital Era* (Institute of Practitioners in Advertising, 2017).

44. Trent Huxley, "Maximizing Your Investment as Online and Offline Ad Efficiency Converge," *Analytic Partners*, April 2, 2019. https://analyticpartners.com/blog/maximizing-investment-online-offline-ad-efficiency/; Analytic Partners, "Digital Marketing Is Good. Digital Alone Is Bad," March 21, 2024, https://analyticpartners.com/roi-genome/2023-roi-genome-omnichannel-report/.

Chapter 3

The Customering Method

If you are a customer management practitioner, or an untrained marketer, I hope the last chapter provided a working knowledge of the formal pillars that form the field of marketing. It is my hope that you will now consider two things.

1. The functions of marketing are specifically designed to achieve market-level outcomes and have been refined over decades of scholarly investigation and practice. They are not "playthings" to be imported into customer management. They belong where they belong, in marketing.
2. The marketing vocation comprises a clear set of management processes and methodologies that require significant knowledge and expertise to execute, which stands in stark contrast to the populist and noisy scattering of CX mantras, all absent a governing model.

The term "customering", as I had initially begun to use it in 2015, was simply a shorthand for "customer management" as distinct from marketing. If one side of the proverbial coin is addressing the wider market, the other side is hosting and serving members of that market who have chosen to interact with the company at the present time. Just as "market" is the root word of marketing, so too is custom, then customer, the root of customering (Figure 3.1):

DOI: 10.4324/9781003513728-4

Figure 3.1 Market and Customering Are Counterparts (Spinley 2024)

About the time that I began to prepare to publish this book, I became aware of another's quite separate origination of the term. That other is Jim Gilmore, one half of the famed Pine and Gilmore duo who together wrote *The Experience Economy*, which I cite in this book. Joe Pine, a friend, told me that they used the term "customering" as an extension of Joe's earlier work on *Mass Customization*. Specifically, they had proposed that there are no markets, only unique customers, and that the ultimate form of engaging with them is on an individualized basis. They had called this customering.[1]

In this chapter, you will find that "individualization" is a core and irreplaceable competency of customering. Of course, individualism has its origins in philosophy,[2] sociology,[3] and political theory.[4] In the customer field, however, I was first introduced to the term by the work of researcher Phil Venville in the early 2010s.[5] For the avoidance of doubt, "customering" is applied here as per my meaning (Table 3.1):

Table 3.1 The Customering Definition

"Customering"	The application of formal customer management. A shorthand term for "customer management". The management of customers as distinct from that of the market. An industrially inspired model. An adjunct discipline to the marketing method.

Throughout the book, you will find the major component parts expressed as industrial discipline, a strident bias to service, an orientation to the individual, and, finally, the periodic select use of experiential tactics (Figure 3.2).

Many will note the narrow use of experiences. Don't misinterpret this; they are both disproportionately powerful and necessary. But they are akin to a drug and, contrary to the common refrain, we must use them under careful and qualified prescription, and as remedy to target needs or ambition only. You should also note that they are hobbled without an unequivocal foundation of service.

Welcome to customering.

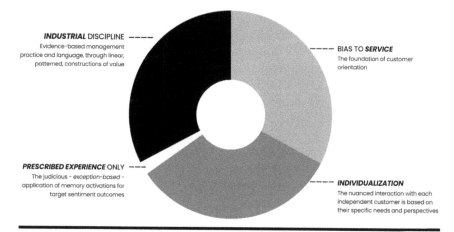

INDUSTRIAL DISCIPLINE ————
Evidence-based management
practice and language, through linear,
patterned, constructions of value

———— BIAS TO **SERVICE**
The foundation of customer
orientation

PRESCRIBED EXPERIENCE ONLY ———
The judicious - *exception-based* -
application of memory activations for
target sentiment outcomes

———— **INDIVIDUALIZATION**
The nuanced interaction with each
independent customer is based on
their specific needs and perspectives

Figure 3.2 The Components of Customering

The Terrain

In among all the noise and hype to arise in the early, indeed the embryonic stages, of the digital era – and most especially in the CX movement – it has been lost on many that advanced customer management is an exceptionally new field in comparison to most.

Across the hallway in the marketing department, the foundations of their work were laid through decades of scholarly and industry endeavor. Marketing has had many great pioneers and scholars – names like Borden, Shaw, Reeves, Ehrenberg, Levitt, McCarthy, Keith, Ogilvy, alongside Kotler and Porter, to the more recent work of Ansoff, Trout, Ries, Shultz, Ritson, Sharp, Romaniuk, Dawes, etc.

But while marketing academia has always incorporated customer concepts to various degrees, their separation as functions of business and research has become essential, even catering for relevant intersections or interdependencies. I work hard in this book to both make their distinction plain and to describe their relationship. I consider that the full implications of the Services Revolution only materialized in the digital era, which made individual customer proximity achievable at scale, and I contend that the real value of this paradigm has been missed by many in academia, and almost entirely by industry.

To understand this, we must start at the turn of the last century, when the world was irrevocably changed. The industrial era de-constructed and re-booted both business and lifestyle for most of the western world. Previously, our agrarian society, raising crops and animals on the land and trading them at market, dominated industry and life. Illustrative of global economies, in 1776 when the USA was founded, over 90% of workers were employed on the land; by 2009 this was only 1.3%.[6]

The industrial revolution replaced fields with factory floors and office cubicles, and in the process we transitioned from a commodities-dominated economy to one based on goods. While this provided consumers with an ability to buy new things, the companies themselves were far more interested in lowering costs via mass production and like efficiencies than in the ideas of market orientation, let alone customer-centricity.

Market orientation, which we discussed in the previous chapter, was, like many of the now foundational pillars of modern marketing, well established by 1990,[7] but true customer-centricity was, in practice, a long way off and remains so – despite its buzzword status. In fact, the ideal of *Mass Customization* within the customer service arena is still not a common operational capability despite its ready availability.

Still, the arrival – and the lessons – of the Services Revolution in the 1950s has proven decisive. For services to be successful as a sustained economic offering, business processes had to shift toward the needs of the customer. That oft-cited quote, allegedly from Henry Ford, that the customer could have any color they wanted so long as it was black, simply did not translate to the world of service. And so, it was in the immediate aftermath of World War Two, as society and its consumers sought easier lives than the first half of the century had offered, that the earliest ideas of customer proximity first occurred at any real scale.

Yet the offerings were largely one-dimensional. While consumers now had more product types that they could buy courtesy of industrial efficiencies, and an increasing range of service offerings as well, the means of access and consumption hadn't changed. They visited a store or a barber shop, for example, or had a sales representative visit them. That, and mail order, was the extent of the customer "channels", and so customer management as we might think of it today occupied its earliest incarnations for a long time and was a largely uncomplicated business. That was, at least, until things started to change in the 1990s.

By this time, the fourth economic offering had started to emerge: "experience". The earliest published work of Pine and Gilmore on the subject, in 1998, looked at the nature of experience as an economic contrast to service, and found that just as products are a customization of commodities, and services of products, experiences were a customization of services. They also deduced that if customization was the transformative upward economic force, commoditization is the powerful downward equivalent. There are often two equal and opposing forces, and so it proved here too.

Interestingly, the greatest force of global commoditization is the internet, and the implications for customer management could not be more apparent. But while the discovery of experience was an important addition to the workings of advanced customer management, it was also to prove a very significant and damaging rabbit hole – not because the theory was wrong, but because the light-headed populism that dominates the CX community had little patience for properly understanding it. Shortcuts are always adopted, and in this case they are extreme. Today, most people in the customer field corral their entire career around the word "experience", from adopting job titles like Head of CX, CX Director, and CXO, to using the term universally without boundary. As a result of meaning anything and everything, it has come to mean precisely nothing.

Consider the "experience management" mantra. While a popular term, it is not one that is supported evidentiarily, and given that disciplinary language is one of the four pre-requisites of professional fields, not one that I believe the industry should maintain. To be clear, experiences are, by definition, a function of human memory, are born of an array of emotional and cognitive processes both conscious and, largely, non-conscious on an individual basis. In short, they are not remotely manageable. Thus, "experience management" is a contradiction terms, not a legitimate field of practice. It is merely a sales slogan, born in a product marketing department.

This is a perfect example of just how non-literate most are when it comes to the role of human experience in the customer management field. In fact, experiences account for only a tiny percentage of interactions between company and customer. Yet most have sought to leap-frog the discipline of service in favor of experience notions, without understanding that experience, as established by Pine and Gilmore in the 1990s, is a customization of the service layer, and that its activations only work well when placed on a foundation of … service! We'll talk about the Customer Engagement Stack[8] in a later chapter.

Indeed, true customer-centricity is birthed in service, which has always been based on the jobs that each individual customer wants to achieve. For instance, if they need to look more presentable, someone might choose a haircut as a job that they need to get done. Making fulfilling that job as effortless as possible is the essence of service. This has remained, and will remain, unchanged. However, when the internet arrived the execution of this core principle began to take on far more complexity.

The exponential rise in internet use between 2007 (1 billion users), 2012 (2 billion) and 2019 (4.5 billion), the rise and evolutions of mobile and social media, all manner of third-party communications platforms (Google, Zoom, WhatsApp, WeChat, etc.) and onto generative AI web applications: all amplified the number and type of touchpoints from a once-analog service paradigm. Such an evolution of connectedness, in such a short period, changed us. As consumer choice expanded, amplified by the anti-social network paradigm, we all became somewhat demanding and opinionated. Brian Solis once labeled this "accidental narcissism",[9] and he wasn't wrong.

Consider that in 1950, 12% of respondents agreed with a survey question that asked if they related to the statement, "I am a very important person".[10] By

1990, before we even entered the digital era of instant gratification, that had increased to 80%. Western society has become more focused on rights than on responsibilities, and so we have entered the period of history that still dominates the customer management field today.

Then, as companies recognized the opportunities of digital technologies, they erected websites, pursued e-commerce, designed new mobile apps, modified backend process capabilities, advanced their CRM instrumentation, applied new marketing automation, and made numerous other capital investments. And yet, as one tactical decision followed another, as the costs increased, and as technology companies surged in both market capitalization and influence, the snowball effect of it all reinforced – or should have – the pressing need to establish more critical management of the field.

Instead, we witnessed the arrival of populism, as described in the Introduction. One should note that this was a time in which traditional twentieth century society was being challenged, and the idea of re-writing the rule book was intoxicating. There was almost a rebellious streak, no better illustrated by the rise of Uber, as an entire generation grasped the "sharing economy" mantra in place of what they saw as old-school business models. It was quite remarkable. The humble taxi driver was derided as if some kind of enemy. Populism tends to do that.

In the same way, the embrace of all things "experience" took hold, in rebellion against the perceived dark lords in cynical ivory towers imposing their will on the masses. There was an underlying value system at play, one in which people wanted a more human, perhaps less corporate business world, and companies responded – albeit, I contend, in shorthand. It has been said that the 2010s were partly defined by people wanting to become more like brands, and brands trying to be more like people. So, we had a business version of "woke-ism" – a term I hesitate to use given the political dynamite now attached to it, but I hope you get the point.

The rise of CX was a part of it all. Many wanted jobs in a field that reflected this newfound humanity, even if much of the marketing-based digital practice has proven to be anything but humane. They were carried along by the idea that digital was the savior of us all, along with UX and "listening" and so on. I should hasten to add that many of these capabilities have a legitimate place, but, like any function, evidence-based methodology and sober discipline is important. Instead, many were over-emphasized and misunderstood all at the same time. As these populist dynamics increased, and the technology continued to arrive at breakneck speed, the wheels fell off. And no one noticed.

While there was an appetite for the wham-bam of *disruption* and *digital* and *feelings* and more, there was no parallel appetite to sanity-test the rhetoric or work toward what established professions would regard as professional standards. Paradoxically, despite all this newfound perceived capability, the industry failed to recognize that serving the customer had become a whole lot harder, and without this sober realization the malaise continued unabated. All were caught in the dynamic, industry associations included. This is the problem with revolutions, of course. Sometimes, in hindsight, evolution might have been better.

The Other Player: Consultants

To sustain any populist movement, there must be enough contributing parties. I have alluded the fast-growing tech sector as one of those, and poorly constituted associations another, although the brush should not be used to tar all. Yet, there is another party involved who supercharged the early misdirection, and who will likely become central to the course correction.

In 2023, a collaboration between a professor at University College London and a PhD candidate at the UCL Institute for Innovation and Public Purpose explored the relationship between institutions and consultancy firms.[11] Their contention is that the over-reliance on consultants:

> weakens our businesses, infantilizes our governments, and warps our economies.

Their book, *The Big Con*, focuses on the impacts of the world's biggest consultancies, which, to be fair, will always have significant impact, good and bad, by virtue of sheer scale. This is true of any global business. Consider Google, Microsoft, SAP, Salesforce, Oracle, or manufacturers like Nike, Samsung, and Apple. Once a certain scale is reached, it is impossible not to make ripples, and it is important to recognize the good along with the less good. Having said that, Mazzucato and Collingwood make an interesting point in respect to what they call, "the confidence trick", which relies on the

> illusion that they [consultants] are objective sources of expertise and capacity.[12]

You may recall that this was part of Adam Smith's criticism of professions way back in 1776. As it stands today, most consultancies have partnerships with select vendors, upon which they build their technology consulting services revenue. This could be seen as a conflict of interest, and at times it certainly is, with many parroting the sales messaging of their partner vendors as if it is management theory. This is problematic. It serves as a kind of wolf in sheep's clothing, because those messages become disguised under banners like "best practice" and are delivered with apparent gravitas from those expected to be independent and expert – a *confidence trick*, giving credence to Mazzucato and Collingwood's proposition.

Eventually, practitioners find themselves unwittingly tenants of the same faulty towers, supporting the contention that consultants have played a role in the rise and failings of the populist CX movement. Inspect job advertisements for consultant positions in the field of "customer" and you will realize how little genuine expertise many firms have in the field, save for vendor-inspired narratives coupled with misplaced concepts like agile and design thinking.

And yet, the relationships with vendors is not the core problem. It is fair and reasonable to gain technology knowledge directly from those that produce it. Instead, the real issue is the absence of industrialized customer management standards in the first place – a gap which is not the fault of consultancies. Consider the case of Deloitte, which partners with accounting software company Xero. Clients understand that this is a commercial offering, and a partnership between the two with a strong value proposition, but they do not confuse that for the actual accounting standards with which they must comply, nor the qualified advice of the accounting profession. While the presence of industry standards makes the distinction plain in the accounting world and in many others, however, this simple hierarchy does not exist in customer management.

Still, some are prone to impose spurious complexity on the field, giving credence to the assertions of Smith, Mazzucato, and Collingwood. Consider the below promotion on LinkedIn from one such organization:

> Journey centricity requires a change in operating model, moving six operational levers in concert, through three phases of transformation.

Aren't you tired just reading that? Thankfully, the truth is a lot less frightening, but the fact that such practice occurs is evidence, again, of the need for an industrial management standard. Indeed, as we take the next step toward one, the global consultancy sector will play a key role in advancing the collective maturity of customer management.

To do so, it seems that we must slow down to speed up; we must separate church and state as it were; and we must replace the common mythologies that have taken root in our most recent history with critical knowledge. It is possible to re-balance the roles of management, practitioner, consultant, and vendor, and to optimize the value of each within a more serious and cohesive industry.

Growth and Loyalty

At this point I want to introduce you to the *Barrier to Churn Principle*. This is one of the most important principles to understand, because it is central to the economic value of disciplined customer management, and the four pillars model.

In essence, the principle asks us to remove the obstructions to our customer's natural bias toward loyalty, noting that loyalty behaviors underpin the economic missions of customering.

To begin with, real brand growth is a consequence of above-average customer acquisition. No brand gains top-of-mind status in its category or dominates market share by reducing the churn of customers. It is always, *always*, about acquisition, with an important though statistically minor supporting role from customering. But – and it's a big "but" – company profit is reliant upon maintained and maximized custom, which means that customer operations must seek to overcome market trajectories (i.e., patterns of attrition) that will otherwise impose a ceiling to the financial performance of the company.

These patterns include the "Duplication of Purchase Law", wherein the customer base of brands in the same category invariably overlaps in proportion to their market share, and the laws of "double jeopardy" and "retention double jeopardy", wherein the customers of brands with less market share typically exhibit less loyalty, and therefore higher customer churn as a proportion of the overall customer base. Compounding that problem for smaller companies is the principle that "attitudes and brand beliefs reflect behavioral loyalty", which means that all customers are more aware of brands they use compared to those they don't, which results in larger brands attracting more favorable attitudes. It is, in effect, a kind of confirmation bias. In short, churn statistics will invariably follow these patterns, unless a company is able to interrupt them in its favor, which is a hint toward the basis of the customer management mission.

Of course we have seen the concept of loyalty programs become popular, but what seems to be intuitively sound is, in fact, not. In practice, the most successful loyalty programs often have little to do with loyalty per se. The program at Qantas is regarded as world-leading and is run as a separate subsidiary business called "Qantas Loyalty". Its real mission, though, is the up-sell and cross-sell of the 12 million people in its database using "data, marketing and analytics",[13] and it has two streams.

The first goal is direct sales to Qantas members of its own and partner offerings, in a range of categories including travel, financial services, retail, health and wellbeing, food, and wine. Its second goal is to sell loyalty program management to other businesses, again in the form of network sales. In truth, airlines have shown little interest in behavioral information and, overall, their customer service delivery is extraordinarily poor. Bafflingly poor, to be honest. It is most certainly not *individualized* as we will discuss in Chapter 4. And so, here we have what many believe is among the most advanced "loyalty" capabilities in the world, and yet the company flounders when it comes to customer engagement.

As for loyalty programs themselves, there is really no evidence that traditional points-based systems drive retention. Instead, people who would have been customers anyway spend at the same frequency as they would have, but now cost the company a lot more to serve. In fact, loyalty programs by their nature tend to attract our most loyal existing customers – which is, of course, counter-productive. Once down that rabbit hole, however, it is very difficult to remove a points system from customers who have grown accustomed to it without wholesale destruction of their trust, and so for many companies the only real option is to maintain them, optimize as much as possible, and look for flow-on monetization tactics in the same way Qantas has.

The irony is that human beings are, as the old saying goes and as social science proves, creatures of habit, which is a great starting point for loyalty. As a 2007 UK study[14] found that

> people are still less likely to adopt what they identify to be the best course of action if changing their behavior means negotiating complex, difficult or unclear choices and options. In short, complexity is a turn-off: it garners procrastination and disengagement.

In other words, our natural state is to be loyal simply because it is easier, unless companies make it too hard (Hint: many make it too hard!). This bias is often leveraged by companies that amplify the cost of switching[15] (actual or perceived) through (a) actual transaction costs, (b) learning costs (the ease or comfort of use may not be transferable to a new brand even if functionally identical),[16] and (c) "artificial or contractual switching costs", such as penalties (although these practices are increasingly prohibited by consumer law). As Sharp and colleagues noted in their paper on the Dirichlet[17] model,

> buyers are busy cognitive misers. They are naturally loyal but polygamously so; their mental and physical availability determines the brands they loyally buy over and over.

Of course, we covered mental and physical availability, the latter of which is also serviced via customering, in Chapter 2. While people won't cease or stall their engagement with a brand in favor of another, or generally wander outside of their personal brand repertoires without cause, there are two factors to keep in mind:

1. All companies suffer churn, and where undisrupted, the majority do so at the typical rate of their category, moderated by the Law of Double Jeopardy, even for comparable global brands.[18]

2. The statistical rate of churn in any given category is, of course, an average. This means that there is an inherent, qualified opportunity to operate at the more positive end of the distribution, and to achieve a rate of churn below the average – which contributes to share and optimizes profit.

Thus, the *Barrier to Churn Principle* is quite simply the systematic removal of the obstructions to our customer's natural bias toward loyalty (or inertia), building on the work of brand strategy and mental availability.

Once achieved we can contemplate experiential activations to inspire upward value in the franchise, but not before. Thus, in the same way that marketing seeks to operate a brand at above-average acquisition, customering must seek to operate at below-average churn. In both business disciplines, the average is the enemy.

Outside of market patterns, loyalty can be positively affected through two layers:

■ World-class, low- or no-friction services, e.g., the customer gets done exactly what they want to achieve with the lowest possible effort, every single time that they engage – thus the brand is "protected".

■ Targeted memory creation, as an exception to the service layer that seeks to create feelings (not mere emotion – see Chapter 6), and memory structures that enhance brand attitudes within the customer cohort, as distinct from the market.

Equally, within market patterns, churn can be increased by a failure to fabricate customer interactions in their favor. Consider Accenture's 2016 study that calculated that churn events due to "triggers" that could have been avoided cost US businesses alone US $1.6 trillion per annum. There is no evidence of improved industrial practice since then. On the contrary, as discussed in the Introduction, plenty of data suggests a continuation, a malaise manifest in the populist movement.

To achieve a churn rate below the average, customering requires a disciplined, repeatable, and scalable management model based on the available scientific evidence, reminiscent of the original values of professions. This is the premise of the four pillars of the customer management model.

Defining The Economic Mission

Having laid out the history and early misdirections of the digital era, you might be forgiven for thinking that all is lost. It is not, and in fact there is a simple progression in all established professions that lights the path:

■ The "mission" informs the "management model", and both inform the "measurements".

Accordingly, you are about to read about the management model, followed by the appropriate measurement and reporting. Before that, however, let me conclude this section by summarizing the economic mission of customer management. It comes in three parts.

Mission 1: Contribution to Growth

Growth, defined as the increase of market share, is delivered through the acquisition of new customers. It is, in nature, the function of marketing. However, every new customer that replaces one lost to the company is only maintaining share, rather than increasing it. In addition, the increased cost to acquire customers, pro rata, means that invariably company margin is diminished. Of course, customer attrition is unavoidable. There is no path to zero: some customers move away, others enter a new stage of life (e.g., no longer require baby products), and others pass away. In fact, the Law of Double Jeopardy shows that two brands of similar size will invariably demonstrate the same rate of churn (larger brands exhibit less churn as a percentage than smaller brands in the same category), but we must keep in mind that all scientific laws are premised in patterns and are generalizations. This means that those patterns may be disrupted in the right setting and with the right tactics. Most obviously, many companies suffer a higher rate of attrition as a direct result of service failure, i.e. they do not erect adequate barriers to churn. Growth is optimized when the marketing function achieves *a rate of acquisition above the average* (primary) and the customering function achieves a *rate of churn below the average* (secondary) (Figure 3.3).

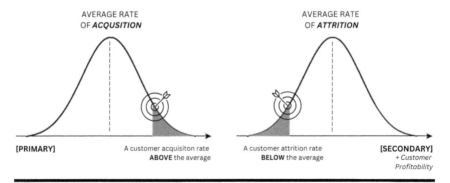

Figure 3.3 Target Growth Model (Spinley, 2023)

It should also be said that the proper design and deployment of customer channels supports another theory of marketing, that being "physical availability" – the ease of brand interaction and purchase – to optimize growth. More on this in Chapter 6.

Finally, we must acknowledge that most studies of churn are occurring in a setting in which global customer management is not professionally undertaken. Consequently, the rate of customer attrition is likely higher than it should be in many industries. Therefore, anecdotally, the opportunity for some may not be limited to the more positive end of the existing distribution but extends to operating beyond it, widening the distribution itself. Irrespective, the first mission of customering is in support of the growth agenda, by maintaining customers for longer. This is also the first input to increasing customer lifetime value (CLV).

Mission 2: Contribution to Profit

As economist Theodore Levitt wrote, the corporate purpose is "to create and keep a customer".[19] Companies seek growth in market penetration because, naturally, more customers should translate into more revenue and eventually more profit. This is, after all, the primary objective of business in keeping with Levitt's statement, even allowing for a triple bottom line.[20] Thus, the marketing vocation was established to "create" the customer base.

Of course, this assumes that those customers can be serviced and maintained, profitably. As we have already discussed, customer management's first goal is to "keep" the customer base, in support of increasing overall market share, and a major additional outcome of that increased tenure, must be a material contribution to company profit. Yet simply keeping a customer does not instantly correlate to them becoming a more profitable one. Dowling and Uncles[21] wrote in 1997 that:

> The contention that loyal customers are always more profitable is
> a gross oversimplification.

Note, however, the word, "oversimplification", which is a hallmark of the populist CX movement today, rather than the word, "impossible". While there is no evidence that the profits of a customer increase over time *naturally*,[22] manufactured methods to incite profitability are found in later chapters.

In practical terms, the contribution to profit is increased as more satisfied customers move from being light buyers during their extended tenure to being heavier– if not "heavy" – buyers through frequency of transaction and transaction value (where category-appropriate). Critically, this is combined with lowering the cost to serve, but not to the extent of customer dissatisfaction or frustration, which becomes counter-productive and invites churn. This is the hole many companies fall into today: over-indexing on self-service is a common digital superstition.

To re-emphasize the notion that existing satisfied customers are important to revenue – and eventually profit – it has been found that the probability of sales conversion increases up to 14-fold when selling to an existing customer compared to a new one.[23] This has been misconstrued by many to mean we should embrace a short-sighted sales orientation, but, errors of execution aside, the principle holds. Analysis within KPMG's 2022 UK Customer Experience Excellence (CEE)[24] Report compared "customer experience performance revenues and profitability", contrasting the performance of those they regarded as the top 100 brands in CEE to the main FTSE 100 index. As they summarize:

> Over a five-year period, the CEE top 100 brands achieved double the revenue growth of the FTSE 100 – an average of 11%, rather than 5.5%.

While the popular Net Promoter Score system is now debunked (see Chapter 9), a comparison by Bain and Company (from whence it came) found in 2013 that, in Australia, the value of a "promoter" was on average about two and half times that of a "detractor" in terms of lifetime value.[25] Bain's much earlier and often cited work in the *Harvard Business Review* famously reported that "[i]ncreasing customer retention rates by 5% increases profits by 25% to 95%".[26] Of course, this is a big range with lots of wriggle room, and most companies would be very happy indeed with the entry point, a 25% bump in profit, but many are dubious about those numbers. To be fair, while they are attention-grabbing, they do enjoy some support.

The "Pareto Law 60/20" documented by the Ehrenberg Bass Institute, the largest marketing science institute in the world, established that around 60% of a brand's purchases come from 20% of its customers (heavy buyers), while the remainder come from the bottom 80% (light buyers). Yes, the traditional 80/20 rule is wrong when it comes to marketing ... Thus, you can do your own maths. Take a sample company of your choosing and calculate the impact to its profit if heavy buyers increased by 2%, 3%, or 5%. It's compelling.

At a unit economics level, it is obvious that the customer acquisition cost (CAC) reads better if amortized over a three-year customer tenure, instead of two, and so great customering also increases profit by lowering costs. Indeed, Murphy and Murphy report that a 2% increase in customer retention has an equivalent effect on profit to cutting costs by 10%.[27] Apart from the revenue side of customer profitability analysis (CPA), the other side of the coin is cost, and our friends at KPMG report that more advanced customer management leaders can reduce overall costs by up to 25%.[28] Equally, Graham Hill of Optima reported:

> Companies with higher-than-average UKCSI [UKCustomer Satisfaction Index] scores have 114% higher revenue per employees, a 7% higher revenue growth rate and 10% higher profits.

Meanwhile, research by Deloitte has found that those rare companies with effective customer programs were 60% more profitable[29] than their competition.

But those are the positive effects. What about the negative, *cost increasing* impact of failed customer service? Well, consider "The Service Profit Chain",[30] which, among other evidentiary sources, suggests that profit is *reduced* as a direct consequence of poor service. It calculates that this increases the "volume, cost and difficulty" of providing future service to affected customers. Likewise, in the UK it is estimated that poor service results in an additional 10% of needless interactions, increasing "friction", the kryptonite of service, and that this costs businesses an estimated £11.4 billion – per month![31]

So, whether your reference is Marketing Metrics, Bain and Co, the Ehrenberg Bass Institute, KPMG, Murphy and Murphy, the UK Customer Satisfaction Index, the Institute of Customer Service, Accenture, or any of the other corroborating analyses such as those offered by the "Service Profit Chain" or Hill, sweating the customer base pays big dividends on the profit line of the balance sheet.

Mission 3: Managing Risk and Value

Lastly, the risk of customer attrition above the average poses significant risk to the business. Such a circumstance means that it is not your company but its competitors that are optimizing market share, and are doing so at your expense. That risk leads to several economic fire alarms.

- Decline of revenue, profit, and, eventually, market cap.
- Adverse impact to the balance sheet and an increased cost of capital.
- Governance escalations.

While marketing and other business disciplines are in the mix here, in the short term this certainly suggests systemic issues in the relationship that the company has with its customers. Left unchecked, these eventually lead to more vocal, and/or public, expressions from those dissatisfied, amplifying individual concerns into group ones that may result in wholesale flight of customers, collapse, or decline of market segments. The costs of dealing with systemic customer issues, including those incurred as part of remediating a corporate reputation, far exceed those of managing the customer franchise risks adequately in the first place. Consider the case of Qantas, Australia's national airline, whose well-documented service failures have seen it plummet from the top handful of operators to 17th on the international airline rankings,[32] and its standing as the country's number one brand to 42nd.[33] Remembering that growth is primarily a function of brand while retention is the combination of brand and engagement, and noting new entrants in the sector, the company is paying the price.

It has also been found that the behaviors of a firm suffering high rates of churn become problematic to its overall decision making and asset prices. As a 2020 study[34] noted:

> Rates of customer churn affect the level and volatility of firm-level investment, markups, and profits. Churn also affects how quickly firms respond to shocks in the value of their growth options (i.e. Tobin's Q).[35]

Finally, if a company sustains a long-term trend whereby its churn rate exceeds its acquisition rate, the financial impost is undeniable. Covenants that it has with financiers will come into focus, as will indicators of insolvency within its financial ratios, something for which directors carry personal liability. Granted, these are extreme circumstances, but a quick glance across busy liquidation practices tells you that extreme does not mean rare.

The Big Proviso: Where to Limit Customer Management Investment

While it may seem counter-intuitive, despite the above the reality is that there are some categories whose growth and profit is mostly – or even entirely – unaffected by customer management. In such circumstances, a company should focus exclusively on brand and distribution (mental and physical availability), with minimal critical lines of service.

For instance, many consumer product offerings are classic examples of what consumer psychologists would describe as "low involvement" categories. They comprise programmed responses for high-frequency needs, usually for products or brands that are well known. Referred to as routinized problem solving (RPS), we use these for purchases that are easy, represent low risk, require low cognitive effort, and are often habitual in nature. These categories will still have an average attrition rate for participating brands, but the distribution that makes up that average will be much tighter, leaving little opportunity to disrupt.

Consider toothpaste. Generally, a buyer picks up the branded product, such as Colgate, that they typically use, almost absent-mindedly as they walk the shopping market aisle. They never deal with the company directly. Rather, the service that they receive is delivered by the grocery store and is provided in relation to their entire shopping visit – from car park to store cleanliness to check out, etc. – and for all the items in their cart, thus abstracting individual products away from prevalence. Colgate-Palmolive (the manufacturer) may provide limited direct interaction options, such as a number to call for defective products, but otherwise it has no interactions with customers at all. Nor do customers want or need it.

For most other categories, though, which have a wider distribution of attrition rates between participants, customer management strategies to disrupt churn patterns become critical to our economic and business measures.

***

In summary, the customer management process prescribed herein seeks to:

- Contribute to market penetration through:
  - security of the customer base.
  - increasing the tenure of the customer base.
- Contribute to company profit through:
  - increasing the tenure of the customer base.
  - contribution to improvement of the ratio between light, moderate, and heavy buyers.
  - lessening the percentage of cost base attributable to customer acquisition.
- Mitigate commercial risk through:
  - delivery of the above objectives.
  - robust measurement and early detections.

Thus, it can be defined as follows:

> The customering mission is to make a minor though strategically important contribution to market share, to mitigate risk to the customer asset, and to materially influence both company profit and values.[36]

With the three-part mission established, we can now prescribe the management model to that effect. A key premise to keep in mind is that there may well be other sub-disciplines, methods, ideas, or measurements, either existing or emerging, that I don't cover or, arguably, cover inadequately, but the foundation – the four pillars of management – is the frame and basis for their application.

Before we begin, let's quickly cover budgeting.

Budgeting

Following the distinct financial objectives between marketing and customering, so too the budget allocation process differs. In the case of marketing the overall goal is, of course, growth, and so the function is one of both strategy (every business must seek to grow) and investment. All investments require a return, measured, eventually, through market penetration and revenue. Considered in the strategy pillar of the marketing management model, this invokes "zero sum marketing", and in that setting, return on investment (ROI) is an appropriate conversation. Even then, there are significant dangers of that metric alone, particularly in relation to brand investment – an issue that we discussed in Chapter 2.

In contrast, there is limited scope for ROI framing in the budgeting process of customer management. Instead, it is better considered as a form of insurance on one hand, and risk management via quality management, on the other. It is, in this sense, the active protection of the most strategic corporate asset, the customer base, operating as a part of the company's system of control.

Customer initiatives that seek to increase custom within cohorts, which is managed in the intersection between marketing and customering, does however invite an ROI lens. More general goals, such as an x% increase to profit, can be fraught, given the multitude of variables that affect profit and the differing calculations therein. That's not to say that tracking the impact to profit by cohort and in aggregate is not important – I've prescribed this as a key objective – but conditioning foundational budget upon it is less so, because this is a downstream financial benefit of properly managing the asset in the first instance, and so companies must first recognize that strategic imperative.

Consequently, firms should be very cautious about treating customering as a calculated venture, whereby each activity or initiative must be funded, or not, via a traditional business case. Instead, like insurance and quality management, it is an essential cost and must have an appropriate budgeting process. Broadly, then, it is neither discretionary nor speculatory. It is a matter of risk tolerance.

Separately, a valid ROI consideration might relate to asset development, i.e., a mobile application. Certainly a new asset must deliver on the necessary functional outcomes or benefits within the frame of the management model, as we will soon explore, and the funding approval should follow that rationale. Even then, however, ROI stipulations that demand arbitrary financial gains will likely undermine the value creation that good design creates downriver of the asset itself, and can serve to weaken that system of control if not managed carefully.

Of course, experiential initiatives should be subject to ROI across a suitable period, following the activation (see the discussion of measurement in Chapter 7).

In contrast, the core capabilities that underlie the use of all assets – such as identification, discernment, decisioning, and orchestration – are indisputable foundation elements of the customer control system, akin to core coverage items in an insurance spectrum, and should not be subject to inappropriate notions of ROI. Fortunately, most of those capabilities can be shared with, and/or amortized across, marketing operations or digital teams.

As a guide, I propose a simple budgeting model – inclusive of technology, human capital, and any outsourcing – based on the core components of a customer management program (Table 3.2).

Table 3.2 Budgeting Guide

Function	ROI-based	Control-based	Hybrid
Central channel agnostic customer identification capability		√	
Core systems of customer intent discernment		√	
Centralized real-time decisioning and channel-less orchestration capability		√	
Channel developments			√
Messaging assets (Promotional)	√		
Messaging assets (Service)		√	
Experiential activations (Refer the MATES test, Ch. 6)	√		
Systems of measurement			√

Given the economic failings of the populist movement, which include funding wildly ineffective practices, this budget model may well deliver savings for some firms. Irrespective, it ensures sharper clarity in respect to budget line types and less scope for waste, and, as you will see in Chapter 8, we should be concerned with the system and business effects of the model, with only limited measurement of isolated elements.

This will all become clear as we traverse the four pillars of the model over the next four chapters, pillar by pillar, until we have contructed the model (Figure 3.4):

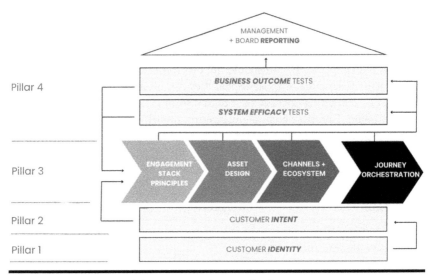

Figure 3.4 Summary of the Customering Method

Notes

1. B. Joseph Pine II, *Customering: The Next Stage in the Shift to Mass Customization* (Routledge, 2018).
2. Carl Gustav Jung, *The Archetypes and the Collective Unconscious* (Princeton University Press, 1969).
3. Zygmunt Bauman, *The Individualized Society* (John Wiley & Sons, 2013); Hans T. Blokland, *Freedom and Culture in Western Society* (Routledge, 2019).
4. Ulrich Beck and Elisabeth Beck-Gernsheim, *Individualization: Institutionalized Individualism and its Social and Political Consequences* (Sage, 2001).
5. On Phil Venville and Thunderhead's Engagement 3.0, see Business Wire, "Research From Thunderhead.com Reveals Bold New Framework for Redefining Customer Engagement in the Digital Era," April 16, 2014. https://www.businesswire.com/news/home/20140416005192/en/Research-from-Thunderhead.com-Reveals-Bold-New-Framework-for-Redefining-Customer-Engagement-in-the-Digital-Era.
6. Bureau of Labour Statistics, *Household Data Annual Averages 2009*, no date. https://www.bls.gov/cps/cps_aa2009.htm.
7. See Ajay Kohli and Bernie Jaworski, "Market Orientation: The Construct, Research Propositions, and Managerial Implications," *Journal of Marketing* 54, no. 2 (1990): 1–18; John C. Narver and Stanley F. Slater, "The Effect of a Market Orientation on Business Profitability," *Journal of Marketing* 54, no. 4 (1990): 20–34.
8. A. Spinley (2022).
9. Brian Solis, "The Accidental Narcissist and the Future of Customer Engagement – Brian Solis," *Brian Solis* [Blog], June 4, 2014, https://briansolis.com/2014/06/accidental-narcissist-future-customer-engagement/

10. Robert D. Putnam, *The Upswing: How America Came Together a Century Ago and How We Can Do It Again* (Simon & Schuster, 2020).
11. Mariana Mazzucato and Rosie Collington, *The Big Con: How the Consulting Industry Weakens Our Businesses, Infantilizes Our Governments and Warps Our Economies* (Random House, 2023).
12. Ibid., publisher's description.
13. https://www.qantas.com .
14. Jessica Prendergast, Beth Foley, Verena Menne, and Alex Karalis Isaac, *Creatures of Habit? The Art of Behavioural Change* (Ernst & Young, 2008).
15. Paul Klemperer, "Markets with Consumer Switching Costs," *The Quarterly Journal of Economics* 102, no. 2 (1987): 375–394.
16. Seo, Dongback, C. Ranganathan and Yair M. Babad, "Two-level Model of Customer Retention in the US Mobile Telecommunications Service Market," *Telecommunications Policy* 32, no. 3–4 (2008): 182–196.
17. Byron Sharp et al., "It's a Dirichlet World," *Journal of Advertising Research* 52, no. 2 (2012): 203–213.
18. Byron Sharp, "Does the iPhone Defy the Double Jeopardy Law?" [Blog post], *Ehrenberg-Bass News*, October 12, 2017. https://marketingscience.info/iphone-defy-double-jeopardy-law/.
19. Theodore Levitt, *Marketing Imagination: New, Expanded Edition* (Simon and Schuster, 1986).
20. The Economist, "Triple Bottom Line," *The Economist*, November 17, 2009. https://www.economist.com/news/2009/11/17/triple-bottom-line.
21. Grahame Dowling and Mark D. Uncles, "Do Customer Loyalty Programs Really Work?," *Sloan Management Review* 38, no. 4 (1997).
22. Werner J. Reinartz and V. Kumar, "On the Profitability of Long-Life Customers in a Noncontractual Setting: An Empirical Investigation and Implications for Marketing," *Journal of Marketing* 64, no. 4 (2020): 17–35.
23. Neil Bendle, Paul W. Farris, Philip Pfeifer, and David Reibstein, *Marketing Metrics: The Manager's Guide to Measuring Marketing Performance* (FT Press, 2020).
24. KPMG, *Value and Values: UK Customer Experience Excellence Report 2022* (KPMG, 2022). https://assets.kpmg.com/content/dam/kpmg/uk/pdf/2022/11/uk-2022-customer-experience-excellence-report-value-and-values.pdf.
25. Katrina Bradley and Richard Hatherall, "The Powerful Economics of Customer Loyalty in Australia," *Bain & Company*, July 29, 2018. https://www.bain.com/insights/the-powerful-economics-of-customer-loyalty-in-australia/
26. Amy Gallo, "The Value of Keeping the Right Customers," *Harvard Business Review*, 29 October 2014. https://hbr.org/2014/10/the-value-of-keeping-the-right-customers
27. Emmett C. Murphy and Mark A. Murphy, *Leading on the Edge of Chaos: The 10 Critical Elements for Success in Volatile Times* (Prentice Hall, 2002).
28. KPMG, "KPMG Global Customer Experience Excellence Research 2020" [Media release], *KPMG*, 3 August 2020. https://kpmg.com/be/en/home/media/press-releases/2020/08/adv-kpmg-global-customer-experience-excellence-research-2020.html
29. Deloitte Research, *Wealth Management Digitalization Changes Client Advisory More Than Ever Before* (Deloitte, 2016). https://www2.deloitte.com/content/dam/Deloitte/de/Documents/WM%20Digitalisierung.pdf

30. W. Earl Sasser, Leonard A. Schlesinger and James L. Heskett, *The Service Profit Chain: How Leading Companies Link Profit and Growth to Loyalty, Satisfaction, and Value* (Free Press, 1997).

31. Anna Tims, "Poor Customer Service Costs UK Firms Billions – So Why Can't They Get It Right?," *The Guardian*, January 30, 2023. https://www.theguardian.com/money/2023/jan/30/poor-customer-service-costs-uk-firms-billions-so-why-cant-they-get-it-right

32. World Airline Awards 2023 edition, announced at the Paris Airshow

33. Andrew Birmingham, "Customers, Hackers and Disintermediation Are Big Long-Term Risks for Qantas as the Flying Kangaroo Makes Big Investments in CX and Digital Transformation Designed to Leave Behind the Gloomy Brand Decay of Alan Joyce's Final Years," *mi3Media*, February 26, 2024. https://www.mi-3.com.au/26-02-2024/customers-hackers-and-disintermediation-are-among-qantass-biggest-long-term-risks-big

34. Scott R. Baker, Brian Baugh and Marco C. Sammon, *Measuring Customer Churn and Interconnectedness* (Working Paper 27707, National Bureau of Economic Research, 2020).

35. Tobin's Q measures whether a firm or an aggregate market is relatively over or undervalued.

36. A. Spinley (2022).

Chapter 4

Pillar 1

Identity

While most literature about customer identity, and the common debates on the subject, deal only with digital interaction, the Identity pillar extends well beyond this limitation. After all, a customer's identity is theirs, just as yours is yours. It goes with them everywhere that they go, including offline channels where it is just as important to be effective at engagement. Identity is the knitted fabric that binds all our interactions.

Indeed, a key principle to keep in mind is that while companies think in terms of their "channels", customers have never heard of them! They go where they want, when they want, and will often interact in more than one way at a time without even thinking about it. For instance, they may check price or delivery information online, even as they stand in the store. They are not constrained by a company's internal preconceptions about its assets, and a firm must be able to recognize the individual as they are engaging, no matter where, or how, and in how many concurrent ways.

And yet, while many claim to understand that identity management needs to apply in an omni-channel way, they usually just mean "digital", or at most, multi-channel. But these terms are not interchangeable. It is a practice that the chief customer officer (CCO) must stamp on given its limiting effect on thought and, eventually, execution. Equally, identity should not be regarded in transactional terms. For instance, it goes well beyond the streamlining of onboarding processes (such as social sign-in etc.) and access management (security and privacy). While these are part of its role, identity is truly foundational to longitudinal human engagement. It is deeply, deeply personal. Customer management teams should have an abiding respect for and understanding of it, and it is no coincidence that it is the first pillar of this model. At the same time, it's important to remember its linear interrelationship with the other pillars, and to guard

DOI: 10.4324/9781003513728-5

against a common problem that we have seen emerge in large and complex consumer businesses: isolation.

This occurs when companies develop their "channel strategy", which invariably means that each channel has a strategy, or is comparative. For instance, some companies talk about establishing insight to determine which channel is the most effective for sales outcomes, allowing the inside-out marketing mindset to dominate. As we discussed in the introduction, customering is an outside-in proposition and corporate attempts to *dictate* customer journeys through "journey mapping" practices have invariably failed. Having a centralized management system is important, but it will not solve the full identity puzzle if the company executes, and dictates, by channel.

From Omni-channel to Channel-less

And yet, despite the failure to yet grasp omni-channel execution, we have already moved beyond it. Today, the most advanced and effective model for customer engagement does not have a channel basis at all. We must become *channel-less*, a concept that is deeply present throughout the four pillars.

Contrary to one of the defining and most damaging myths of the vocation, customers have almost no interest in an "experience". Instead, they are concerned with getting done what they want to get done. They interact where it is the most convenient for them, or as per their habit. It doesn't matter whether that is via the web, a chatbot, SMS, email, cell phone app, contact center, store, or within the third-party ecosystem: WhatsApp, iMessage, Skype, Slack, and so forth. All that matters is the quality of the interaction and the ease of the outcome. In short, channel strategy (multi or omni) is about the business, not the customer. My dear friend the inimitable Paul Greenberg is widely known as "the Godfather of CRM" for his pioneering research and writing in the field.[1] An acclaimed industry analyst and author, he put it best when he said:

> The essence of the channel-less approach is … to understand and serve the needs of your customers from their perspective.

To achieve this though, you will need to nail down the foundational pillar: Identity.

The Identity Lens

Having established the principle that identity operates across all customer driven interactions, let's now zoom in on the function. Most companies start and end their thinking about identity within the frame of access management and security (and, more recently, consent management). However, these are only a portion of the Identity pillar. Others have begun to connect classic access management with the "Customer360" mantra, which is itself a valid concept but one that has been watered down and, to date, has missed the mark by some margin. That watering down comes from the prevalence of considering only historical transactional data and any customer-volunteered preferences. Yet there can never be a full view of the customer, as implied by "360", without an understanding of their intent, and the behavioral paradigm more broadly. At its very best, Customer360, as it is mostly described, is more like Customer180. To remedy that, identity is critical.

Think about your everyday life. The way you interact with another person is entirely oriented around your understanding or perception of who they are. From stranger to someone you have met once before to a casual acquaintance – perhaps a friend of a friend – to a regular in your social network to a close friend, a best friend, or a partner – this context affects how you relate to each "someone".

There are also contextual and environmental layers in play. Is this person a colleague at work, did you meet them on a holiday, are they a parent of child that plays with your son or daughter, are they someone you chat to on the sideline of weekend sports, are they an ex-partner of a friend, and so on. Their "identity" in relation to you is the definitive starting point for how you choose – or choose not to – interact with them. The same applies between company and customer.

Now, a word of caution. There is no room for silly notions of customer love or deep abiding emotional connection between company and customer. This is populist nonsense that simply does not reflect the reality of how people think about companies. Brands are tiny, tiny, tiny specks in our memory structures. Yes, those specks can be powerful, but specks they are and that is all. Customer management can reinforce a brand's position within the customer franchise but does not exist to create one. I'll cover this in Chapter 7.

So now, let's get practical. The first challenge to emerge since the proliferation of channels and touchpoints – and the more powerful pursuit of channel-less value creation – has been how to identify an individual no matter where, when, or how they appear to us, and, equally, to protect their privacy in the process.

The operational disciplines of the Identity pillar are fourfold:

- Capture status.
- Stitching.
- Privacy.
- Systems.

Capture Status

Quite naturally, we can't progress in any concept of identity management if we are not first capturing it. Classifying the nature, or status, of the identity must occur at the point of capture to enable the first nuanced interactions to be formed. As we discussed in the introduction to this section, a person's identity is relative to the principal, and in this case a customer's identity is relative to us, as a company.

And so, the first discipline of the identity pillar is not merely capture, but capture statuses, which are typically as follows (although you will encounter alternative terms for the same):

- Unknown.
- Recognized.
- Verified.

"Unknown"

An unknown customer is exactly that. A person has presented themselves, but we do not know who they are. Perhaps they have walked past the store or lingered in one of its aisles before leaving. Perhaps they have browsed the website, either as a prospective customer who does not yet have credentials or as an existing one who doesn't log in during their visit.

We know that they are there, because of patterns in the data or witnessing their arrival, but that is all we know, so our interaction with them is limited to template messages, static content (such as web pages), or proforma interventions most typical in the clumsy use of marketing automation: if this, then that, if the customer looked at this product on this page, then send them this message. It is a brute force, unintelligent, and yet default approach for many brands which make a very big, and dangerous, assumption: that we should hit customers with sales activation-based content irrespective of the central element in the equation, *the customer*. In these cases, it never occurs to the business to understand why that person has visited and what it is that they hope to achieve.

Yet it is important to understand that the fact that we may not have identified a customer does not mean that we can't engage with them in a more contextual manner. While we may not know who they are, we can still infer some aspects of their intent in order to activate alternative interactions – both of which are covered in the following sections of this chapter. We make those inferences by observing component activities.

A scenario used as an example throughout this chapter is the customer who first searched on Google for a particular product or category. That search took them to a set of results in the form of Google ads, from which they selected an option, clicked on it, and arrived on a landing page. Many companies already know that they can see that a visitor arrived via this pathway (found in the UTM parameters), and so already know the broad context of the visit. The user is still unknown, but we can start to interact with them based on their intent, albeit with limitations. Still, unknown visitors represent low attributable commercial value.

"Recognized"

The next stage is when we are able deduce the likely identity of a customer, even though this has not been verified by the customer themselves.

For example, in a web instance a person may *navigate to* the login page of the "My Account" functionality, or *navigate past* a newsletter sign-up form. If their browser had previously cached their username and password for that website, causing an auto-population of one or more fields, then even though the customer themselves has not completed the log in and registration, the presence of appropriate technology will make the association.

The same concept might apply in-store, where someone who has downloaded the mobile app is recognized by the same background technology in combination with Wi-Fi infrastructure, either through the app itself or the MAC address of the phone. And again, if someone calls into a contact center the number they call from may be recognized in the system before they have even had their call answered.

It is possible in all three examples, and others besides, that it is still not the person that the system recognizes at all. In the web scenario, it might be someone else in the household who has borrowed the laptop. They may not be, for instance, the bill payer. In the store example, a teenager may be shopping with his mother, and while her phone is recognized, he is the primary customer. And in the contact center, again, someone else may call from that same number, rather than the main account holder.

"Verified"

Once the web visitor enters their password, the store visitor engages with staff or the point of sale, or the person calling the contact center provides their credentials, their status advances from recognized to verified.

The trigger for verification is a definitive cognitive action that is explicit, rather than deduced. From a customer perspective, there is an expectation of value trade that comes after entering personal information, providing a password, or otherwise supplying evidence of one's identity. It is not functional in the sense that identification has been confirmed, but it is intentional, in that the customer is seeking an exchange. Customer management leaders need to be very clear on this point though: an exchange does not immediately mean a sales transaction.

Unlike marketers who are all about acquisition and conversion, true customer management is all about serving the need of the customer first and foremost.

This is not, as many presume, anti-sales, because when a brand interacts with a person based on that person's context and needs, they exhibit a far greater propensity to convert. Indeed, Mittal et al.[2] found that

> a positive association of customer satisfaction with customer-level outcomes (retention, word-of-mouth, spending, and price insensitivity) and firm-level outcomes (product-market, accounting, and financial-market performance).

In summary, the verified status of the identity allows companies to associate a visitor with all manner of other information about that unique individual. Their ability to discern intent, and therefore to arbitrate the next logical interaction, is increased many times over. And as if to supercharge the effect, the customer themselves has demonstrated a current desire for those interactions. As you can see, as we advance the status of identification we are also able to recognize an advancement of engagement and of economic progression.

A case in point: a USD60B pharmaceutical giant saw an 18× increase in conversion of profiles from unknown to known status. The resulting value, measurable financially, from such increases is always profound. Indeed, the progression of identification, its initiations, and value outcomes might be illustrated as follows (Table 4.1):

Table 4.1 Identity Status

Status	Triggers	Uplift to value of subsequent interactions
Unknown	Patterns in data only	Marginal
Recognized	Customer keys[3]	Moderate
Verified	Exchange	Optimized

Stitching

We have established that when someone visits your brand – in whatever channel that might be – their identity is going to be either unknown, recognized, or verified. But that is only true for each visit, or, to use a web term, for each session. Their status may well be different in *different* sessions, even visiting the same website.

I may have browsed "apples" anonymously in one visit but have been recognized when I read the page on payment terms. Those sessions may have been a week apart, a day apart, or could be occurring at the same time, with more than one browser open. It gets even murkier. What if yet another session was open on my cell phone, and I had logged into my account, and thus I was fully verified in that instance? And what if I then stood in front of a sales assistant in the store and asked, not about apples, but about bananas?

In all instances, my status of identification is entirely different. What "session", and therefore what status, should the company apply to its interactions with me? This is a good question that is almost never asked. The blunt force use of marketing automation rarely seeks to resolve this, nor the reality that all those various visitors are actually the same person, and it certainly won't attempt to deduce the interrelationship between the sessions or visits.

Instead, it will just spit out separate template sales intervention messaging to each session, within each channel. Transported into a human relationship context, this is the equivalent of having a coffee with a friend that you have known for 20 years in the morning, only to find that they have no idea who you are when you see them at the bar. Why? Because they only know you in the café "channel", not in the bar "channel". In short, it is a form of corporate dementia, and it kills the functional relationship between company any customer. It also diminishes the preconditions of human trust.

And yet, there's more. So far, we have covered the scenario of entirely different customer sessions or visits, where the same customer is seeking to achieve different outcomes while occupying entirely different capture status in each instance. But we are still just talking about one customer interacting with one company.

Now take that same unresolved complexity and apply it to a situation where there is a group of companies under the same ownership and customer management regime. Perhaps one sells shoes of all types, another is a casual fashion brand, a third is an upmarket fashion retailer, and yet another offers financial products for shoppers (e.g., hire purchase or store credit). What if the same customer who is causing all those headaches for one brand is exhibiting similar behaviors across two of the others? Can identity be managed as a group? Even if they only interact with one of the four, can their identity be harnessed to serve their needs in the others?

This is why stitching is so important in the modern era.

Stitching works by recognizing the data pattern of an anonymous (unknown) user, and associating it with sessions and visits that have become recognized or verified. Instead of disparate interactions, the company – or companies, assuming customer consent – can now discern that this is the same person and can uplift the interactions based on that understanding. In addition, it means that the company or companies can now begin to see the entire journey of the customer, without limitation.

Stitching also relies on various customer keys, which can be present at any stage of unknown, recognized, or verified, and such as those in Table 4.2.

Table 4.2 Customer Keys

Unknown	System generated unique tracking identification number
Recognized or Verified (examples only)	Email Cell phone number Device identification Account number Reference number Credit card

As tricky as these sound, it's even worse. For instance, sometimes a customer might use another device, one they don't own. Nevertheless, that is the challenge that stitching must solve.

Overall, this essentially takes different parts of the same map and puts them together, enabling the business to make decisions on how it interacts with that individual customer based on the full map instead of separate component parts floating in a context-free zone. This is extremely important to understand, and critical for customer management leaders to embed in their organization, because without a full picture of each customer, it is impossible to deduce and serve their intent – the next pillar of the customer management model.

Cyber and Privacy

In today's world, identity can be a contentious area. Many contemporary grievances and debates take place under the broad headline of "privacy". But privacy fatalism is not new: on Friday the 13 July 1341 (yes, you read that right), Isabel Relict complained that John Trappe, owner of an adjoining property, had broken windows through which he and his servants could see into her garden. She won her complaint and continued a litigious battle for privacy with no fewer than three other households, according to records from the London Assize of Nuisance.[4]

More recently, but still as far back as 1890, the threat of the Kodak camera had US attorneys Louis Brandeis and Samuel Warren so worried that it inspired their famous law review article, "The Right to Privacy".[5] In the 1920s laws were passed to deal with the ethics of wiretapping as phone technologies emerged, with many proclaiming the "death of privacy",[6] as they have often since.

Still, the digital era – which has only been upon us from the mid 2000s and is still in embryonic form – has hastened and heightened the risks to individuals and expanded the scope of the debate surrounding privacy. Certainly, the practices of digital advertising – many of which are still prevalent at the time of writing – will be looked back on by history as an evil propagated in our digital immaturity. The fact that it is also largely fraudulent, and very often totally ineffective, will be looked back on with even more bemusement. One of the issues to arise from all of this is that of third-party cookies (as distinct from the secure proprietary type) to track interactions, not to benefit the customer but for the sale of their data, or the use of it in ways that they did not consent to.

It goes without saying that the security of personal information is paramount. At the outset of the global COVID-19 pandemic in 2020, the volume of compromised personal records spiked by over 270% year-on-year to nearly 16 billion records in the first half of that year,[7] and in 2022, for example, Australia suffered major breaches to national brands Optus, Medibank, and others,[8] resulting in a wave of new regulation and criminal sanctions imposed on company directors. Other parts of the world also approach the issue of governance, or malpractice, with the same vigor.

The actual cost to companies is often not available, but when Marriott International told the market that attackers had stolen data on more than 500 million guests in 2018,[9] it reported costs of more than US $44 million in the first quarter alone, separate to the US $25 million fine imposed by the UK Information Commissioner's Office.[10] I am not aware of any study of the impact on its brand or direct and indirect revenue loss suffered, but even without such data, we can assume additional losses to those noted above. Consequently, we have seen the rise of more secure identification controls, such as protecting customers at registration, authentication, and during in-session digital activity (timeouts etc.) and, of course, multi-factor authentication and the like.

Compliance and Consent

I won't visit in any detail the complex and significant information security management implications that surround this area. For a small portion of my career, I helped to run an information security consultancy firm with strong technical (ethical hacking, etc.) and governance practices. The latter helped organizations with compliance to various standards, most commonly:

- The principles-based ISO 27001.
- The prescriptive PCI DSS standard.
- Various government data classification-based information security regimes.

Globally, the rise of stringent data protection regulations such as the General Data Protection Regulation (GDPR) and the California Consumer Privacy Act (CCPA) have been shown to significantly increase business costs. In fact, a study by the Oxford Martin School, involving a large sample of companies exposed to GDPR in literally dozens of countries and industries, found that it reduced corporate profits by 8% on average, and sales by 2%.[11]

While this might be seen as an unnecessary impact on corporate performance, it is a partly a consequence of the morally wayward behaviors of marketing and CX practitioners, misusing personally identifiable data and funding media outlets and technologies with less than honorable records. If the buying public wasn't put in danger in the first place, lawmakers would not have to regulate such extensive protections. That doesn't mean that the practical implementation of GDPR and its ilk isn't unnecessarily onerous for business, or that most consumers haven't noticed. Indeed, there may be a robust case for both arguments, but marketing and customer management leaders are hardly in a credible position to make them. Whatever your view, they are now part of the terrain we must operate in.

In any event, industry responses such as Google's depreciation of third-party cookies and Apple's Intelligent Tracking Prevention made responsible data collection critically important, for both compliance and performance reasons. Remedies include the adoption of best practices related to first-party data collection, identity capture and stitching, and wider techniques such as pseudonymization, anonymization, and clean rooms, none of which I will write about here – they are well-trodden subjects.

Many firms believe that empowering customers with explicit consent processes – such as selecting options for how their data can be used upon arriving on a website – fosters transparency and trust. In my experience, most customers would prefer not to have the headache. They really don't want to spend their time reading about their options or checking boxes about the use of their data, the nature of which they don't readily understand anyway – and they certainly don't want to do it for every company they deal with, over and over, ad nauseum. This generates more friction, not something consumers like very much! Watch this space for aggregators.

It's a challenging issue, but the terrain is the terrain. In the current environment companies are forced to present those interfaces, and so consent has been a major emergent factor for customer management. One thing has become clear, though: gaining explicit informed consent relies on an inherent value exchange with customers, and that has several implications, most notably that some customers will not value the exchange ...

In that instance, companies might rely on "legitimate interest"[12] to present their offers, although often in reduced form. Having lost the third-party tracking cookies that had been the basis of sales personalization, especially in areas like re-targeting, these regulations have bitten. And thus we return to the need for better value in the exchange for customer consent.

The problem is that operational marketing teams, with a heavy bias toward sales conversion tactics, are not philosophically or capably oriented to the vastly more nuanced customer engagement challenge this issue embodies. And customers feel it. Emarsys found that nearly 50% of customers only want to hear from marketers "occasionally", while 20% do not want to hear from them at all.[13] I believe those numbers are in truth much higher, but they should grab your attention as is.

Customer data, and the consent of customers as to its use, is clearly a customering matter first and foremost, with marketing interests a downstream benefactor. In fact, a study by Cisco found that 19% of customers have left companies over data misuse,[14] and so consent management now forms a very contemporary element in resolving the *Barrier to Churn* principle. Mastering the service bias and the interaction model holistically, as described in these chapters, is critical.

Other Factors
Brand Size

Higher market penetration, together with the associated attitudinal bias toward prior usage, means that existing customers of larger brands will have a higher propensity to do the work associated with giving and managing their consent. Indeed, all customer operations are easier in larger brands with greater penetration, than they are in smaller ones with less. That's just a fact of life, and it plays out here too. It also means that if you are running customer operations for a smaller company (although this still holds in larger firms), you really do have to ensure that the interaction model is on point. It may also mean that if you're a smaller company, a seasonal partnership with a larger one might help to boost consent.

Experiential Tactics

In the interactions section of the book I will take you through the Customer Engagement Stack, two layers of which are managed by the customer team: Services and Experiences. The latter are memories, which are colored by the connected emotional dimension, and can therefore cause shorter term behavioral outcomes. For example, creative gamification might be a way either to create positive emotion just prior to asking for consent, or to make the process of giving it more enjoyable – or, more realistically, less painful.

The Trust Curve

Companies must understand that information exchange is a gradual or staged process for human beings. We don't go on a first date, for example, and start sharing our financial information and our deepest fears. Exposing ourselves to vulnerability only occurs to the extent that trust is formed, and this happens over time. The same principle applies here. Once someone has an account for example, it is easier to ask for other information. Customers have already crossed the threshold of giving you some information, so doing it again is less of a hill to climb. Equally, it is sensible to incrementally seek information over time, mimicking that human trait, rather than asking for all of it all at the same time. The latter not only carries the risk of running ahead of the trust curve, but also increases the cognitive load (effort) on the customer and the likelihood that they will abandon. This concept of obtaining information gradually, rather than all in hurry, is often known as "progressive profiling".

Incentivization

Value exchange may also invoke, in some settings, the use of incentivization tactics. An e-commerce site may offer free shipping on the next purchase in exchange for additional consents and associated information. Factoring in an offer or a campaign might be an area to collaborate on with the marketing department. But a word of caution. Customer management is not the domain of marketing. You must guard against marketing's promotional mindset overtaking the nuance of the customer mission. I refer you, again, to the trust curve, and remind you that the impacts of customer lifetime value go well beyond campaign short-termism. Treat your customers, and your interactions with them, with the greatest care.

Individualization

According to Pew Research,[15] 80% of American adults claim they are asked at least once a month to agree to a privacy policy, while another 25% claim that this happens almost daily. It has become akin to the imposition of never-ending customer surveys, and consequently companies, through sheer clumsiness as much as anything, are reaping the unfortunate fruits of customer fatigue.

It is important that you are only asking what you need of each individual customer, and nothing more. For instance, if you have both retail customers and wholesale customers, your needs from each may be different. Don't have a set template that becomes irrelevant to some. More granularly, consent may differ by customer cohorts, which, unlike marketing segments, are dynamic and behaviorally based. Being able to engage around the capture of consent with the same rich nuance as you would on any other aspect of engagement is critical. Always remember that each customer is an individual, and so we can optimize customer consent if providing the correct path, customer by customer, based on their individual intent. We will cover this in the next section but the lesson here is to have a library of options available within the customer interaction model, not an internal inflexible policy. Lastly, managing consent is a universal activity that applies across all subsequent channels and touchpoints. Never impose internal channel management siloes on customers. This is true of all aspects of customer management and obtaining consent is no different. Manage centrally, apply globally.

Systems

We all interact with typical identity management systems – possibly every day. This happens every time you log into a website for your grocery shopping, or to check when your utilities bill is due, or purchase concert tickets, or when you checked your feed on your social media account. Perhaps you completed some banking via a mobile app and received a one-time verification code via text message. Quite typically, identity management systems are built for digital channels only. In the commercial software market they are part of a category known as Customer Identity and Access Management (CIAM).

CIAM tools solved many of the problems that emerged in the very early days of customer websites, where customers we subjected to:

- Being forced to create an account and password just to browse a website.
- Offensively long disclosure requirements of personal information (for example) within the initial registration process.
- Disparate, limited, or unavailable access depending on device.
- Forced re-authentication at every new session irrespective of context, e.g., when using the same location and device.
- Being "channeled" to the contact center in order to reset a password.
- Having to create different accounts for different websites and apps of the same company, or to use different services of the same company.

While such errors hark from the early days of the web, it is astonishing how common many remain today. There is really no excuse. Even as more recent developments in authentication have entered the arena, such as face recognition on your smart device, most companies are still mired in channel siloes and are unable to address a customer consistently.

Clearly, poorly executed identity management introduces needless friction and reduced utilization, and thus diminishes the downstream engagement opportunities. When considered in the interactions model (Chapter 6), all service touchpoints must carry no, or low, cognitive load. In other words, they must be frictionless or near frictionless. Some systems, like a few of the customer data platform (CDP) vendors and the more advanced journey orchestration vendors, have identity management capabilities built in.

For instance, one vendor has a capability it calls the Adaptive Engagement Profile (AEP), which is a data repository that stores proprietary customer identifiers as well as their associated journey behavior, and then maps all that data about recognized customers (as described previously) back to systems of records (like a CRM) through their data adapters. Then, when it's time for that platform to orchestrate a customer conversation, its own decision engine references the AEP to create conversations that are relevant and specific to a customer, whether unknown or recognized.

It is best that tools such as this map back to existing systems of record that house that data, so that the risks associated with personally identifiable information are mitigated, along with those associated with sensitive data replication. It is also important to note that some of the vendors operating in the CDP space – a banner under which there is an increasingly diverse set of offerings – have developed customer identity and consent management capabilities in their platforms, and these are always advancing. Today, CIAM offerings and the like typically manage for a balance between and across three dimensions:

■ Technical security of customer accounts.
■ Management of both privacy and consent.
■ Compliance with regulatory mandates.

But, as the above examples attest, the most advanced systems of customer engagement – specifically orchestration capability, which we will soon discuss – now incorporate identity management capabilities and are designed to integrate with dedicated CIAM capability to balance security and compliance with engagement. We can certainly expect more convergence in these areas (Table 4.3).

Table 4.3 Summary of Identity

Function / Discipline	Description
Capture Status	Discerning the customer identity as relative to the company: • Unknown. • Recognized. • Verified.
Stitching	• Applying the capture status across sessions and channels. • Applying the multiple, disparate capture status per customer across sessions and channels, and customer need. • Leveraging the capture status across brand (within a group).
Cyber and Privacy	• Regulation. • Application of management systems for control of customer data. • Customer consent.
Applicable Systems	• Customer identity and access management. • Customer data platforms. • Journey orchestration capability.

Notes

1. Paul Greenberg, *CRM at the Speed of Light: Capturing and Keeping Customers in Internet Real Time* (Elsevier, 2001).
2. Vikas Mittal et al., "Customer Satisfaction, Loyalty Behaviors, and Firm Financial Performance: What 40 Years of Research Tells Us," *Marketing Letters* 34, no. 2 (2023): 171–187.
3. A customer key is an identifying element such their name, email, mobile number, account number, username etc.
4. "Misc. Roll DD: 5 Nov 1339 – 15 Dec 1346 (nos 349–399)," in *London Assize of Nuisance, 1301–1431: A Calendar* (London, 1973), 85–98. *British History Online*, no date. https://www.british-history.ac.uk/london-record-soc/vol10/pp85-98.
5. Samuel Warren and Louis D. Brandeis, "The Right to Privacy," *Harvard Law Review* 4, no. 5 (1890): 193.
6. A. Michael Froomkin, "The Death of Privacy?," *Stanford Law Review* 52, no. 5 (2000): 1461.
7. https://securityboulevard.com.
8. Edward Kost, "13 Biggest Data Breaches in Australia" [Blog post], *UpGuard*, updated 19 January 2024. https://www.upguard.com/blog/biggest-data-breaches -australia.
9. Nicole Perlroth, Amie Tsang, and Adam Satariano, "Marriott Hacking Exposes Data of Up to 500 Million Guests," *The New York Times*, 1 December 2018. https://www.nytimes.com/2018/11/30/business/marriott-data-breach.html.
10. Carly Page, "Marriott Hit with £18.4 Million GDPR Fine Over Massive 2018 Data Breach," *Forbes*, 30 October 2020. https://www.forbes.com/sites/carlypage /2020/10/30/marriott-hit-with-184-million-gdpr-fine-over-massive-2018-data -breach/?sh=a7a6be5e4b02.
11. Giorgio Presidente and Carl Benedikt Frey, "The GDPR Effect: How Data Privacy Regulation Shaped Firm Performance Globally," *CEPR*, 10 March 2022. https://cepr.org/voxeu/columns/gdpr-effect-how-data-privacy-regulation-shaped -firm-performance-globally.
12. Activities where personal information is demonstrably necessary for the processing of business operations. This requires that the company only conduct those that maintain the rights and freedoms of affected individuals (GDPR), and to inform them.
13. Emarsys, "The Great Retail Race: New Research Reveals Expanding Disconnect Between Customer and Retailer Perceptions," *Emarsys*, 16 October 2023. https://emarsys.com/press-release/the-great-retail-race-new-research-reveals-expanding -disconnect-between-customer-and-retailer-perceptions/.
14. CISCO, *Generation Privacy: Young Consumers Leading the Way. CISCO 2023 Consumer Privacy Survey* (CISCO, 2023). https://www.cisco.com/c/dam/en_us/ about/doing_business/trust-center/docs/cisco-consumer-privacy-report-2023.pdf.
15. Brooke Auxier et al., "Americans and Privacy in 2019 – Concerned, Confused and Feeling Lack of Control Over Their Personal Information," *Pew Research Center*, 24 October 2023. https://www.pewresearch.org/internet/2019/11/15/ americans-and-privacy-concerned-confused-and-feeling-lack-of-control-over -their-personal-information/.

Chapter 5

Pillar 2

Intent

There is a reason you have never walked into a hardware store and had a salesperson immediately accost you, "Hey! You need to buy this shovel!" Clearly, they have no idea of who you are, what you need, or why you walked into the store, information without which they are unable to curate the appropriate interaction.

This seems too obvious. And yet, if we transpose this scenario to the digital world, many companies are trying to shovel their shovels down our throat the moment we enter a website. They have a promotion on product X, and so that is what the banner promotes, or the chatbot promotes, or the pop-up promotes, or the follow-up email promotes, and so on. Many use what they see as a more advanced mode, in which they apply triggers to inform messaging. This is called personalization but it isn't, really – because it has nothing to do with the wants or needs of the *person* and has everything to do with the sales ambition of the company.

Instead, our goal as customer management leaders must be to engage customers on their intent, first and foremost, consistently with a bias to service.

Jobs to Be Done

As we discussed in Chapter 2, the Jobs To Be Done (JTBD) framework was originally conceived in the pursuit of corporate innovation, and marketing professors teach it in MBA-level curriculum for use in strategy functions. The legendary Clayton Christensen who co-wrote the book *Competing Against Luck*, said that

DOI: 10.4324/9781003513728-6

executives often fail because they study the wrong product and customer data, which leads them to unwittingly design innovation processes that churn out mediocrity.

This could not be more on the money, not just for innovation or marketing but also – and more so – when it comes to customer management. Companies are constantly working with the wrong data. Perhaps this is symptomatic of having so much of it at a time when our understanding of it and artificial intelligence are still so young.[1] This is certainly true of those that conflate marketing with customer operations and, to be fair, those that do stick to their lane. The overuse and misuse of surveys, an unhealthy homage to software company jargon, and the analysis of historical transactional data without contextual inputs are just three examples. Wrong data, wrong data, wrong data. Christensen was, and is, right.

In 2021, research company Hanover[2] asked consumers why they chose new brands. Half of all respondents said they've done so because they had a new need and found a brand that met it. A "need" is almost always framed by the job the customer wants to get done. And yet I submit, with great respect to both innovation management and marketing, that it is in customer operations that JTBD has potentially the greatest impact. As Christensen explains:

> When we buy a product we essentially 'hire' something to get a job done. If it does the job well, when we are confronted with the same job, we hire that same product again. And if the product does a crummy job, we 'fire' it and look around for something else we might hire to solve the problem.[3]

In other words, companies need to home in on the job the customer is trying to get done when taking on the customer management function – which is another way of saying we must understand their intent. This is an entirely different mode to dictating design patterns to sell something, the dominant mindset today. This, of course, is the basis for "customer journey maps", as they are commonly called. These maps, however, look more like nice, tidy, linear process diagrams rather than depictions of realistic – and messy – human behavior. They are works of fiction, based, again, on desired outcomes such as sales, conversions, acquisition and so on, not on the needs of the customer.

In contrast, when service design is properly based on JTBD, it ensures the customer's intent is determinant of each of the interactions that they encounter. When a utility customer is moving house, what is the real job they need to be done? When a new banking customer is taking out a loan, what is their context, and what is the job they really need to get done?

A customer's jobs are always multi-dimensional. More than purely functional, they routinely involve dominant sociological and psychological dimensions that inform and color the job itself. This means that the context in which a customer approaches a given job can be entirely different to that of another customer approaching the same job. Thus, again, beware of linear process methodologies disguised in the language of "journeys", which are simply not credible in the cold light of day. Equally, I caution against the dangers of applying averages. Human behavior is not divisible, so also beware of personalization hacks. More on that later.

The original godfather of JTBD, Tony Ulwick, wrote the highly successful book *Jobs to Be Done: Theory to Practice*.[4] He proposed that to gain deeper insight into a customer's needs, companies should stop focusing on the product and the customer in transactional terms, and instead aim to understand the underlying process – or "job" as Christensen would later term it – the customer is trying to complete when using a product or service. He went on to suggest, powerfully, that instead of companies obsessing over their own measures of success (e.g., sales short-termism),

> they need to understand what fundamental measures of performance actual customers use to measure success.

This is one of the truly essential tenets of customer engagement, and it requires that we apply an "outside-in" model to our operations. Using JTBD helps to translate that notion from a philosophical position to operational execution. It should be noted the model offers very real commercial benefits, reinforcing that service execution is a fuel for long-term sales results.

As a case in point, Ulwick's consulting company, Strategyn, first used the JTBD model for medical device company Cordis Corporation. Within two years Cordis launched 19 new products, all of which became number one or two in their category, and Cordis's market share increased from 1% to more than 20%.[5] Its stock price more than quadrupled. While this is a marketing example, it certainly reinforces the power of JTBD, compelling customer management leaders to recognize intent as foundational.

The Dimensions of Intent

Our individual intentions are, of course, subject to our very particular psychology, which in turn is affected by a range of external and internal factors ranging from social influences that evolve over time to stimuli that occur in any moment. Translating this to repeatable management requires a capability that considers each dimension.

"Why" over "What"

Context is the first key to understanding a person's intent. Consider the man who rushes home in the middle of the day, a look of desperation on his face. He flings open his front door and there, standing on the other side, is his wife. She turns and looks at him. She doesn't say a word. Neither does he. They embrace.

Is this a story of newly-weds, apart for the first time since their honeymoon, desperate for each other's presence? Or is it a story of sadness, the news of the passing of his wife's dear grandmother, sending him home to her? Or has their doctor called to seek a conference on the prognosis of their sick child in hospital? Perhaps, instead, they have won the state lottery?

All those scenarios fit equally well with the visible actions, the "what", and so it should be clear that this surface information is entirely inadequate to determine what is happening, and what to do next. Understanding the "why" is critical.

His rushing home, his sense of urgency, his flinging the door open, his quick embrace of his wife, are all easily viewable actions, but without their context they are useless. It is the same with customer management. Like it or not, it is a job that requires a more nuanced approach to humanity than does marketing. This isn't to say that market diagnostics is an easy task – not by any stretch – but mass-market dynamics are ultimately generalizable and divisible into segments. This is their very nature. Engaging with the weird and wonderful human species, one by one, however, offers a distinct challenge. It poses an inherent test for those who manage, and those who use marketing technologies, to interact with customers. The trigger-based activation for campaigns or messaging so commonly applied using these technologies is very dangerous and often very destructive of value. Why? Because those using it concern themselves only with the "what", and rarely with the "why".

In truth, customer context needs both, and while the "what" may be easy to recognize, unearthing the "why" is only possible by understanding the majority, if not the entirety, of the customer journey. Even then, we must understand that the fullness of their journey may include interactions with third parties or across wider ecosystems of which we do not have visibility. By and large though, we can ascertain the customer "why" far more clearly than is common today.

By way of example, if someone calls the contact center of their telecommunications company right after they have run a speed test on their home internet connection that provided poor results, there is a high probability that the reason for their call is related, yet most companies never deduce a correlation. Contact center managers often have "journey map" pinned to their wall that starts with the inbound call. They have no interest in or ability to connect the prior actions of the customer and are only concerned with the "what" – that the customer is calling – almost never with "why" it is that they are doing so.

Just think about the operational enhancements if they did:

- They could route the call directly to the right department or agent rather than putting the customer through the standard triage process.
- This would lower the time on the phone for the customer.
- And lower the cost to serve incurred by the company.
- They could insert logic into the tree of the IVR, again reducing the time on the call for the customer, and or automating as much of the resolution as possible to the benefit of both parties, but most importantly, the customer.

More mature companies wouldn't wait for the customer call at all. They already know the customer ran a speed test and that the result was poor. Why would they defer service when poor performance is potentially threatening the tenure of that customer? Instead, they raise a ticket immediately to resolve the internet speed and send a text message to alert the customer to the fact that they know there is an issue, and that they are already working to resolve it.

There are a range of other actions that a truly customer-centric telecommunication business would take. If you work in the field, you can probably imagine some, but hopefully my point is made: it was not that the customer wanted to call the contact center that was primary, it was *why* they wanted to do so that was at the heart of it all. It was, in other words, all about customer intent.

Time

While customer engagement occurs over time, it is made of up of an ongoing series of interactions that are nuanced, self-contained, and yet, in some circumstances, can affect downstream intent and interactions.

Equally, we must also factor in decay; advanced capabilities will do this by using out-of-the-box algorithms. The concept of decay simply recognizes that an interaction, or set of interactions, that occurred in the past may not be at all relevant to the interactions that are occurring today.

Behavioral and Unstructured

The observation of actual human behavior always offers the most powerful insights. In research terms, this is called, "ethnography".

Ethnography can be defined as "the first-hand experience and exploration of a particular social or cultural setting based on 'participant observation'".[6] And that's perfect, because it means that we, the company, must participate – or interact – with them, the customers. Ethnography focuses on work in the field, observing either collectives (societies, communities, social groups, etc.) or individuals – which is central to customering. It seeks to explore, and understand, the situational settings of the subjects, going beyond other human influences to include environmental and cultural factors.

Now, many are quick to consign areas like the social sciences to the too-hard basket. It is a field, after all, that most in business circles haven't studied and aren't all that interested in. There can be little patience for that attitude among customer management people, however, because there is no escaping that customers are indeed human beings. If one has no interest in how humans operate, make decisions, and interrelate within different settings, then, frankly, they are not a fit for the job. Others who claim an interest but argue that the social sciences are difficult to translate into industry might be interested to know that it has done, and for a long time now. For example, ethnography has been used for many years in shaping healthcare systems, policy, and even nursing as a profession.[7]

More broadly, there are examples where incorporating insights from behavioral sciences has led to better implementation of programs to reach the most marginalized. To take one example, a project in Kenya was trying to encourage the chlorination of water to prevent deaths from diarrhea. Public education campaigns to encourage people to add chlorine to their water had failed, but removing behavioral barriers through a simple intervention – deploying chlorine dispensers at the same location people were already picking up their water – increased the uptake of chlorination by 53%.[8]

Herein lies the lesson. Customers are less prone, especially in the age of overcommunication, to respond to a *campaign*, something that is targeted *at* them, than they are to a change in *environment*, something that happened *with* them.

The value of this approach, the observation of behaviors, is supported by substantial evidence. In fact, ethnography is a long-established methodology, having originated in the early 1800s. Its roots can be traced back to colonization of the "New World" when anthropologists became interested in exploring races and cultures outside Europe. The primary focus was to study "primitive", unindustrialized peoples and cultures using written description and records, and later photography.[9] Ethnographers typically spent months or years conducting research, during which they were present among but "detached" from those they were observing.

Being "detached", in this context, means that researchers must observe their subjects *without being influenced by their own beliefs and values*. This is an important principle in customer management. It means that we start with them, not with us, or with an agenda of acquisition, conversion, etc. Too many impose a value system on the outcome of the "research" irrespective of the actual customer behavior, and there is no better example of this than poorly executed surveys dripping with bias. This is not a new issue. Traditional ethnographic research relied heavily on researchers' ability to explain communities' richness and complexity, a challenge faced by marketers today, and it was argued that their findings were often influenced by their own "preconceptions and prejudices concerning cultures other than their own".[10]

The common problem today is that no matter the research undertaken, the bias to interpret everything as either additive to, or diminishing of, the sales agenda is prevalent – and crippling. Once we cauterize that infection from our own businesses, we come back to the question of how to deploy the power of ethnography in customer operations.

There are two answers.

The first, is that ethnography plays an important role in designing customer assets, such as website and mobile apps and the like. I will talk about this in the interaction section of the book. The second has more to do with the behavioral tendencies and flows that occur when customers encounter, involve themselves with, and eventually – or at least hopefully – engage with the channels we have made available to them. That's what we will focus on here.

Now, behavioral scientists study the common patterns in how people make decisions, but customer management leaders don't have the luxury of conducting a three month study, or something more longitudinal, analyzing the data, experimenting, establishing hypotheses and testing them, before finalizing a set of findings for possible activities in a customer program. All that has wider value, but that is the role of academics. Instead, our mission is to engage with customers in real time, when and how they are choosing to do so. Sure, we may have a body of research that underpins some of our work, but interaction management lives for and in the moment.

So, how do we couple the power of ethnography as the most valuable source of customer insight, with the demands of real-time engagement? And how do we do so repeatably, and at scale?

Operational Ethnography

In the section that looked at identity, we talked about "stitching" – the capability that enables the identification of an individual, across their various statuses (unknown, recognized, verified), by *stitching* them all together to represent an individual person. Well, stitching is a foundational component of the advanced function of customer observance (ethnography). Once we know who is doing what, and our eyes are opened to the nuance of their individual journey(s), person by person, this ultimately enables individualized interactions – as we will soon discuss.

Of course, the CX movement immediately defaults to surveys as the best way to establish a person's intent, satisfaction, etc. But "remembered satisfaction" is quite different to "live satisfaction" at the point of receiving an interaction.[11] The act of inserting a survey at the point of interaction is counter-productive, because it actively imposes friction in precisely the location that we do not want it. This is why observational techniques are so important. Operational ethnography, whereby we obtain very significant behavioral insight and inferred sentiment, requires no additional friction and is not tainted by the memory variables inherent in reported satisfaction or other impressions.

Beyond this individual insight, we must also make business decisions based on the aggregate. Fortunately, customer journeys can be observed at both levels. This is often called "journey visualization" and when you see it in action for the first time, you quickly realize why traditional "journey mapping" is almost entirely redundant.

Real Journey Visualization

It is critical to understand that the below illustration (Figure 5.1) is not the typical left-to-right staging of a traditional journey map: there is nothing dictated or linear.

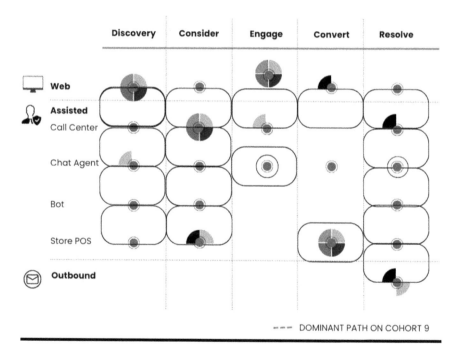

--- DOMINANT PATH ON COHORT 9

Figure 5.1 Cross Channel Journey Visualization

While you might see terms such as "convert", these are merely the selected labels, which can vary. What is important to note is that all touch points are mapped to customer jobs and stages, and the data is only then populated in the form of journey flows as customers interact with them. In other words, the map is drawn bottom-up, if you like, by customers themselves as they interact directly at every single touch point. This is dynamic and real-world data that requires no customer preference research or anything like it. Instead, companies simply watch the actual behavioral journeys unfold right in front of them. There is nothing theoretical.

Another way to think about this is that it is a "real" customer journey map, not a contrived, inside-out process based on a sales orientation or notional personas, nor does it require focus groups or other forms of qualitative testing, or quantitative measures, given that we are already dealing in real data. It is like watching a nature documentary, observing the animals – i.e., customers – in their natural habitat. You are dealing in actuals, and can respond accordingly, rather than seeking to drive customers down a run like cattle and through company-ordained decision gates.

Such practices are not optimal, but let's park that contention for a moment because we are dealing with the discernment of intent only at this stage, nothing more. In this instance, the map is exactly that. There is no activation yet, and no presumption or bias toward sales. We are simply mapping the actual behavioral terrain, customer by customer, by behavioral cohorts, and in the aggregate. This informs both immediate and deferred actions.

Of course, if you can only see from one eye you will suffer distortions of perception. The same is true of customer channels and so we must deploy sensors at every touchpoint. Think JavaScript tags on the website, APIs to in-store systems (POS, WiFi, etc.), call center management systems and IVRs, CRM systems and service applications used by mobile service agents, speech, text analytics engines, and from pixel trackers and SDKs within mobile apps, and external information sources such as geofencing services, weather apps, etc. There is no limit to that which can be ingested, and so long as it can be, it must be. Companies that don't sense every single touchpoint will not understand the full map and its intersections, and will therefore miss aspects of context, diminishing the ability to discern intent. However, those that are in possession of this customer insight are well ahead of the majority.

No longer does a firm have to experiment to understand customer propensities, nor does it need to develop static left-to-right "maps" that, held up against the cold light of chaotic human behavior and across complex channels, no longer reflects actual journeys anyway. This is a big subject, that I know will confront some, and I'll deal with the demise of traditional journey mapping more fully later in in the book, but for now, it is important to recognize that:

1. This was inherently based on the "average", which is the direct opposite of individually nuanced engagement.
2. Even the applied average was not reliable because it wasn't derived from "actuals" (i.e., real journeys).

In contrast, visualization based on the combination of stitching and real human behaviors, enables us to understand a range of scenario investigations. The below is by no means exhaustive but provides some illustration. At the aggregate level, companies can:

- Interrogate points of progression between stages of customer and company value.
- Correlate journey characteristics with customer jobs.
- Isolate points of regression and explore common paths to that point.
- Identify propensity for behaviors based on variables in "journey-to-date".
- Profile all journey abandonments (not just the cart!).
- Review dominant paths by job, cohort, and virtually any other variable.

In addition, a customer management practitioner might inquire of their platform:

> "Show me all customer journeys that originated from the Google ad ID 12345, arrived on the landing page, engaged the chatbot, but abandoned the web asset at the information page, and called the contact center."

If you work in the field, you will recognize that this is a particular query that might be used to resolve call deflection[12] issues for a very specific cohort. This level of granularity and accuracy was unprecedented in the industry, but has revolutionized the capture of customer insight broadly, and customer intent specifically, for those that use it. Of course, in addition to sensors at touchpoints, a good engine will also ingest transactional data more commonly associated with a CRM or data platform, and in doing so, practitioners can gain even more granularity in their queries, by adding (for example):

> for all known customers with a CLV under 100 and churn propensity score over 20.

And/or:

> for all customers with a mobile plan and a preference for the iPhone.

While these queries use natural language they still aren't entirely natural, and will seem somewhat cumbersome compared to generative AI use cases. Still, the variables are almost limitless. Visualization places in the hands of customer management leaders, tangible, real data, evolving in real time. Moreover, it frees up chunks of time spent on surveys and focus groups and statistical analysis, and all the other means of research assumed necessary to derive a perception of journey, not to mention all the budget tied up in that process. Of all the sources of insight, this is the most powerful and the most useful – and, given that the tools used to obtain it are often the same as those used to activate it, easily the most actionable. We'll talk more about that in the orchestration section in the Interactions pillar.

Now consider the power of being able to detect, in genuine real time, the warning signals that might precede a customer's potential attrition, well beyond the obvious common examples of purchase patterns, complaints or key words used during interactions, etc. What if you could perceive nuanced product use, unobvious or complex journey constructions with a high propensity for downstream churn outcomes, specific combinations of customer asset interactions, and so on. Visualization enables much richer, and much earlier, detection not just of churn risks but of opportunities for service optimization, which we'll soon discuss. This is all based on the ability to discern intent.

Journey Research

While journey analytics is among the more advanced capabilities, it is complemented by journey research, and in that order. The initial concepts of journey mapping and service design were not supported by hard data and so companies had little option but to use dubious inputs (e.g., surveys – see "self-reporting" later in this chapter – and workshopping). This combination of bad data inputs to inform equally bad practice was predictable. For instance, the traditional journey map, according to Graham Hill[13] of Optima,

> creates an unrepresentative, unrealistic, and unimplementable understanding of customers and their behaviour. The widespread use of these maps has damaged the professionalisation of service experience design.

But today's technological capability has solved these problems. Data lakes containing information about customers, their contracts, their contacts, and their real-time consumption data are commonplace. Sadly, though, this is all most companies analyse customers on, never realizing that they are missing another "c" – their *context*.

Enter journey analytics, Sankey diagrams, and live visualization as earlier described. Now we are starting to see the actual journeys that real customers take to get their jobs done. However, while journey analytics will tell you everything you need to know about the journeys customers undertook, they are less effective at telling you about why they took them. It is true that we can infer some intent from the journey, but not *all* intent, and we remain blind to aspects of their journeys that involved other companies.

And so, the use of journey analytics to inform targeted, not broad-brush, journey research is often the optimal combination for discerning customer intent. This might include very carefully constructed approaches such as:

- Customer or user interviews.
- Direct observation.
- Contextual inquiry.
- Diary studies.

Text Analytics

One area to emerge in the 2010s is that of text and speech analytics. Most commonly, these are used post-event, such as complaints or elicited feedback; this is not without merit, but isn't as effective for understanding the in-the-moment intent of a customer. Applying this capability earlier is an area of opportunity.

Using natural language processing (NLP) helps companies understand the explicit communication of customers. NLP is an interdisciplinary field that draws upon text analysis, computational linguistics, artificial intelligence, and machine learning. It helps computers to "read", "understand", and then to "replicate" human speech. If captured in real time and not just as part of a feedback process, this offers another conversational source of interaction and enables an equally real-time reaction on the part of the company, as we will discuss in the next section. However real-time interaction, especially but not exclusively, leans heavily on the ability to deal in nuance if it is to offer any confidence that the customer's intent is properly understood. NLP can be a very useful input because it seeks to decipher the linguistic use and the context behind the text, but it can't operate in isolation of the wider journey context.

Paying attention to customer comments has always been important, especially unsolicited comments. Done properly, it can identify the key "jobs" where any problems occurred, the in-scope touchpoints, and particular gaps. However, more advanced journey visualization capability acts as a short-cut for much of this work, and a source of validation.

Conversational

One of the great opportunities that remains largely untapped is the ability for direct, conversational engagement between company and customer. In its peak expression, this mirrors the way the everyday people communicate with each other. If you want to check on what your electricity bill is going to be this month, why can't you just text your provider?

- "Hey Origin, what's my bill so far?"
- "Hey Aarron. $267 – with four days to go".

Now this is, of course, an interaction, which we will be discussing in the next section, but as we have seen with the visualization of observed behaviors, conversational interactions are also a source of insight. Consider what the above conversation might begin to suggest to us. For instance, is the customer is under financial distress?

Of course, SMS, or text messaging, is a medium in which the tone is set by those who use it, and for the most part it is used within family and social groups, which has established it as a medium of informality. No one texts using formal language, and even the norms of grammar have increasingly become optional – so much so that educators have worried about the habits it forms in young people. This extends into other messaging apps, such as WhatsApp, or Facebook Messenger, or even the more business-minded LinkedIn messaging. By extension, it's an opportunity for companies to interact in a setting that is inherently more conversational than anywhere else, certainly in terms of customer channels.

Another conversational medium, albeit one that is less informal than messaging applications and SMS, is chatbots. Of course, many bots are really just basic engines serving up pre-scripted content without any ability to deal with customer nuance, and in such instances no tone of voice deployed within the content will make up for its inadequacies in mimicking human conversation. Other companies use the interface as another means by which their contact center can engage with web visitors without them having to change "channel" or make an inbound call, and as such there is a human being typing away at the other end of the exchange. This is, of course, a much higher cost to serve, but the former and cheaper alternative nearly always creates customer frustration. Of course, as the technology improves, particularly through the application of generative AI, the two draw closer together.

Irrespective of the technology, however, we know that when human beings can interact in ways that are more natural to them, they are prone do so more often and/or more openly, which in turn generates more contextual insight.

Conversational Insight Combined with Behavioral

Conversational insight adds further context into the journey flows. If someone abandoned a journey at a particular point, and if this was preceded by a conversational interaction, discerning their intent is easier, although not definitive, as we have direct communication. An important point to keep in mind is that what people say and what they do are very often different things, and so having the ability to observe their actions, pre- and post- conversation with the company, can be illuminating. Unfortunately, many companies accept certain feedback as gospel, when the even the behavior of those that have given it suggests a different reality.

Consider again the conversational interaction over the current electricity bill. If this indicates that the customer is under financial distress, your journey visualization might show them exploring flexible payment terms on your website. Combining a conversational interaction, perhaps via a messaging app, with a set of otherwise seemingly isolated activities can provide a richer behavioral basis upon which to confirm a customers need.

Self-reports

The least powerful method for establishing customer intent is, ironically, the most common, the least understood, and the most error-ridden. If you recall the pages on market diagnostics, surveys are properly used as a quantitative tool to give scale to findings established using qualitative methods. Well, the same attraction to scale applies here, but the default assumption – that to understand human behavior, all we need do is ask about it – is not an enlightened one.

The resulting survey spam is ineffective and problematic. Companies prescribe their use immediately after a sale, during onboarding and support interactions, and as soon as possible for product feedback. A range of other surveys (NPS, CSAT, etc.[14]) are also sent regularly over longer periods of time, and the sheer volume is negative. Globally, the arrival of "survey fatigue" among consumers is growing and response rates are declining. This is no surprise. Consider that the movement also advocates sending a survey to every new customer and then either quarterly or bi-annually to track their trends. Now, add up all these periodic and triggered surveys, and then multiply that annual figure by the number of companies of which any individual is a customer, and you will see how totally out of hand this has become from a customer perspective. However, it is not just the volume of surveys that is the problem. It is their very nature.

The "observer effect",[15] first postulated in the field of physics, establishes that changes occur in an observed system simply from the very act of observation. Its parallel is the "Hawthorne effect," coined by John R. P. French,[16] in which human behavior is reactively modified in response to the subject's awareness that they are being observed.

Instruments such as surveys, which are disruptive and intercessory in nature, alter the environment and can inherently have this effect. In short, they almost always degrade the journey; as author Roger Dooley[17] notes:

> The mere act of trying to measure customer experience changes that experience, almost always for the worse.

Remember that our goal is to discern intent, which requires a level of observation of the behavioral, but it is very important for those who work in the field to understand that when it comes to customers self-reporting techniques are largely unfit for this purpose.

Issues with Self-reporting

The flaws of self-reported data are well understood in the social sciences world. There are many reasons why self-reporting is plagued by unreliability. One is the phenomenon is of "post rationalization"[18] –when we ask someone why they did a certain thing, they will often construct a reason that makes sense to them, even if they didn't in fact do the thing that we have asked them about. One of the reasons humans do this is that we often can't recall doing something if it was a low-cognitive activity – and even if we remember doing it we usually don't know *why* we did it, which is the nub of the issue behavioral research is trying to address. So when we are asked about our actions we will often accept the premise of the question on face value, assume that we did whatever we are being asked about, and then rationalize why we must have done it. Some believe that social desirability bias[19] plays havoc here too. Operating both consciously and non-consciously, this bias prevents us from simply saying "I don't know", especially when we are talking about our own behavior – instead, we quite literally imagine ourselves doing it, overlay a supposition of why we must have done so, and report it as if fact. It's not as insidious as a conscious lie. We are genuine in our reasoning. But it's still not true.

Despite this, many CX programs run such lines of questioning and then seek to act on the flawed datasets that the answers generate. Some even trigger active APIs sending noxious data directly to customer-facing staff or to the systems that they use, automating its distribution. As the techies would say, GIGO![20]– or, as Rory Sutherland says in his book *Alchemy*:[21]

> Solving problems using rationality is like playing golf with only one club.

But this is just the tip of the iceberg. In another example, this time from the health sector, Saul Shiffman of the University of Pittsburgh's Department of Psychology found that the diaries of health patients (i.e., after the fact) did not prove accurate recording of simple objective events like smoking.[22] In fact, he said, people often fail to accurately record simple events into their memory, let alone report them. It is just not there for recall.

In the same report, two other scholars made telling comments. First, psychologist John Bargh of Yale University remarked:

> It's difficult for people to accept, but most of a person's everyday
> life is not determined by their conscious intentions and delib-
> erate choices, but by mental processes put into motion by the
> environment.

And Wendy Baldwin of the NIH[23] Office of Extramural Research noted that

> observational and experimental studies have shown that there are
> barriers to accuracy at every stage of the autobiographical report
> process: perception, the state of the self, encoding and storage of
> memory, understanding the question being asked, recalling the
> facts, and judging how and what to answer.

Indeed, self-reporting has a range of accepted validity problems. For instance,
in the same way that patients may exaggerate symptoms to make their situation
seem worse, or conversely under-report the severity or frequency of symptoms in
order to minimize their problems, customers are more prone to negative sentiment for a range of perception-based reasons. If they complain more, might they
obtain a favorable offer, or a freebie? If they are more compliant, will they find
more favor? And if they really don't have a position on the question, how have
they interpreted or psychologically reacted to the nature of the question itself,
or its wording?

This last point was reflected by the Ehrenberg Bass Institute in relation to the
"usage drives attitude" bias, finding that consumers know *and say more* about
brands that they use (or use more) than others, and so larger brands always have
higher scores on surveys than smaller ones. Penetration, and usage bias, combine
to produce this effect.

Likewise, there are problems with the mechanisms of memory encoding and
recall.[24] Remembering is a reconstructive task and typically suffers from a range
of distortions, including the bundling of events, the tendency to "telescope"
them (loss of perspective as to proximity in time), and to bring them forward
from their actual chronological place, possibly based on other events that are
bundled into the overall memory.

Also problematic is the evidence of *mood-dependent memory*[25] – namely, that
because memory is reconstructive, not merely a computer-like readout of your
brain's data, it is inherently affected by mood states. Thus, if a person feels poorly
or is in a low mood state when questions are asked, for example, their answers
will be more negative, while if they feel good their answers will tend to be more
positive. Of course, a person's mood state is reflective of a range of factors –
not just the interaction or stimuli that is occurring or has just occurred (e.g.,

a visit to a website or service center), but also the macro influences in their life such as other forms of stress and concern, or sources of contentment, happiness, excitement, etc. Compounding matters, it has been found that men and women emphasize different sources of information, which affects memory and recall.[26]

The fact is that most decisions are made in sub- or non-conscious states, affected by complex factors therein. It has been suggested[27] that as much as 95% or 96% of our decision making occurs this way. In summary, self-reporting is ineffective as a means to determine intent.

Remedies for Self-reporting

It is important to note that there are methods that can mitigate some of these validity issues, usually in terms of the sample size; these methods have varying reported effectiveness but none of them resolve the foundational problems. Nor, of course, do they address the inherent profile differences between people who respond and those who don't (i.e., selection bias).

It is fair to counter that many practitioners simply don't understand how to best construct surveys. Alan Nance, president of XLACollab in Florida, notes:[28]

> Most surveys are poorly constructed, unscientifically fabricated, and with questionable reporting accuracy. A survey is only help-ful if it is anchored in separate sources of empirical data.

Other theoretical and scientifically proposed remedies include helping the respondents to reconstruct the past more accurately by asking questions that are structured according to the way in which the events are likely to have been encoded. But this theory struggles to find a home in practical terms. It is impossible for a researcher to know what sequence, unique to the individual customer and their context, informed their memory structures.

In scientific circles, "validity" refers to whether a study measures what it claims to measure. Surveys are often found to lack validity, for a number of reasons, and one way of assessing their validity is to compare the results of the self-reporting with another test. This is referred to as "concurrent validity".[29] Of course, this other test has to be on the same topic and applied in the same context and time, which is not always possible – and even where concurrent validity is confirmed, it is still only *perception* of memory, and does not escape all of the issues briefly discussed in this section.

There are also a range of tools that can be used to address the problem of respondent bias. Most commonly these involve the use of "constructions" to minimize respondent distortions, such as the use of scales to assess attitude, measure personal bias, and identify the level of resistance, confusion, and lack of adequate response time, etc. Stripping out any leading questions helps remove bias from both questioner and respondent, and open questions allow respondents to expand upon their replies. Ironically, one of the favored approaches to confirm a survey's validity is by using observation strategies, which, as we have already established, are a more powerful and accurate source of customer intent than any other – which poses the question of why the customer management community starts and ends most of its work on "insight" with surveys in the first place. Part of the answer is that most programs are not tethered into a governing management framework such as the four pillars, and so they are not actually seeking to understand intent to inform interactions in a programmatic manner. The other aspect is the undue influence of software vendors, as previously discussed.

Actionability

Compounding the issues of self-reported data is the nature of successful interactions themselves. As we will discuss in the Interactions pillar of the management model, these must be delivered, or offered, in the customer's context. One of the dimensions of context is *time*. For any interaction to be the most valuable to both customer, and by extension the company, it must occur in the customer's moment of value.

In fact, if it's in service of a live customer journey, it must meet the Doherty Threshold,[30] which states that a customer's psychological engagement soars when a computer and its users interact in 400 milliseconds or less (i.e., with close to zero discernible lag). Neither must wait on the other.

Surveys, by their very nature, do not enable anything resembling a subsequent real-time interaction. Of course, this is fine for market research or product feedback, but if your goal is engagement you can't afford the lag. Surveys are, by default, non-actionable as a means of high-value customer interaction in relation to the customer's live context, with the exception of sending an email, which, even if delivered quickly, will be read if and when the customer chooses to do so.

In summary, self-reported data is:

■ Reliable for non-time-critical and high-cognitive research (e.g., product feedback).
■ Defective as a means of behavioral insight and real-time engagement.
■ Unreliable in the discernment of customer intent.

As a guide, the typical use cases of surveys is summarized in Table 5.1:

Table 5.1 Survey Effectiveness

Use Case	Business Area	Effectiveness	Notes
Market Research (Quant)	Marketing Diagnostics	●	Scaling qualitative research findings to market sizing (see Chapter 2).
Brand Metrics	Marketing Measurement	◐	Consumer surveys are one method within a range.
Product Feedback	Marketing Measurement	●	Surveys work well for high-cognitive (rational) use cases such as product feedback. See the marketing's tactical pillar.
Brand Health within Customers	Customer Measurement	◐	See the upcoming chapter on Measurement: part of testing brand health within existing customers, related to memorability of experiential activation.
Asset Design	Customer Management	◐	As part of initial design research. High-cognitive only.
Behavioral Insight	Customer Management	○	Not appropriate. See section on self-reported data.

Summarizing the Capture of Intent

The goal of this section was to understand the most effective ways in which we, as a business, can discern our customers' intent, as a lubricant to better and more fruitful engagement with them. To that end, I summarize the usefulness of the various methods discussed as follows, noting that the combination of journeys and the conversational data within them is most powerful (Table 5.2).

Table 5.2 Insight Variables

Insight		Application		
Source	*Description*	*Asset Design*	*Channel Design / Iteration*	*Real-time Interaction*
Behavioral / visualization	Longitudinal observation and ethnography.	◑	●	●
Conversational	Unsolicited, casual (e.g., SMS, advanced chatbots, etc).	◔	◔	●
Elicited / self-reported.	Predominantly surveys	◑	◔	○

As the right-hand columns of this table indicates, the value or detraction of insight is always manifest in the resulting interactions that impact customers, such that the business value is increased, or decreased. So then, let's look at the Interactions pillar.

Notes

1. Aarron Spinley, "The Big Problem with Big Data," *Forbes*, 7 March 2022. https://www.forbes.com/sites/forbescommunicationscouncil/2022/03/07/the-big -problem-with-big-data/?sh=f8e1ba540a31.
2. S. Jacques, *2021 Trends in Shifting Consumer Behavior* (Hanover Research, 2021). https://www.hanoverresearch.com/reports-and-briefs/2021-trends-in -shifting-consumer-behavior/?org=corporate.
3. Dina Gerdeman, "Clayton Christensen: The Theory of Jobs to Be Done," *HBS Working Knowledge*, October 3, 2016. https://hbswk.hbs.edu/item/clay-chris- tensen-the-theory-of-jobs-to-be-done.
4. Anthony W. Ulwick, *Jobs to Be Done: Theory to Practice* (Idea Bite Press, 2016).
5. Strategyn LLC, "Cordis Corporation Stock Surges 6X after New Product Releases," *Strategyn*, no date. https://strategyn.com/jobs-to-be-done/cordis-case -study/.
6. Lee M. McDonald and James A. Sanders, *The Canon Debate* (Baker Academic, 2001).
7. Mildred H. B. Robertson and Joyceen S. Boyle, "Ethnography: Contributions to Nursing Research," *Journal of Advanced Nursing* 9, no. 1 (1984): 43–49; Edward V. Cruz and Gina Higginbottom, "The Use of Focused Ethnography in Nursing

Research," *Nurse Researcher* 20, no. 4 (2013): 36–43; Sheria G. Robinson, "The Relevancy of Ethnography to Nursing Research," *Nursing Science Quarterly* 26, no. 1 (2012): 14–19.

8. Michael Kremer, Edward Miguel, Clair Null, and Alix Zwane, "Chlorine Dispensers for Safe Water," *Innovation for Poverty Action*, no date. https://poverty-action.org/impact/chlorine-dispensers-safe-water.

9. Gemma S. Ryan, "An Introduction to the Origins, History and Principles of Ethnography," *Nurse Researcher* 24, no. 4 (2017): 15–21.

10. David M. Fetterman, *Ethnography: Step-by-Step* (3rd edition, Sage Publications, 2010).

11. Tore Pedersen, Margareta Friman, and Per Kristensson, "The Role of Predicted, On-Line Experienced and Remembered Satisfaction in Current Choice to Use Public Transport Services," *Journal of Retailing and Consumer Services* 18, no. 5 (2011): 471–475.

12. Call deflection is a common goal of companies to deflect customers away from their contact centre, which represents a high cost to serve, and instead seeks to keep them on self-service (low cost) channels.

13. Graham Hill, "Rethinking Service Experience," *LinkedIn*, 2019. https://www.linkedin.com/feed/update/urn:li:activity:6820709258250743808/.

14. Net Promoter Score and Customer Satisfaction.

15. Also known as the Heisenberg Uncertainty Principle.

16. Jessica M. Utts and Robert F. Heckard, *Mind on Statistics* (Cengage Learning, 2021), 222.

17. Roger Dooley, *Brainfluence: 100 Ways to Persuade and Convince Consumers with Neuromarketing* (John Wiley & Sons, 2011).

18. Martina Lind, Mimì Visentini, Timo Mäntylä, and Fabio Del Missier, "Choice-Supportive Misremembering: A New Taxonomy and Review," *Frontiers in Psychology* 8 (2017): 2062.

19. Allen Edwards, *The Social Desirability Variable in Personality Assessment and Research* (The Dryden Press, 1957).

20. "Garbage in, garbage out."

21. Rory Sutherland, *Alchemy: The Surprising Power of Ideas That Don't Make Sense* (Random House, 2019).

22. John Garcia and Andrew R. Gustavson, "The Science of Self-Report," *Observer*, 1 January 1997. https://www.psychologicalscience.org/observer/the-science-of-self-report.

23. National Institutes of Health.

24. Justin Storbeck and Gerald L. Clore, "Affect Influences False Memories at Encoding: Evidence from Recognition Data," *Emotion* 11, no. 4 (2011): 981–989.

25. Penelope A. Lewis and Hugo D. Critchley, "Mood-Dependent Memory," *Trends in Cognitive Sciences* 7, no. 10 (2003): 431–433.

26. François Guillem and Melodee Mograss, "Gender Differences in Memory Processing: Evidence from Event-related Potentials to Faces," *Brain and Cognition* 57, no. 1 (2005): 84–92.

27. Gerald Zaltman, *How Customers Think: Essential Insights into the Mind of the Market* (Harvard Business School Press, 2003); C. James Jensen, *Beyond the Power of Your Subconscious Mind* (Waterside Publications, 2012).

28. Alan Nance, "XLAs Are the Magic Linking Pin for Employee, Supplier, and Customer Experience Management," *HRM Outlook*, November 7, 2022. https://hrmoutlook.com/xlas-are-the-magic-linking-pin-for-employee-supplier-and-customer-experience-management/.

29. Kassiani Nikolopoulou, "What Is Concurrent Validity?" *Scribbr*, 10 September 2022. https://www.scribbr.com/methodology/concurrent-validity/.

30. Walter J. Doherty and Ahrvind J. Thadani, *The Economic Value of Rapid Response Time* (I.B.M. Corporation, 1998).

Chapter 6

Pillar 3

Interactions

PART A - Foundations

Having discussed how we establish and delineate individual customer identity and then discern the markers of specific intent, with the latter building on the former, our linear customer management model now takes us into the resulting interactions, served on an individualized basis.

Indeed, that concept, *individualization*, is central to effective customer management and you will learn much about it in this chapter, noting that it is a far more powerful and advanced capability than mere personalization. But it is not the only key concept we must understand to deliver our customers an optimal set of contextually charged interactions, and to extract the business value on offer when we do.

In the same way that people only tend to notice campaigns and promotions, and not the vast body of work that constitutes the marketing discipline, so, too, most only ever notice customer interactions, without ever understanding the underlying foundations. These are the pathway to genuine customer engagement, which is itself the pathway to the economic benefits of customering. Thus, it must be done properly, and soberly. Paul Greenberg coined the most technically literate and considered definition of customer engagement in his highly influential book *The Commonwealth of Self Interest.*[1]

> Customer engagement is the ongoing interactions between company and customer, offered by the company, chosen by the customer.

DOI: 10.4324/9781003513728-7

While succinct, there's a lot packed into that sentence including consistency of the interrelationship, the dimension of time, the constraints of what can be offered, and the ultimate power of the customer to choose and define value.

This is broadly corroborated by scholars[2] who consider engagement to be a psychological state, a "set of actions that go ahead of capital investments and are generally defined as a customer's moral expression that has any brand, firm, or person focus, above purchases, concluding motivational intentions",[3] and argue that customer engagement is found "to incorporate affective, cognitive, and behavioral aspects, uncovering its multifaceted perspective".[4] Taking from academia and applying it through operational principles requires an appetite for the nuance of actual engagement, instead of transactional shortcuts that misappropriate the term. In one example, Thunderhead, the UK research and technology company to which Greenberg was an adviser, proposed:[5]

> Customer engagement means an on-going, value-driven relationship between a customer and an organization which is consciously motivated according to the customers reasons and choices.
>
> Engagement is built through the ability of the customer and the organization to derive value from the relationship over time (note that the value taken by the customer and the organization need not be equal or the same type).
>
> The value obtained at each point of interaction is co-created between the customer and the business.
>
> Only the customer can determine value – but it is dependent on the ability of the business to create a context at each point of interaction in which value can be created.
>
> The ability of the business to enable value creation over time builds trust, and the accumulation of trust, and mutual and shared knowledge, builds engagement.[6]

Essential points:

- Engagement reflects the psychological and motivational state on the part of the customer.

- Engagement is not the same thing as involvement (a common misapprehension, as is use of the word engage as a synonym for interact).
- Time matters: engagement is built over time, and this is why the customer journey is so important.
- Engagement can be managed. Experiences cannot.

This chapter will start by introducing you to the Customer Engagement Stack, comprising the offer, service, and experience layers, and exposing their unique characteristics and economic attributes in the customer engagement equation. It will introduce choice architecture and the non-linearity of journeys – not to be confused with traditional journey mapping – and review channel ecosystems, asset design, and then, most critically, the live orchestration necessary to bring it all together.

Executed as described, companies can become responsive, anticipatory, and adaptive organisms, each touchpoint a mere limb on an intelligent body, cohesively serving the customer mission and its economic goals. While they seem foreign and futuristic, rest assured all components and capabilities in this section are readily attainable and affordable – and have been for quite some time.

Applying the Customer Engagement Stack

When companies are defining their interactions pillar they should be very deliberate about whether each interaction is a service-dominant one, or whether it should induce memory. In truth, how a customer engages with a company is also dependent on a third and foundational element, which is the product or offer integrity: does it do what I purchased it for? Can I rely on it every time I use it?

As we discussed in Chapter 2, product development is a function of marketing, not customering, but I will briefly cover the wider frame of offer integrity to the extent that it provides context to the overall perspective of the customer (not the market). Customer management leaders, however, *do* have direct control of the interaction pillar, and so the service and experience layers are imperative. Let's start with a summary Table 6.1.

Table 6.1 Engagement Stack Delineations

Interaction Type	Characteristic	Outcome
Offer Integrity	Reliability	Baseline consumption
Services	Involved (friction-light) to engaged (via trust)	Ease of desired task completion
Experiences	Engaged Friction/drama-heavy	Memory creation

It is important to note the each has different impacts and leaves a different impression on the customer. Nevertheless, I acknowledge that many use these terms broadly and will often combine them. For instance, the concept of *servicescapes*[7] refers to the "service experience". My contention is that a more defined use of both terms is important given that the characteristics and economic distinctions between services and experiences have been established, and if our goal to manage effectively we are best to maintain them as separate functioning components of the customer interactions model (Figure 6.1).

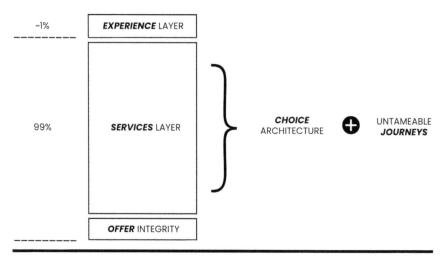

Figure 6.1 The Customer Engagement Stack (Spinley, 2024)

Offer Integrity

It goes without saying that we care whether the thing we are buying works as we expect it to. In general terms, companies cannot overcome fundamental issues with the integrity of their offering through creative brand strategy, service design, or experience. If the running shoes give you blisters, you only care that your feet are sore. If the new car breaks down, or the window wipers never work, or it leaks oil, no amount of funky activation can save the day.

Now, in the context of an engagement stack, when we talk about offer integrity, we are lumping together all the elements that occur pre-service:

- Offer reliability.
- Brand attributes.
- Marketing communications.
- Fit for purpose.
- Price point.
- Availability.

You might argue that we are talking about the product, pricing, and distribution components of marketing's tactical pillar, and you'd be right, except for the added dimension that we are contemplating how they impact an actual customer as distinct from the wider market. For the purposes of the Customer Engagement Stack, these are all lumped into the concept of "offer integrity", which is foundational and forms the beginnings of customer engagement.

The role of the actual product (offer) to overall value, via customer use, across the lifetime of that product cannot be overstated. In this regard, it could be argued that the summary Customer Engagement Stack diagram as shown above is misleading. For example, the ratio is expressed differently for brands in the entertainment sector. For these types of companies, their core offering is an experience itself.

Equally, companies in categories such as industrial wholesale must have a heightened regard for offer integrity. In this case, the actual use of the product is always critical. If you buy a new oven, for example, you will use it every day, which is far more than you will interact with its manufacturer, or even with the retailer. In these settings, you might weight offer integrity at 98% of the engagement stack, and service, given its limited role, might be weighted at 2%, with no experience executions at all.

This is an area that would benefit from research, but even in these offer-intensive categories I propose that the overall ratio of 99+% – comprising offer integrity and service as illustrated in the diagram – is almost certain to hold, and that only the proportions within that 99+% will alter. Irrespective of the final mix, the diagram seeks to confirm to customer operations teams, who do not manage the offering, that the service layer is their dominant imperative, albeit with reference to, and informed by, offer integrity. As this book is focused on customer operations, I'm not going to dwell on this topic, but it is important to understand that the elements of any stack rest upon each other.

The Services Layer

Customering teams should regard the service layer as the most critical element of the stack. It requires the most nuance to execute and, because of the many lazy shortcuts of populism, it is where most companies fail. A focus on service may seem contrary to the idea that everything should be about experience, but that reflects an industry that is less than literate in both.

Indeed, the word "experience" has come to mean everything, and consequently to mean nothing. I contend that we do not have that luxury. As discussed at the outset of this book, if customer management is to embed an industrialized operating model – and one day aspire to the level of a profession – it must pursue markers that include disciplinary language. Buzzwords and distractions have their place – at music festivals and street parties. That's the stuff of weekends. From Monday to Friday, if we are serious, we don't deal in them.

Time Well Saved

In their book *The Experience Economy*,[8] Pine and Gilmore refer to services as "time well saved". It is the perfect description. Way back in the 1950s, when the Services Revolution was first occurring, it reflected the demands of a post-war middle class seeking an easier life. Convenience was in its infancy as a category, but a consumer shift was well underway and today services represent between 70% and 80% of GDP[9] in developed nations. We are no longer content to labor away combining different products to gain an outcome when, in the shape of a service, we could just buy that outcome.

"Time well saved".

It is that same underlying principle that informs a company's service layer to customers today. Paying your utility bill is not something that you wish to remember. You want to log in, get it done in as few clicks as possible, and get back to your life. Even better, you want it paid by automatic bank payment so you aren't even aware of it.

Transactionally, an average customer spends time online, researching an offering, long before they come into a store (if there is one) to buy. In equal and opposite measure, they may visit stores to verify size and color in person before looking for the best way to buy online (price, retailer preference, delivery terms, etc.). They may visit several competitors and know more about the options than most salespeople. But paradoxically, while contemporary consumers desire more knowledge pre-purchase they also have little patience for research and will rely on brand salience as a heuristic. Yet while the customer intent is to save time, companies have responded, largely by accident and absent an informed strategy, in the very opposite fashion.

As the Hick-Hyman Law establishes, the time it takes to decide something increases with the number and complexity of choices. And so it becomes an important design principle that we limit the number of scenarios or choices presented, if any are presented at all, so that the level of cognitive effort is reduced. Another common construct that is relevant here is Occam's Razor (also Ockham's razor), a problem-solving principle that when presented with competing hypothetical answers to a problem, one should select the one that makes the fewest assumptions. Again, the service characteristic of being frictionless, or at least low-friction, is reinforced.

Despite this, the rise of mercenary sales tactics and journey interruptions (e.g., annoying chatbots and messaging) has rendered website visits an often-painful activity for customers simply because their latent needs are ignored, or never even ascertained, with coherent service delivery becoming the casualty. A research series[10] by the company Customology reveals the impact of this type of behavior on customer trust:

> [C]ustomers are increasingly annoyed by what they perceive to be a pushy sales stance ... 71% find the approach to sales by brands too aggressive. This figure is up 10% (from the 2020 report).

World-class service is always characterized by how quickly, and easily, the customer gets done what *they* want to get done. The Jobs to be Done framework is central. We discerned the customer intent based on that premise, and now, we seek to serve them to achieve that via service interactions, on the same basis.

Through our marketing apparatus we have established brand, made promises, and presented our offering. Now, the customer management team must host those that respond, or return, just as store attendants have done for decades. How can I help you? – followed by providing the very thing that the customer wants. And so, the services layer, now presented in contemporary terms across potentially hundreds of channels and touchpoints, can be described as follows. It:

- Is characterized by low or no friction.
- Does not create lasting memory.
- Is essential to execute well in order to "earn the right" to create experiences.
- Is the layer that has the most impact to the creation and sustenance of customer trust.

The Service Layer Is Central to Customer Trust

Many vendors, commentators, and consultants talk about "customer trust" but only in very broad terms. Most have no substantive understanding of the subject and make a myriad of ill-advised claims.

The study of trust offers great opportunity for insight and technical application, and the key principles for customer operations staff are not complicated. There is often a false narrative that if a company protects service characteristics (e.g., throttling or suppressing triggered promotions, etc.) it will have a negative effect on sales when, in fact, the reality is quite the opposite.

"Trustability Is a Capitalist Tool"

This is a quote from the duo of Don Peppers and Martha Rogers, who wrote the book *Extreme Trust*.[11] In it they speak to the inherent value exchange that occurs when we act in a customer's best interest: the formation of trust. They are right. Trust plays a central role in customer retention, eventual share of wallet, and then lifetime value. In fact, there are robust academic arguments that trust is an equal if not stronger factor than satisfaction on retention.[12]

Yet many companies are fighting in highly competitive markets that simply don't trust them, and while some likely know it, they still haven't invested in understanding how to pursue that trust and de-risk their customer asset in the process. If they had, they would understand that, in fact, they are their own worst enemy. Contrary to so much of the silly sloganeering that surrounds the topic, trust itself is a non-conscious human reaction.

Of course, there are macro – anthropological – forces at play as well. In the last couple of decades we have seen a massive collapse of trust across society. Our engagement with brands and institutions has evolved to a point that marketing messages, or brand promises, are no longer accepted as the gospel they once were. We reject with equal distaste spin-doctoring from companies and governments alike. In fact, such is the phenomenon that it has become a matter of global concern, as highlighted in September 2018 when UN Secretary-General António Guterres, said:

> Our world is suffering from a bad case of "trust deficit disorder".
> Trust is at a breaking point. Trust in national institutions. Trust
> among states. Trust in the rules-based global order.[13]

In addition to the general shifts in society, driven in part by technological change and the rise of issues such climate change, we have seen major events such as the Cambridge Analytica scandal[14] further rock our already rocky boat. The evolution of social media into more a dystopia than a utopia, and the unchecked moral hazard of the digital advertizing model that funds it all, has hastened the trend. The policy discord around the world and the growth of reactionary politics in the West during this period is, perhaps, the poster child for trust's collapse – and demonstrates its relationship with populism.

And yet many studies describe trust as a paradoxical issue as it relates to modern society. On one hand we need it more than ever; on the other, there are fewer natural opportunities for it to evolve.[15]

Economists and sociologists have nominated trust as a "lubricant in managing uncertainty, complexity, and related risks".[16] It has been found to lower transaction costs and to increase "spontaneous sociability",[17] and can play a "critical role in enhancing knowledge creation and transfer within the organizational context",[1819] corroborated by Kramer in 1999[20] – all findings supportive of the premise that customer service is fundamentally about relational transfer and trust between company and customer.

This underscores that customer management is facing a generational challenge and shines a light on its need to understand trust more critically, instead of reducing it to yet another lazy and uninformed buzzword. So, if it is both a device for staving off society's rumblings and a "capitalist tool", as per Peppers and Rogers, how then do we embed trust creation in our customer operations? Well, work by scientists in Poland has explored trust from a psychological perspective.[21] Kosonen, Blomqvist, and Ellonen write that trust

> [r]eflects the security one feels about a situation because of guarantees, safety nets and other structures (structural assurance), and the belief that things are normal and customary and that everything seems to be in the proper order (situational normality).

This is key. It provides the operational tenets for calibrating customer operations to the creation of trust, and it all resides in the service layer. Let's break that down.

Structural Assurance

The first tenet of the above definition, structural assurance, is a very straightforward concept. It simply means that the thing that we want to rely on is, in fact reliable. Consider the humble chair. We sit on chairs at home, in the office, and at cafes. We drop into seats in taxis, airplanes, at conferences, and in stadiums. Chairs hold us up. We don't question this, and this simple truth is called "structural assurance".

Situational Normality

This, too, is a very straightforward concept, and it builds on the first. It is not enough for chairs to hold us up, for us to trust them to do so. They must *always* hold us up, and because they *always* do, that simple truth is never tainted.

This is called, "situational normality".

Of course, if there was a moment where that structural assurance was tainted, the truth, and our knowledge of it, is damaged or lost. If the outcome is randomized in some way, or even if a chair collapses on us just once, we will not – at least for some time – sit again without thinking about it. We have transitioned from a sub- or non-conscious act, where the preconditions are met for us to feel safe and we trust in the structure upon which we are about to sit, to a state in which we must engage our conscious mind and assess risk. The very instant that a chair fails you, your inherent trust in that structure is undermined. The condition – or the contract, if you will – is broken. What Kosonen et al. found is that both the above elements must be present, consistently and without fail, to form and, critically, to sustain trust.

Other Evidence

There is other strong corroborative evidence for this. Consider the work of Mayer, Davis and Schoormans,[22] who state:

> "The trustor's propensity is an expectancy held by an individual or a group that the promises or statements of others can be relied upon".

More specifically, their model of trust is broken into four dimensions: ability, benevolence, integrity, and trustor's propensity, which they describe as follows:

> Ability is that group of skills, competencies, and characteristics that enable the trustee to have influence within a specific domain. Benevolence is the extent to which the trustee is believed to want to do good to the trustor, in addition to focusing on his own profit. Integrity represents the trustor's perception that the trustee follows a set of principles that the trustor finds acceptable.

Consider and compare this language with that of Mayer et al., and note the critical element of benevolence – "to do good for the trustor" – or to act in the customers' interest, as we have discussed. This is the essence of service. Yet, this must be made routine or, as per Kosonen et al., situationally normal. In fact, a later study[23] has shown that "ability" – our capability and competence – affects trust over twice as much as benevolence or trustor's propensity. We must be, and be seen to be, effective. Equally, habit forms via the "habit loop":[24] the "cue", the "routine" (actual behavior), and, finally, the "reward", which is repeated (situational normality) (Figure 6.2).

Let's return to the transition, where the conditions for trust are broken, from sub- or non-conscious, to conscious. We always want our customers, who are prompted by a want or need to interact with our company, to do so without fear or concern. The moment someone must assess risk, we have erected a barrier between them and us.

As an example, I am – or at least I was – a platinum member of a high-profile airline, having routinely flown all around the country, the region, and globally on several occasions. Yet, even while holding that highest of status in their loyalty program, I hated, and I mean *hated*, it whenever I was faced with the prospect of calling their contact center. The hold times were, and at the time of writing still are, the most hideous and soul-destroying waste of time I have encountered, compounded by the fact that a good portion of the time, they are unable to help me anyway.

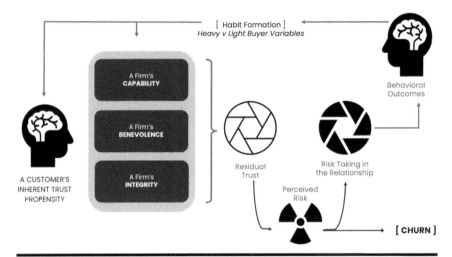

Figure 6.2 Customer Trust Model (adapted from Mayer, Davis and Schoorman, 1995)

Once, I spent close to three and half hours on hold waiting to see if I could transfer some of my points to my mother-in-law (to be) – because the website was not clear – to be told that it "might" be possible, and that they would call me back to confirm. They never did. On another occasion, after waiting for over 90 minutes, an automated voice confirmed for me, as if I didn't know, that hold times were very long that day and encouraged me to call back later, before the line was unceremoniously cut off. To this day, I detest the prospect of having to contact that company and others like them. That mental process, the assessment of risk to my time and my emotional equilibrium versus the low likelihood of a satisfactory outcome, is a case study in the neurological collapse of trust, customer by customer by customer.

Usually, as when a chair collapses, this only needs to happen once to affect a customer's sense of safety, but at companies like the one I have just described there is no structural assurance and no situational normality at all. Whether an isolated events or an entire system failure like my airline friends, this is where the services layer, rather than being a frictionless and forgettable state, becomes a memorable experience for all the wrong reasons. When this happens, it has direct negative consequences for both brand health among customers – which, given the Law of Buyer Duplication, means customer churn and direct consequences for customer lifetime value, both individually and in the aggregate.

We'll talk about how to measure all this in the next chapter, but let's flip from the negative of our case study to the positive. It turns out that when we design and execute a world-class service layer, we embed the optimal conditions for human trust by default. It's kind of a buy one, get one free scenario. From a customer perspective the implications are obvious:

- Information is easy to obtain.
- The contact center answers the call quickly.
- Customer service teams understand your needs.
- Response times are fast.
- Opening times are consistent.
- Nothing is too much trouble.

What Kosonen et al. found is that both elements must be present, consistently and without fail, in order for trust to form and be sustained. Here's the simple progression of value, paraphrased from Peppers and Rogers:

- You want the customer to generate the most value for your organization.
- The customer will generate radically more value for your organization when they get more value from you.
- The customer gets the most value from you, and thus returns more value to you, when they feel that they can trust you to act in their best interest.

This last point – to act in the customer's best interest – is critical, but so many companies make fundamental operational errors that leave customers with no option but to conclude that they aren't doing this. For example:

- If you have an e-commerce website, don't make a "click and collect" promise if it isn't connected to real-time inventory, supply chain, and delivery data. If you don't know where the product is or when it will be there, they can't know where to pick it up!
- Don't have any customer-facing systems that are intermittently available or crash under load. We saw this a lot when demand spiked during the COVID-19 pandemic. Companies that take shortcuts will get caught out.
- Don't deploy outbound sales reps, instore sales assistants, or contact center staff who don't have immediate access to critical information that the customer will obviously need.
- Speaking of contact centers, don't make people sit on hold for hours. Don't transfer them between multiple departments. Don't ask them to verify their identity over and over. And don't play them a recorded voice over while they wait, telling them to go to the website instead.
- If a customer is owed a refund, give it to them, unsolicited – in fact, preferably before they even know they are owed it. And never, ever ask them to "apply" for it!

While such examples are obvious, they are also un-obvious, going by the mountain of evidence that they are commonplace. All of this leads to one simple conclusion: by and large, companies have no sense of the proper customer mission and its component parts. This, above all else, is why customer trust has been in free-fall, inhibiting customer lifetime value, destroying company profit, and increasing risk in the process.

Given most customer interactions occur here in the services layer, the mission is to support customers to get their jobs done, both constantly (structural assurance) and without fail (situational normality). When we do that, we create the conditions for customer trust.

Empathy and Compassion

While an extension of the principles of trust creation, the practical expression of empathetic and compassionate service delivery stands on its own as a quite powerful force. This triggers the *service recovery paradox*, whereby resolving a problem valiantly improves customer advocacy. The act of resolution is more powerful than the initiating problem, which indicates that a more proactive, rapid, and visibly *empathetic and compassionate* service response, triggers longer term trust and indeed and retention – and sometimes word of mouth.

Most organizations don't have the knowledge or capability to enable empathetic customer interactions on a systemic basis, or at scale, but this is critical to the service interventions that make all the difference when something has gone wrong.

If organizations had mastered this capability, it would have been made highly visible during the global pandemic of 2020 and beyond. Instead, evidence of the opposite was everywhere. In fact, the UK Customer Experience Excellence study cited earlier reports that customer satisfaction is at its lowest since 2014, with a 2022 score of 7.09. Interesting, it specifically attributes this to a reduction in empathy. Similarly, the Institute of Customer Service, also in the UK, reports[25] that customer satisfaction (CSAT) is at its lowest since 2015:

- Organizations have taken longer to resolve complaints and more problems remain unresolved.
- Each of the 13 UKCSI sectors has lower customer satisfaction than a year ago.
- The impact of bad customer experiences is often most acute for customers with low levels of financial well-being.
- From the perspective of customers, the leading issues organizations need to improve are making it easy to contact the right person to help, employee behaviors and competence, and website navigation.

Just look at the scope for practical empathy and compassion in these bullet points. And yet, when we consider the explosion of commercial customer technologies in that same period – to 11,038 at the time of writing[26] – it is apparent that the issue is not one of capability but, rather, of an underlying competence gap in the field and the lack of a necessary bias toward service.

Service-dominant Logic (SDL)

You may recall when we discussed market diagnostics, that the principle of "market orientation", is distinct from product, sales, or adverting orientations. Well, in a similar vein, albeit with an entirely different lens, is the idea of goods-dominant logic versus service-dominant logic. The premise is that while marketing inherited its model of exchange from economics, which was, thanks largely to the industrial era, based on goods, there is more value derived from the outcome of the exchange – in particular, the *service* that is obtained by the parties. This concept, "Service-Dominant Logic" (SDL), is a framework drawn from behavioral economics by Stephen Vargo and Robert Lusch,[27] who contend:

> The fundamental component of economic exchange is service, not goods. A service is a specialised competency that is applied for the benefit of the company or the customer by the other. True value is co-created by company and customers and is customer centric in nature.

Before we go any further, it is important to stop anyone before they scurry off down a rabbit hole. Many in the industry see terms like "co-create" and instantly conflate customer operations with notions and methods that hail from agile development methodologies. Don't make that mistake! We are not building products here, and we do not require focus groups and feedback models as is the populist tendency. Instead, the concept being addressed, is *value creation via exchange*, which of course requires more than one party and which, by default, is always therefore "co-created".

If I sold my car to someone who wanted to buy it, we co-created value together because I attained a monetary outcome, which was aligned to my intent, and they got a new car of a specific type, which was aligned to theirs. We did not, however, co-create the car itself. See the difference? I hope so, because your customers are not involved in co-creating the interaction model that you serve to them! What it does mean though, is that your model should be based on their intent as covered earlier in this chapter, which is of course, where there is most mutual value.

In short, SDL is summarized as transitioning from one orientation (goods) to another (services). We're not going to cover SDL in any depth in this book. There is a mountain of literature on the subject, which we don't need to replicate here. Suffice it to say, the SDL concept is a powerful one but, unfortunately, it does suffer from some confusion, partly due to its origins – which are of course, marketing. The fact that the concept frames itself around "service", which we know is an outside-in proposition (they come to us with a need: we serve them), not an inside-out marketing one (we serve our own need), can be a source of confusion and discussion – for instance, some have referred to SDL as "service marketing".

It seems obvious that this is a contradiction in terms, and I would caution against this phrase, if only because of the thinking that it encourages. The mindset and methods involved in marketing do not co-exist in service. One (sales) is the pursuit of a company goal; the other (service) is in support of theirs. The attempt to blend these disparate perspectives into one shorthand management approach simply does not work as a general rule. "Service marketing" is language that further conflates the market and marketing methods with customers and customering methods – the dangers of which are a key theme of this book. For instance, consider the language proposed in this 2010 paper (authors shall remain unnamed):

> Market driven management customer centricity.

Respectfully, this is word salad. The former does not inform the latter. No doubt, SDL has its main use in marketing. It looks at how to create the most value for the company through re-constructing the point of the transactional exchange. For example, Theodore Levitt famously remarked that

> [p]eople don't want a quarter-inch drill, they want a quarter-inch hole.[28]

The drill of course, is goods-dominant, and companies believe that the value is created in the manufacture and supply of the drill itself. In contrast, the customer obtains the most value from the hole that it creates. If this is starting to sound a lot like the Jobs to be Done framework, good! It's very much the same philosophy. Let's leave SDL there; suffice it to say it has a valid place and is a useful reference.

The Service Relationship to Sales

As discussed already, there is a distinct difference between acting in the customer's best interest and on their intent, versus acting in service of a sales objective. Based on this, there is often a false assumption, that if a company prioritizes service characteristics it will have a negative effect on sales. In fact, the reality is almost always the opposite, and for two reasons.

Engagement Increases Sales Propensity

Customers are more likely to spend, and to repeat-spend, when they have a higher state of engagement. As we have discussed, the goal of the services layer is to consistently deliver on customer intent, and thereby establish the conditions for human trust. We have also discussed the role of trust in repeat custom – as Rogers and Peppers put it, "trust is a capitalist tool". Later, I will talk about the role of customer management in brand health in the customer franchise as central to customer lifetime value. When taken cumulatively, there is sound evidence that the services layer, over time, increases the propensity of customers to buy more, or more often, or with greater security of custom, or all the above. Remember, our goal is a rate of churn below the average.

For the avoidance of doubt, the evidence for service as foundational to sales is well established. In any selling scenario, the salesperson's ability to listen to his or her prospects is important because the relational perspective of the buying decision process requires "dyadic" communication, meaning the bi-directional interaction between two people.

Customer relationships, company to customer, are essentially nurtured through empathetic communication and resultant actions, being services, which in psychology literature is well documented to be processed cognitively as a feeling of love.[29] Studies into the quality of information supplied to a customer, one of the tenets of service, has also been found to have a direct linkage to performance.[30] Equally, there is plenty of empirical research that supports the linkage between customer satisfaction and greater repurchase intentions[31] and to actual repurchase.[32] Such studies have also shown that overall customer satisfaction is a function of the company performance in various factors that are important to customers. Note the operative reference: *important to customers.* Establishing a high-performing service layer, predicated on customer context, is essential to customer satisfaction and, therefore, to custom.

There is also the concept of "service activations", which operates both in the long term as described above, and with potential for near-term commerce outcomes. For instance, a telecommunications company that identifies an internet outage to an area, might choose to provide additional cellular connectivity free of charge during the outage and to proactively notify the affected customers. The service responding to the problem becomes central to the relationship, rather than the problem itself. The propensity of those customers to respond to a subsequent promotion the following month is likely to be higher than if the company chose to do nothing during the outage.

Financial services company Klarna deployed a multi-lingual AI assistant to serve its 150 million customers in routine needs like managing returns and refunds. Launched in February 2024, by April of that year it was 25% more accurate and 500% faster than a human agent and is projected to increase profit by US $40 million[33] through a combination of savings, retention, and improved sales propensity.

Amazon provides another example. I am someone who buys books, mainly on business, and I often do so through Amazon. A few years ago I bought a title that wasn't immediately available, and it was placed on back order. About a month later, I received an email from Amazon advising me that book had been dispatched and that the unit price of that title had dropped by 19 cents. My account would be refunded that amount. At first, I was incredulous that they went to the trouble for such a small amount, but then I realized, that as a result I felt like I could really *trust* them. The cynics might say that they did it on purpose, and that the price for my loyalty was a whopping 19 cents! Maybe they're right; either way, the act of service – providing a refund I didn't even know I was due and would never have known about had they not told me – certainly had a positive effect on my future custom. The quality and timeliness of the information, and the fact that it was a company acting in *my* interest, determined my sentiment.

Of course, when we serve our customers well – most especially when it creates delight and becomes an *experience* – it can have the effect of releasing the chemical oxytocin. Credited for the rise of neuroeconomics, Dr Paul Zak[34] stated:

> I now consider oxytocin the neurologic substrate for the golden rule: if you treat me well, in most cases my brain will synthesize oxytocin, and this will motivate me to treat you well in return.

A high-functioning service layer doesn't only operate pre- or mid-sale but post-sale as well, and can serve to safeguard revenue. For example, consumer psychologists describe "high involvement" categories as those which involve more complex problem-solving by the customer. When we buy a new car or a house this naturally attracts some anxiety, and we tend to experience post-purchase cognitive dissonance, wondering if we did the right thing. Using the service layer to provide reassurance is a critical execution for brands that occupy these high involvement categories. It can protect the sale during any cooling-off period and ensure happier, or at least less stressed, customers. It is certainly not a time for cross-sell messaging, as many companies are prone to do, such is their sales orientation and their triggered marketing automation.

But as compelling as these types of isolated use cases may be, there is a more systemic sales benefit derived from mastering the service layer. In 2022, I gave a presentation at an industry conference with Brendon Power of Telstra, Australia's largest telecommunication company. Telstra had embarked on a program of customer engagement using journey orchestration capability across its consumer division.

- Long-term scope: all consumer channels.
- Ambition: real-time arbitration and orchestration.

At the time Telstra was probably that country's most advanced customer engagement company in terms of that capability – which is, as we will discover later in this chapter, a critical capability to delivering service layer excellence at scale. Said Power:

> It was interesting. We kind of flipped this thing around. What we learned is if you can build something [that is designed] not to sell, you can do just about anything [to enhance selling].[35]

What he was saying is that it is much more nuanced (i.e., harder) to master the management of serving customers based on their intent, but as Telstra progressed its ability to do so it realized that this more advanced operational capability afforded it far more effective means of activating sales outcomes, as ironic as this seems. Of course, we always knew this to be the case in the pre-digital world, where sales assistants would ask, "How can I help you", not "What can I sell you?", but we lost that along the way. Companies like Telstra have rediscovered that, powered by the correct use of digital.

Now, as you are reading this, it is very important not to misconstrue what I am saying. We are not just talking about more system-advanced ways to activate promotions, offers, triggered messaging, email interceptions, etc. Companies that do this are taking marketing's inside-out business agenda and imposing it on the customers it is supposed to be serving. The indoctrination with "data-first" approaches bears much of the blame, having become code for importing mercenary practices from the world of digital advertising, into service channels, a space where trust between brand and customer is supposed to form. Such a brute force mode is certainly much easier than identifying and discerning intent and then arbitrating and orchestrating meaningful interactions, but it doesn't do much for customers. As per Telstra's experience, a heightened ability to realize sales benefits starts with a more judicious, contextual, and therefore far more effective interaction model based in customer intent, and with service as its bedrock.

Service Affinity with Loss Aversion

When executed properly, customer service operates in alignment with the customer's need as the primary goal. That means that we must understand their drivers broadly and their context narrowly. In discerning their intent, we have resolved the narrow (micro) element, but let's discuss the broad (macro) element. All human beings share a set of commonalities that transcend cultural and sociological influences, and one of these commonalities is our universal aversion to personal loss. This is perhaps one of the most fundamental premises of behavioral economics, alongside "Prospect Theory"[36] – how people make decisions when presented with alternatives that involve risk, probability, and uncertainty.

Loss aversion[37] is a cognitive bias resulting in the tendency for individuals to avoid losses in preference to acquiring gains. If we are always acting in the interest of our customer, part of the service imperative is to engage with them on that basis, whenever appropriate. As you will see, when we do, we enhance the relationship between service and sales, and we serve the mission of customering in the process. Melina Palmer, who teaches applied behavioral economics at Texas A&M University, provided a simple example of loss aversion, which I borrow here.

> On the way out the door one morning, a person grabs a jacket that they haven't worn for a while. To their delight, they discover a $20 bill in the inside pocket. You can relate to this, can't you. It feels pretty good, and they have a little buzz, but it's not something that they'll get too excited over or run to tell their friends about. Now imagine that another person is invited to an event that only takes cash. They figure that they should take about $100 with them, and so stop by an ATM to withdraw the money. When they stop to pay for parking and open their wallet, there's only four $20 bills. One is missing! They pull the wallet apart. They pull the car apart. Maybe they'll even accuse the bank of short-changing them, and going forward, they'll remember it every time they use that parking lot. You can relate to this as well, can't you. That gnawing resentment of losing money.

In one scenario, we are up $20, which isn't profound monetarily but it's nice, if not memorable. In the other, we are down $20, which also is not profound monetarily, but it is horrible, evokes upset, and *is* memorable. In fact, research has found that the pain occasioned by a loss is double the pleasure enjoyed from a gain – so, using Palmer's example, if someone loses $20, they'll need to gain $40 to get back to neutral. You can see how the economics play out. Enter customer service.

For example, ask yourself why most loyalty programs operate on the promise of gain by offering points on future transactions, and why online businesses add an incentive to buy using add-on value, like a gaining a free pair of socks with a purchase of shoes? If loss is a stronger driver of behavior, why do we lean toward gain? Well, the answer, as in just about every facet of popular CX, is that untested but trendy intuition outweighs actual education.

When we frame our service to customers on their terms, inclusive of their need to avoid a sense of loss, we can begin to realize value creation that serves the mission. To illustrate the point, I'll return to Palmer for another wonderful example, this time, of loss aversion in action.

In the banking sector, the card issuer receives "interchange income" every time a card is swiped, which is great for the bank because they get to generate revenue without having to charge their actual customer. US readers might have received promotions at some point in which if they swipe their card twenty times in a month they receive $50. It's a reasonably compelling offer, but while people report wanting to take it up, statistically it doesn't convert as much as you might expect. Says Palmer, "What if you flip it around?"

What if the financial intuition sent out a promotion advising customers that they have *already* loaded $50 into your account, and that if the customer uses their card 20 times this month, they get to keep it? Instantly, through this act of observed service, the customers psychology will tend toward taking a "perceived ownership",[38] when people who own a good, or start to believe that they own it, tend to evaluate it more positively will want to take steps to protect it. A key to this is the ability to "see" it as real, rather than notional or potential. In the case of the banking promotion, the customer already "has" the $50 – they can literally see it in their current balance (though not their available balance) – and so it has transitioned from potential to reality, psychologically at least.

This perceptual dimension, one of existing ownership, is material to invoking our customers' aversion to loss. And so, as service logic has always dictated, we start by giving, the notion whereby we proactively add value. We do not wait. Service is inherently proactive, hence its shared characteristics with the workings of loss aversion. Combined with increased customer propensity, this is why service is a lubricant for sales, not a speed bump – but only when it is properly understood and executed in the proper, mutual context of the business and the customer.

So, how do you frame your service interactions with customers, particularly around communications asset design? Keep this in mind as we explore that subject in the coming pages. You should also bookmark this page and refer to it when you read Chapter 8, the collision of marketing and customer management.

The Experience Layer

Only at this stage, having laid a foundation that is biased toward service, are we able to leverage the experience layer. The power of human experience, of memory and of the emotion that is resident within it is astonishing, as we will soon learn. Bad experiences can drive people away from brands – sometimes forever – while great experience can create deeper preference or specific behaviors. The proper use of the experience is akin to a scalpel, or a homing missile, seeking out specific targets, but to know when and how to apply this layer, we must first understand it.

For most companies, the idea of emotionally charged brand advocacy in the exaggerated form often depicted by the CX movement isn't remotely possible. However, there is evidence that there is a bias toward brands that we have already chosen ("usage drives attitude"), right up until the brand breaks our trust or imposes unacceptable friction. Yet, in scenarios where a customer does exhibit advocacy, it is almost always on the back of an instance of delight (surprise), or other experience dimensions.

However, for all the talk and despite its use of the word on repeat loop, the industry invariably misses the boat on this subject, and by some margin.

It is a paradox that despite the vast number of people talking about experiences, particularly "customer experience", literacy in the subject is so low. Executives with titles such as customer experience director or CXO, and those with roles such as CCO or CMO, etc. who use the term just as liberally, are almost universally unable to articulate what an actual human experience is, how it is formed, or what the implications are for brands and their customer interactions.

In this section we will talk about exactly what a human experience *is*. We'll start with the economic attributes of experience and, later, we'll also look at how customer experiences can be applied as part of our interaction model. As the last sentence indicates, a big takeaway from this section is that unlike services, which are table-stakes across all customer operations, experiences are very tactical in nature. In fact, given the low level of maturity in most customer operations, I regularly advise my clients to park the experience layer entirely while their organizations grapple with the foundational disciplines of the model, namely service. As the Customer Engagement Stack suggests, it is a *stack*. Experience, as a customer strategy, can only work if the foundational layer of service is in place and in optimal working order.

Firms that rush to experience without mastering service invariably diminish the health of their brand in the customer franchise. First things first, as they say ... but once that competence is established, experience is a mighty powerful tool.

The Economics of Experience

In the economic progression, experience is the customization of services, and we pay more for it than we do for services (which is more than we pay for products, which is more than we pay for commodities). Indeed, Lee Kaplan's study of the relative performance of companies between 1960 and 2010 found that those she identified as "experience brands" (referring to admission-able entry) outperformed their peers in one of the other economic offerings.

In the study, the price of commodities was found to rise at the rate of infla-tion, which was to be expected, while the price of goods broke away from commodities early in the study period, which broadly correlates to the rise of middle-class incomes in the corresponding timeline. Service industries, which had their real launch pad in the 1950s, continued a steep upward incline as con-sumerism shifted toward convenience. But, as you can see in the figure below, brands that established experiential offerings via preferential or elite status mod-els, or as a separate chargeable offering in and of itself, saw significant growth from around the turn of the current century. It is clear that these attributes can have significant economic upside (Figure 6.3).

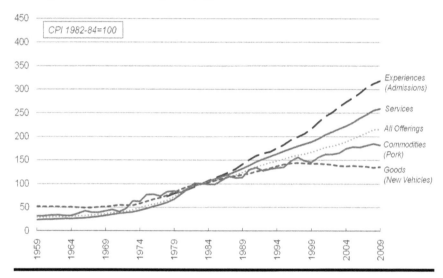

Figure 6.3 US Consumer Price Index by Economy Offering (based on Lee S. Kaplan's analysis, 2020)[39]

So, the economics are compelling on face value, but what exactly is experi-ence? Isn't everything an experience? If not, why not? How do we make the operational distinctions, and what do we need to understand if we are to deliver them to customers for such returns?

Experiences Are Memories

This is quite probably the best shorthand description for experiences. When we encounter an interaction or stimuli, we react with an emotion or a potential feel-ing (I'll explain the difference shortly). The presence of that *emotion* permeates less understood, psychological reactions, such that it may traverse our limbic system for storage in memory. The presence of *feelings* increases the likelihood of that occurring.

But we don't just store the cognitive knowledge of the interaction. We also store the sentiment attached to it. In this way, compelling experiences are never neutral. They are either good, characterized by the more positive reactions, or they are bad, characterized by negative ones.

A principal challenge for memory theorists has been to establish the exact neurocognitive processes that impact the mnemonic fate of our interactions.

We know that everyone consumes and reacts to interactions differently, even when the interaction is shared. How that interaction is recalled, and whether it is recalled at all, is subject to the individual who is processing it: their mood state, current feelings, attitudes, biases, and pre-dispositions (such as the presence of current goals or "jobs"), all occurring alongside cognitive/mental processes both conscious and unconscious. But this is a surface explanation. Indeed, the neuroscientific discovery of the non-consciousness, as deeper than unconsciousness, and undetectable by consciousness, stands in contrast to our default belief that we know ourselves, control ourselves, and that our consciousness is dominant. In truth, we can't, we don't, and it isn't. The renowned neuroscientist Antonio Damásio[40] wrote that this was

> reversing the narrative sequence of the traditional account of consciousness by having covert knowledge of life management precede the conscious experience of any such knowledge.

In other words, our non-conscious self is not informed by our conscious self. It is, in fact, the other way around: we operate mostly in accord with a "covert knowledge of life". That knowledge is, of course, informed significantly by memory. Damásio continues:

> What we normally refer to as the memory of an object is the composite memory of the sensory and motor activities related to the interaction between the organism and the object during a certain period of time.

Here, he is referring to the way that neurons behave as they map and mimic parts of the body, something we won't get into here – I'm not clever enough – but a central theme is the interrelationship between a person (the "organism") and external objects, or events.

As touched on above, part of that memory creation relies on emotion, but that doesn't mean that it is conscious, as is the common misunderstanding. Beware marketing and customer technology companies, and wide-eyed CXers, who talk about trading on human emotion. If they were talking about targeted experiential strategy, and they meant feelings, they would be partially right, but they aren't, and even if they were, the common waffle on this subject does not comprehend its dimensions. Radical over-simplification, leading to the creation of false narratives and ineffective practices, is a hallmark of the populist movement.

Instead, it is useful to understand that emotion is, logically when you read it, from a *motion* – which is to say, a reaction in the body to an object or event (i.e., something happens *to* us) – and is a biological reaction for survival. This harkens back to the idea of our "covert knowledge of life". This functions automatically and we are blind to it, until it begins to register in our conscious minds in the form of *feelings*. And so, emotion occurs without us knowing it! We are only aware of our feelings, which might be described as an extension of emotions – and indeed only some of our emotions, the remainder of which remain unknown to us, and yet are material to how we behave.

Keep this in mind when I talk later about why customer surveys are fraught with bad practice. To take it another step, the feelings that we have are only our perceptions. So, there are distinctions between emotion, feelings, and perceptions. Here is how Damásio explains that:

> While emotions are actions accompanied by ideas and certain modes of thinking, emotional feelings are mostly perceptions of what our bodies do during the emoting, along with perceptions of our state of mind during that same period of time.

There are two physical dimensions to emotion: "arousal", the intensity of the body's physiological response, and "valence", an evaluation of whether something is positive or negative. Our feelings are a construct based on those dimensions.

As you can see, this is not a trivial subject, and my summary of it is about a quarter-inch deep! Yet hopefully it has illustrated that the ability to remember the past depends on ridiculously complex neural processing set in motion – including *e*motion – at the time of an event. Moreover, numerous studies have shown that this is deeply individualistic. In their work on "episodic encoding",[41] Paller and Wagner write about the link between "sensory inputs to the internal representations that are interpreted or comprehended".

In short, both interpretation and comprehension are dependent in each individual dealing with those inputs. It is, therefore, personal. Another study[42] explored how seventeen different people watched and verbally recounted a television episode while undergoing functional neuroimaging. It found that

> All 17 participants accurately recounted the major plot points of the episode. However, when we zoomed in to examine people's memory shapes in more detail, we also noticed that each person

appeared to distort the shape of the episode in a unique way. That told us that each participant was remembering, omitting, and/ or distorting a unique set of low-level details about the episode. Our findings suggest that people's memory systems place different importance on different types of information.

Again, memory is formed dependent on the individual.

In the marketing world, brand management is all about salience – which is to say, it is about building memory structures in the minds of those who make up the market. Creative agencies working with a strategy brief for a brand look to use emotional concepts, central to memory creation, as they relate to the target or mass market.

A good example is humor: think "Waassup?" by Budweiser in the 1990s. Another example is a sense of pride and familiarity: think "We Still Call Australia Home" by Qantas. Brand building relies on memory. This has significant complexities, but one might argue that it is a more straightforward proposition compared to the challenge of leveraging memory – aka experiences – within the more nuanced world of customer-level operations.

Equally, to do so on any consistent basis can become very expensive. Nevertheless, given the power of experience, it does offer disproportionately positive outcomes when you get it right, when it's intentional, and when it's designed with sober, deliberate objectives in mind. Indeed, one of the most important roles of *targeted* experience is the *targeted* reduction of churn.

Brains and Heartbeats

Given the propensity for mental shortcuts, it is difficult for a company to truly immerse customers in any form of content. They first must pay sustained attention, and then become emotionally connected. Attention is associated with dopamine, but emotional connection is a trickier proposition, as we have discussed. At a chemical level, it comes from the brain's release of oxytocin, and in combination these literally change the way that your heart beats. This isn't about the rate, but about the changes that occur in between each beat, as per the ground-breaking work of Professor Paul Zak cited earlier.

Atmospheres

One of the defining hallmarks of the physical world, and therefore physical channels, is the atmospheric conditions that cannot be replicated in digital settings.

In late 2023, academics Chloe Steadman and Jack Waverley, and contributors from Manchester Metropolitan University, published a book[43] on the relationship between atmosphere and consumption, building on earlier work by

Phillip Kotler (who wrote their foreword). They explore a range of impacts to human perceptions and behaviors as effected by the multi-sensory environments that have been designed for them. Examples cover a range of contexts from retail and pop-up stores to music festivals, tourist spaces, town centers, sports stadiums, amusement parks, food and drink, urban squats, and seaside piers. It is compelling reading.

I have long contended that the widespread notion of "retail innovation" is largely unfulfilled, and that there hasn't been true model-changing reinvention since Wanamaker[44] and Sears[45] in the nineteenth century, the introduction of product liquidation by Morris Anderson[46] in the 1990s, and Apple's digital accounts[47] in 2002. Almost all retailers miss significant opportunities to craft unique atmospheres, instead holding fast to accepted merchandising mechanics behind brand-based veneers.

I don't advocate total creative freestyling divorced from the positioning of the brand, but for some at least, there are paradigms that remain unexplored. For instance, could a home hardware retailer create walk-through renovation spaces complete with a materials manifest, instead of just presenting unrelated products in aisles? If you doubt the power of atmospheres as experiential activations, there is good material on the subject. In the meantime, consider the following short case studies.

EXAMPLE: FOOD SERVICE

Located directly opposite a popular nightspot there is a late-night kebab store in Perth, Australia. As the music fades and the lights come on in the early hours, patrons head across the road for something greasy to end their evening. But this is no normal kebab stand. Known far and wide, it borders on the iconic for its many customers. Once inside, standing in a queue, the fun starts – before they have even ordered.

"And what the #$&k do you want?!", bellows the middle-aged Greek man from across the counter.

The theater begins. The customer returns fire. "I'll have 'the works,' you lazy old #$&k".

The whole store is in on it, the laughter is infectious, as amused patrons anticipate the next zinger.

"Yeah, I bet you will! Looks like you need the works in more ways than one, you ugly #$&k!"

And on and on it goes. It may not be a family-friendly activation, but the simple food service has been turned into a festival of cussing-based insults – enjoyed by its target customers. This example is instructive in another way. In an age of digital devotion, it reminds us that old-fashioned "analog" human-to-human interactions in a physical space offer dynamics that digital interactions can only dream of. They can be more nuanced, sharper culturally and colloquially, and are often the most powerful avenue for both service and unique experiences.

EXAMPLE: HEAVY MACHINERY

Case Construction is a US company that sells heavy earthmoving machinery. Like virtually all participants in the vehicle retail sector, they have a vast showroom staffed by a knowledgable sales team, all immaculately groomed in company attire. But unlike so many of their peers, they have sought to add genuine experience to their service layer.

In the north woods of Wisconsin, you will find their Tomahawk Experience Center. Here, prospective customers literally play with the equipment. It's essentially a gigantic sandpit where executives revisit their childhood, racing massive machines around obstacle courses and competing to make the biggest pile of dirt. And it works. According to Pine and Gilmore, from whom this study is borrowed, the showroom closed sales at the industry average 20%, but the Tomahawk Experience Center closes at nearer 80%.[48]

Readers should note that only some of the service layer has been customized to create experiences. The balance – things like the quality of information, support packages, responsiveness of the finance team (and so on) must be world-class or the experience, no matter how novel or delightful in the moment, will be defeated.

Applying the Peak

The "peak-end rule" is a recognized psychological heuristic that changes the way we recall past events. This stems from work in the psychology of judgment and decision making and behavioral economics by Barbara Fredrickson and the late Nobel Laureate Daniel Kahneman.[49] They found that the presence of peak moments (such as surprises), and in particular the way something ends, has a disproportionate effect on how we remember it.

Researchers think that this is largely due to our recency bias, though there are other factors at play. For instance, if we have a wonderful three-week holiday but the airline loses our bags on our return home, our memory of the entire holiday is diminished. The same applies in reverse; for instance, when people end their exercise at a lower intensity, they are more likely to feel positive about doing future sessions.[50]

So, if we end a journey positively, even if the balance of the journey was less good, it will improve the sentiment with which it is recalled, and if we end it poorly, even when its balance was good, the sentiment is diminished. Naturally, then, a focus on how interactions, jobs, or journey flows finish is an extremely powerful tactical tool for customer management leaders, even applied judiciously to the most benign of customer jobs.

Of course, people must notice something first, before processing it for recall, and so sometimes designing for attention at the outset can also be important for experiential customer outcomes. The Von Restorff Effect predicts that when multiple but similar objects are present, people will notice the one that differs the most from the rest. This hints at a bookended approach to the experiential asset in journey design. We ensure contrast at the outset to attract attention, and we ensure a highly positive end state to optimize the way it is recalled.

And so "the peak" goes beyond the premise of feelings only (e.g., surprise) to the mnemonic fate of our interactions, including contrast and the point at which the event of stimuli occurred in context of the wider journey. This is informative. Specifically, if companies deploy experiential interactions into their customer journeys, there is work to be done to understand how to execute the tactic. Both emotion and contrast are difficult to sustain because all things normalize, which speaks to the more tactical, short-term nature of experiences compared to the foundational nature of the service layer. Experiences are, therefore, an inflationary force or an escalation of cognitive engagement. Put another way, they are the exception, not the norm, which is their superpower.

The Role of Memory in Loyalty

Remember that the mission of customer management is to maintain an attrition rate below the average, and that we are therefore always seeking to erect a barrier to churn.

You will recall the typical market patterns that we are working against, specifically the "Duplication of Purchase Law", the laws of "double jeopardy" and "retention double jeopardy", and the principle that "attitudes and brand beliefs reflect behavioral loyalty". In short, the deck is stacked against us, and the role of customer management is to mitigate those forces for the betterment of the financial performance of the company.

After ensuring that we eradicate friction from all service interactions, the next step in that process is the targeted creation of memories. In short, we remove the scope for negative emotion throughout, and then occasionally activate positive feelings using the peak.

There is also value in another law of marketing science, namely the Pareto "60:20" Law. Contrary to the more commonly accepted ratio of 80:20, this states that around 60% of a brand's purchases come from about 20% of its customers, while the balance (circa 40%) comes from the remaining 80%. We can deduce two things from this.

The first is that so long as we maintain a world-class customer service layer – which is still a stretch goal for most organizations – then these heavy buyers (the 20%) are likely to remain as such, allowing for natural attrition (category exit, etc.). The second is that the light buyers (the 80%) will more naturally overlap their purchases with competing alternatives, and so once the service layer is properly established experience tactics may come into play to increase the preference of this group. This starts to overlap with the marketing mission to some extent, and we'll cover that intersection in the next chapter.

Among light buyers however, there will be various sub-groups. Some may be identified through the market segmentation process, and exploring this with the marketing team might highlight market segment/s to focus on. A better approach will be to identify behavioral customer cohorts that emerge though the application of the techniques designed to understand customer intent, especially ethnographical approaches related to journeys. Armed with this information, customer management teams can start to explore experiential asset design, or experiential journey models, that are specific to those cohorts based on very targeted points of value (not necessarily purchase). Remember, experiences are expensive to deliver, and so this kind of choiceful-ness is both more effective and most cost-effective. It will improve both the business case and the measurement. And, most importantly, it is a valuable tactic in our pursuit of a churn rate below the average, in the aggregate as well as in revenue and profit measures.

For instance, the CMO of a neo-bank once told me that she wrote a hand-written message to each new customer in the early stages of growth. Early customers of neo-banks were often anti-big banks and part of a "movement", and they loved the personal sense of connection. While some of her colleagues argued that this wasn't scalable, she regarded the human element in a digital-only bank as essential. It was, as she put it, one the best customer retention methods available to the business. Applied as a sales technique, the bank could have targeted customers of an entry product as part of inciting positive emotion (and therefore memory) to increase their propensity toward higher value offerings.

The MATES Test

Experience is not the foundation of the customer field but a tactical addition to either reinforce sentiment or inspire new behaviors. Before embarking on an initiative, I have found that there are five useful decision criteria (Table 6.2).

Table 6.2 The MATES Test

	Criteria	Explanation
M	**Maturity** of the service layer	A company should not usually progress to experiential tactics until it has mastered the service layer. Where we find ongoing friction in service channels, there is not an adequate platform upon which to activate experiences.
A	**Access** to funding	Experiences are typically expensive to deliver, and many organizations simply don't have the adequate resources or funding. As a priority, budget should always resolve the service layer first, and depending on the maturity of that capability, may still be in a corrective investment cycle that consumes all available funding.
T	**Transactional** profile	This test looks at where customers are interacting with the brand and asks if there is a "stage" upon which an experience can be delivered. For instance, when you buy Heineken you are likely picking it from a shelf in a liquor store. There is no interaction with the company Heineken itself, and so there is limited opportunity for an activation. Compare that with a visit to Heineken factory in Amsterdam. Here there are direct interactions, and the entire visit is geared around the experience. Same product, same company, but an entirely different transactional profile. Sometimes, creativity outside of existing channels is required.
E	**Execution** skills	The execution test simply asks if you have the experience design and delivery skills necessary to pull off target activations. Of course, you can outsource this need, and therefore it becomes part of the funding test. Either way, great experience (memory) design can often require a combination of skills from research, hypothesis, project management, creative, and technical competencies relative to the type of experience.

(Continued)

Table 6.2 (Continued) The MATES Test

	Criteria	Explanation
S	**Sanity** check	Many organizations think that they must deliver customer experiences without ever assessing if this is the case. The Sanity test simply asks whether doing so will achieve any value for both customer and company. This test may be satisfied for a range of reasons, depending on the experience that could be contemplated. One company I worked with decided that it would send all new customers flowers after a house move. They knew that their customer processes needed to improve and so they leveraged the peak-end rule to make sure that the final part of the process ended positively, which they believed would lower the risk of churn of those customers by 7%. Experiences don't have to be Hollywood productions! Of course, there are activations at the other end of the design, delivery, and cost equations. ROI can take many forms, and so the main point is to make sure that everyone is clear about the objective and its rationale.

Summarizing the Stack

For customer management leaders, there is generally little to no control over the offering(s) the company presents to market. Most typically, this occurs in – or takes key inputs from – the marketing department (if the company knows what is good for it), and/or with strategy and R&D teams, or specialist product and offer management teams. Customer management should be focused on the service and experience layers of the stack within the customer franchise.

Of course, there is scope for the final ratio between services and experiences to vary based on the specifics of the category and or the company itself. For entertainment brands, experiences are the product itself, but the services layer remains critical. A family trip to the movies can turn sour quickly if the bathrooms are not cleaned, if the café is dirty, if the ice-cream bar is closed. Each component service enables the end experience. And so, while the ratios may differ, even in this scenario it is the service layer that:

- Is foundational to customer outcomes in general.
- Enables any experiential product or experience-based customer activations.
- Represents the largest portion of interactions between company and customer.

Not only has this not changed in the digital era, nor as a result of the misguided "experience-everything" mantra, but during this period it has become even more critical, owing to the rise and rise of channels, touchpoints, device proliferation, and journey complexity. As consumer choice has increased, many focused on the technologies and lost sight of the customer. Had they maintained a customer focus, they would have noticed that despite all those new touchpoints and perceived customer mayhem, the dominant customer needs remain as old as business itself. The customer:

- Is looking for information.
- Needs to pay their bill.
- Is making a product comparison.
- Wants to know the availability.
- Is researching alternatives.
- Wishes to make a complaint.
- Is using the product or service itself.
- Wants to make contact.

In the main they are not seeking out an exciting or otherwise emotional moment, and despite all the rhetoric about experience, brands rarely provide anything that rises to the standard of being one anyway. So, the foundational and primary layer of customer interactions is always services. Indeed, mastery of this layer is the most difficult and requires discipline, but not any more so than other fields of business. It only has the appearance of a mountain-too-high to those that lack the know-how – which, I hope, this book helps to resolve. In any event, if you are not inspired to master the service layer, you have no hope of delivering effective experiences, and no place in customer management at all. None. It is, after all, critical to resolving the Barrier to Churn Principle, which is central to the business value attained by the function. Assuming you understand this, and that you have both the relevant business context and capabilities to create experiential activations, the question becomes:

when designing customer-facing assets or interactions, are we providing a service outcome, or are we seeking to embed memories?

PART B - ASSETS AND CHANNELS

Asset Design

Having laid the foundation for you to think about when constructing and evolving your customer interaction model, and, in particular, service versus experience dimensions, let's now take a look at the first step in that execution: asset design (Figure 6.4).

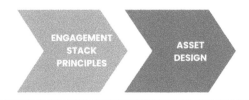

Figure 6.4 Interactions Progression: Engagement Stack to Assets

When we talk about individual asset design, it is always useful to maintain a lens on the role that the particular asset plays in service of the overall customer journey. As the Hick-Hyman Law has established, the time it takes to make a decision increases with the number and complexity of choices and so, for example, it is entirely appropriate for an app that is being established as part of the company's loyalty program to adopt a service-dominant design imperative. In that case, it seeks to be low friction, possibly with limited target functionality, and to provide customer value by way of utility. The app for a superannuation company might only provide a savings balance, the history of contributions and fees, and perhaps a direct connection to the customer service team. It maintains a tight scope and seeks to serve highest utility needs of the customer, which is likely to drive the greatest level of adoption.

Another asset might be more experiential in nature. For instance, 3CS is a snowboard and winter apparel brand. Some years ago, it launched a consumer mobile app called *Rise&Fall*.[51] In essence, the app gamified the mountain experience (as if skiing or snowboarding wasn't already a natural game state!). Visitors to selected slopes would find themselves prompted to download the Rise&Fall app through onsite promotions. The idea was that upon downloading the app, they could register as an informal contestant and compete against other visitors to the mountain to reach the fastest velocity, how many G forces they could pull, the longest hang time, etc. All users received a voucher with a discount on 3CS products, and those who "won" a category gained social status and higher discounts as a reward. Its downfall, I contend, was that it was treated as a campaign (advertising agencies tend to do that) rather than a means to longitudinal engagement, and so its true promise was never realized. Still, it received an award at Cannes Lions in the Mobile Craft Category. As you can see, this is an experiential asset with no real utility (service) value, and offers a contrast to the superannuation example.

The third option is a combination, where a single asset can have both service and experience dimensions in play. But this is where many get unstuck. The rush to combine features and functions is a common pitfall. Never forget that the way that a person's psychology consumes a service attribute is different from an experience, and how the asset combines the two elements is not a trivial matter. For example, operators in the arts and crafts sector deal with hobbyists and enthusiast buyers. When working with a client some years ago, research had shown up two significant market traits:

- It was very community-minded and socially oriented.
- It exhibited a propensity for hoarding favorite materials.

So, the team created a "My Stash" section on the website where customers could digitally hoard much-loved products, and a "My Story" section where they uploaded videos or stories about making things – kind of a "how-to" for their co-crafters to share in.

These experiential journeys, leveraging those propensities, were designed to look and feel completely different from the promotions, catalog, and cart (e.g., transactional) sections of the very same website. Even the style guide was different, albeit maintaining essential brand codes. For customers who invested time in the experiential spaces of the website, the sales volume increased. This is a great example of the stack – services and experiences – working together within a single channel.

Of course, instead of designing for both experiential and service journeys within the website (or any other channel for that matter), another brand may have decided to make the website a transactional service only and use experiential concepts in other interactions. For example, many B2B companies and consumer brands will find themselves with a stand at a trade show from time to time, or with activations at community carnivals or expos, and use some interactive physical competition that rewards participation with exclusive products or free swag, exclusive access, etc. The competition and the social buzz is the experience. They design the show stand "asset" accordingly. It takes time. It is fun, elicits emotion, provides contrast, and is memorable. Then, the exclusive barcode they get for participating takes them straight to the checkout website page preloaded with their goodies. All they do is hit "confirm". That's the service: it is not fun or memorable, and yet is essential.

Again, this is the stack in action, but in a dual channel or dual asset setting. Extrapolating this concept out across multiple assets – and, of course, channels – is about the totality of the customer perspective or journey, not just one asset in isolation. Always keep in mind that for the most part, the first and primary objective is to support customers to achieve their desired end state.

The Thin End of the Wedge

In the early years of the 2010s, when smart devices were only just arriving and the opportunities (and implications) were very much embryonic, we saw a range of projects that involved some level of stealth. In fact, I am confident that we still do.

For example, one large retail mall released a single feature app that, if shoppers activated it when they entered the mall, allowed them to access extremely fast WiFi-based internet access. It was a clever offer because, at the time, public WiFi at malls and airports and the like was very poor quality due to technology constraints. Most thought it a simple act of differentiation against other malls in the area, and it was, but not primarily. Buried in the app, which stayed on and ran in the background, was code that enabled the mall's marketing team to see where their shoppers went after their shopping visit was concluded. Using geofences, the main objective was to see what surrounding suburbs those people returned to, and thereby deduce the mall's market penetration, suburb by suburb.

This may not be viewed favorably by some in today's privacy-leaning society, in the main because the customer never consented to being tracked (not that they do on Facebook I might add), but it was nevertheless effective. As one outcome, the mall sponsored a prominent sporting club in an area that seemed to have less penetration. All due to an app that, to all appearances, was nothing more than a route to free and fast WiFi.

Another example is provided by the team at 7-Eleven in Australia. In 2010, it acquired 295 gas stations from Mobil, taking it up to 482 fuel outlets across the eastern seaboard and about 18% of the market. At the time, the perhaps well-founded perception of the Australian public was that gas prices seemed to spike in the weeks leading up to long weekend public holidays, which was compounded by the near-constant volatility in the price generally. And so, in 2016 the company launched its customer app, "Fuel Lock".[52] Customers could now lock in their gas price days in advance of filling up, using a 7-Eleven digital wallet. They simply selected a voucher for the type and volume of fuel they would like to purchase and were guaranteed of that price at the bowser. This addressed the growing concern about price gouging and enabled customers to feel that they had more control. It went on to win Canstar's Most Satisfied Customer Award.[53]

But again, this was the thin end of the wedge. As much as increasing share of the fuel market was an important objective, the downstream effect of doing so was that more people were buying products from the convenience store at the service station, which is, after all, core business: *convenience*. The company could just have run promotions, an offer on a loyalty app, or some other obvious initiative, but instead a more strategic, all-of-customer mindset was applied. The complexities of doing so were pronounced – from hedging wholesale fuel prices through to process modification at the point of sale – but the behavioral change sought required nothing less, and it remains one of the more intelligent pieces of contemporary strategy in recent years.

Value Collision

Both the examples above represent companies that seek to collide strategic objectives with customer needs via asset design, and both contemplate use within multiple channels (Figure 6.5).

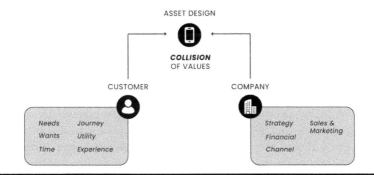

Figure 6.5 Collision of Value (Spinley, 2019)

The "Rise&Fall" app mentioned earlier also had some aspects of strategy, initially anyway, that were not immediately obvious. We know that visitors to mountain are often a seasonal excursion, and so one hypothesis was to allow the "gifting" of points, from one visitor to another. The idea was that someone like me, who is a terrible skier and would have received very few points anyway, could gift them to my neighbor before she went up the mountain and maybe do better than I could. What many don't see is that the process of gifting requires that my neighbor sign up and, in the process, become someone that the company could recognize (refer section on Identity), and migrate toward becoming a customer, and potentially an engaged one. And of course she might on-gift points herself, or at least tell her social circle about her acrobatics on the mountain, further creating word-of-mouth benefits or the brand.

Concepts like gifting are an example of a tactical play that so many companies miss the opportunity for because they are too focused on a narrow transactional lens for their designed assets. It is too easy, as well, when talking about asset design, to rush into tactical disciplines without first addressing the broader customer imperative.

Touchpoint Assets

There is a lot of literature about user experience (UX) design, and indeed it is a bona fide field requiring significant expertise, such that I will only cover it briefly here. Nevertheless, there are some key messages to take away.

Firstly, it is a discipline that is properly located in the interactions pillar of customer management. It should, therefore, have regard for the critical and enabling data that flows from the previous pillars of identity and intent, and for the context of the wider customer journey. Of course, "experience design", one could argue, is poorly named. Many of the assets that emerge from the process do not provide experiences at all, as we have discussed.

UX design seeks define what the user will encounter when interacting with the asset. Some people conflate this with product development, but while it shares various elements, this is much broader than design only. Instead, maintaining a focus on asset design governed by the customer management pillars overall offers better business outcomes. In any event, design decisions are driven by research, data analysis, and test results rather than internal preferences and opinions. In this way, it is one of the few legitimate areas of research that should be undertaken in customer operations.

Kept in focus, asset design will most often apply ethnographic research, seeking to identify and prove (or disprove) assumptions, find commonalities across target audience members, and mental models in context of their needs or goals.

It is also important not to confuse UX design with mere user interface (UI) design, which is only one element of the discipline. The former also includes dimensions such as user perception, usability, desirability, and asset performance. That last word, *performance*, is an important one. It encompasses everything from security and stability to areas of functionality that extend beyond the front end of the asset itself. For instance, in an e-commerce setting the way that stock availability or supply chain conditions impact delivery is just as important, if not more so, to the overall user outcomes as an appealing UI. Remember what I said in the section on services, where we discussed how human trust is formed and sustained? Well, poorly performing assets will very quickly degrade that relationship, so asset designers and builders must have all the elements in place, not just a sexy UI. This work will typically include:

- User research.
- Visual design.
- Information architecture.
- Interaction design.
- Usability.
- Accessibility.
- WCAG (Web Content Accessibility Guidelines) compliance.
- Human-computer interaction.

As a conceptual discipline, UI's roots are in human factors and ergonomics,[54] which since the 1940s has focused on the intersection of machines, humans, and the context of their environment. It was Donald Norman,[55] a professor and researcher in design, usability, and cognitive science, who coined the term "user experience" in 1986:

> I invented the term because I thought human interface and usability were too narrow. I wanted to cover all aspects of the person's experience with the system including industrial design graphics, the interface, the physical interaction and the manual.

As you can imagine, the arrival of the digital era, particularly the explosion of the internet and rise of apps, has escalated the discipline well beyond anything its earliest practitioners (or Norman, I would imagine) could have ever envisioned. Asset designers use a range of tools in their work, from user modeling (e.g., personas and archetypes) in order to frame how they approach groups in precise ways, to interactions framework and screen layouts and flows (e.g., wireframes and sketched or printed prototypes, etc.), along with parallel visual design processes and specific "visual language". They'll use flow diagrams, specification and tech docs, websites and applications, mock-ups, presentations, and videos; whatever they deem the most appropriate methods to refine, communicate, and collaborate with stakeholders.

In addition, asset design teams should be concerned with several well-researched laws and principles that you might now find familiar, including:

- **Hick-Hyman Law**: the time it takes to make a decision increases with the number and complexity of choices. User flows must therefore be intuitive and require as little cognitive load as possible.
- **The Choice Paradox**: allied to the Hick-Hyman Law, and compounding its implications, the choice paradox states that too many consumer choices can cause decision paralysis or abandonment.
- **Parkinson's Law**: any task will inflate until all of the available time is spent.
- **Doherty Threshold**: this requires that all interactions between computer and user are returned within 400 milliseconds.
- **Law of Least Effort**: even in its resting state, the human brain uses over 20% of the body's energy and so we display a tendency to take the path of least resistance in pursuit of an objective (Table 6.3).

Table 6.3 Example Digital Asset Register

Asset Type	Purpose	Function
Phone app	Loyalty	Utility
Phone app	Activation	Experiential
Web app	Multi-purpose	Either, or both
Chatbot	Customer information	Utility
Smart watch	Customer information	Utility
Wearables	e.g. Health sensors	Utility

Messaging Assets

Quite aside from distinct touch point assets, all companies have a range of messaging assets, the majority of which tend to be promotional and sales-oriented. Take a visit to almost any website and the dominant messaging is of this nature. Consider banners and pop-ups, designated landing pages, and communications that are triggered based on an action, such as the messaging that occupies an email or SMS.

And now ask yourself this. How aligned to the customers intent is that dominant messaging logic? How oriented to an act of *service*, rather than an act of sale, are most assets?

This is one of the fundamental areas of weakness in today's typical customer operations department. It lays bare the basic error of a movement that assumes some benefit is derived from sending surveys purporting to care for the customer's perspective, whilst subjecting them to multiple unsolicited intrusions and incessant sales pitches. In the main, the movement, along with wayward martech administrators, fail to understand that invasive sales techniques and survey disruptions are counter to the customer's journey(s) of choice, and their subsequent level of engagement.

It is important, at this juncture, to re-affirm that sales messaging is entirely valid and, indeed, necessary, and its use requires only tempering. In addition, let me re-state that sales effectiveness is heightened where successful service precedes the message. There is strong evidence for this. For instance, Salesforce Research[56] found that

> 89% of consumers are more likely to make another purchase after positive customer service.

Service messaging assets have three dimensions:

- Firstly, they lower the friction involved for a customer when completing a job that they wish to get done. You will recall this from the section in which we explored the attributes of service, *time well saved*.
- Secondly, they enable both responsive and pre-emptive interactions.
- And thirdly, because they usually *continue* a customer journey, message assets must be designed for different touchpoints assets, enabling the conversation to flow no matter the customer's journey flow (Tables 6.4 and 6.5).

Table 6.4 Example of Sales Messaging Assets

Asset Type	Purpose	Content
Email promotion	Sales	Conversion
SMS promotion		
Promotion banner		
Web app pop-up		
Phone app pop-up		
Re-marketing message		
Instore signage		
Digital instore signage		

Table 6.5 Example of Service Messaging Assets

Asset Type	Purpose	Content
Email information	Service, Invitation, Update, Query, Confirmation, Nudge	Customer-dependent
SMS information		
Web banner		
Phone app pop-up		
Web app pop-up		
Chatbot		
Digital instore signage		

Consider a telecommunication customer who has renewed their phone plan with a new iPhone in the last year. A homepage banner that promotes the same product is entirely out of context to them and can generate a negative sense of distance from the brand. Equally, if they have indicated possible financial distress through late bill payments or visits to the flexible or deferred payments webpage, then suppressing any sales activation at all, in favor of support or assistance, is far more relevant to that individual.

Irrespective of the type of messaging, if any, that the company presents based on the specific characteristics of each customer, it must be able to traverse channels. Never forget that while we may have divided our businesses up by channel, and budget, and authorities, etc., our customers don't care. For example, just because a customer signaled their potential financial distress through conduct in an online setting, they may now be engaging on their phone app, or instore, or through the contact center. The company must have the ability to continue the conversation, and therefore messaging assets – including systems for frontline staff – must be designed in various formats that enable their expression wherever the customer is.

Taken together, all assets – both sales and service – form a library that must be centrally managed and maintained for relevancy in every relevant channel format.

Not an Island

This, albeit extremely brief, summation of the field seeks to do two things. Firstly, it pays homage to these critically important disciplines and, secondly, it locates them within the interactions pillar of the management model, where they must operate as one part of the wider whole. Even when the development of touchpoint assets, and both sales and service messaging, are designed and iterated with customer conversations in mind, no asset is ever an island unto itself. Too often, contemporary asset design sits disconnected from overall customer management strategy and suffers as a consequence.

Ecosystems and Channel Platforms

It is easy to underestimate the number of touchpoints customers may encounter as they interact with a brand. Recent human history has witnessed a wholesale revolution in the societal use of technology. Internet users reached one billion in 2007, two billion in 2012, 4.5 billion in 2019, and 5.35 billion in January 2024.[57] Cloud computing, which enabled consumer applications, hit the mainstream in 2012. Smartphones became our "first screen" in 2015 with monumental societal impacts,[58] and social media reached 3.8 billion users in 2018, and is now well over 5 billion. Finally, device proliferation took off across the various operating systems and ecosystems (Figure 6.6).

Figure 6.6 Interactions Progression: Stack to Assets to Channels

In fact, from an average of just 2–4 channels in 2002, a study by Google in 2018 found that the average consumer journey (then) involved between 20 and 500+ touchpoints and this continues to evolve. The arrival of the metaverse, Web3.0, and digital marketplaces, etc., suggests that channel spread is not going to reduce any time soon. But it's not just the company-owned and managed assets that are within the scope of our customers' lived experience. There are always wider ecosystems that influence their perceptions.

For example, my favorite gin is manufactured outside of Melbourne, in a charming town called Healesville. The Four Pillars Distillery – not named after this management model sadly – is an amazing place to visit, with an eclectic and creative range of gins available to sample and its entire brand dripping with the earthy, underground qualities usually reserved for the craft beer industry, all combined with the undeniable sense of premium quality. Allied to a great brand, its product has won too many world awards to list, and its fame well exceeds the influence of its own channels. This, of course, is what great brand marketers seek to achieve: salience (or fame), and with as much earned media as possible. But it can be a double-edged sword. In 2023, the company was sold by its original founders to Lion, a corporate giant of the industry. Suddenly, those underground qualities were diminished in the minds of some, even if the product itself, its small-town story, and its brand codes haven't altered at all.

These are challenges for the marketing department, rather than for customer management, but the same principle applies. Just as brand sentiment is affected by externalities, so too are customer journeys. For instance, a customer who is searching for information about different types of running shoes may talk to friends and conduct web searches, join a running club, or read blogs. None of these occur within company-owned channels or assets, and therefore, aside from the company's wider branding and positioning program, it has no real influence. This mirrors life. You may be a great football player, but you don't control the playing field, or the weather conditions.

However, while this is important to understand, it only reinforces the need to focus on how our model responds when people choose to interact with the company. It must be world-class at identification, at discernment of intent (notwithstanding ecosystem influences), and at context-rich and responsive interactions.

Channels

The digital communications revolution has spawned unprecedented customer choice, affecting consumer dynamics like never before. The resulting focus on channels has been, and continues to be, the driving force behind many digital superstitions within the movement.

At the turn of the century, companies might have offered a store (or store network), but not always the option to telephone customer service, or in a B2B setting they might have had phone sales reps. By today's standards, the range of ways in which a customer could interact with a company was constrained to say the least, and so it is a quite natural response to seek some regaining of control.

However, the truth is that all this proliferation and customer choice now means that the company no longer "owns" the customer journey.

What is interesting is that, despite the arrival of vastly increased opportunities for customer interaction and significantly more advanced technological capabilities to do so, we still think of channels in a one-dimensional way. Let's consider the industry that is the most customer-facing of them all: retail.

There are very few sectors that celebrate their customer experience peers like the retail industry. Gala events and ritzy award ceremonies dispersing lavish praise on an almost monthly basis. We've all seen the social media pics: glammed-up guys and gals at the photo wall, euphorically hoisting a trophy and screaming down the lens in triumph, their digital agency in toe.

"It's been a tough year", they gush. "I love my team".

Among all the hype, an insistence, both underlying and in-your-face, that retail is the unquestioned leader in all things customer and digital. However, in more recent years there is a strong case to be made that there is little to support this claim – which is a pity, because once upon a time retail businesses were indeed the standard bearers.

John Wanamaker's famous department store was founded in 1877. "The Grand Depot"[59] was six stories of clothing and dry goods in Philadelphia, and the birthplace of price tags, forever changing the dynamic of customer service. Then, in 1888, Richard Sears launched his first catalog, which eventually ran to 1,985 pages! Goodness knows who read the whole thing, but for the very first time customers trusted products they couldn't examine in person, paving the way for online shopping over a century later. Originally, "outlets" were only used to sell excess or damaged products to company staff, but in 1993 Morris Anderson opened the first factory outlet to the public. Product liquidation was born, a concept that contemporary deal sites like Amazon, eBay, Groupon, and Catch translated into those online sales. Then, in 2002, Apple became the first mass retailer to give consumers access to digital purchases anywhere in the world by logging into an account. This was remarkable, if only for the fact that it was a full decade before cloud computing became mainstream, so the thinking was, for the time, truly progressive – and it changed the industry forever.

Through these types of landmark innovations in retail, emergent channels have been a theme, and while all recent hype is about digital expressions, the management of related change should not be so foreign. Consider the following:

- **1876**: Alexander Graham Bell patented the electric telephone, eventually paving the way for modern customer service, eradicating the need for lengthy travel to learn about, buy, or get help with products, or to arrange repairs, etc.
- **1960s**: the Private Automated Business Exchanges (PABX) arrived and was thereafter increasingly deployed to handle large call volumes, which enabled the arrival of call centers and, eventually, contact centers.

- **1965**: the first host-based electronic mail program, MIT's CTSS Mail system became – you guessed it – email.
- **Early 1980s**: interactive voice response was invented, which allowed companies to develop logic trees that customers could navigate through verbal commands, "yes", "no", or other key words, like "bill".
- **1980s**: databases started to be used to store customer information, which evolved into one of the fastest growing software categories of all time, Customer Relationship Management (CRM), dominated by Salesforce and its (then) novel cloud model post 2000. It further evolved as an essential enabling capability in sales and service channels, as well as help desk, which in turn was revolutionized by companies like ServiceNow.
- **Late 1980s**: Quantum Link created On-Line Messages (OLM) for the Commodore 64 which, believe it or not, paved the way for instant messaging as we know it, and eventually for live chat.
- **Early 1990s**: the internet …
- **Mid-1990s**: loyalty programs, and the communications channels that they required, grew in popularity off the back of CRM: credit cards, frequent-flyer miles, discounts, and points systems.
- **1998**: Jeremie Miller invented Jabber/XMPP, the open-source technology that earliest incarnations of live chat software were built on. It was in the same year that LivePerson, the first ever commercial chat service, was launched.
- **Mid-2000s**: the arrival of the online help desk was pioneered by companies like Zendesk, Freshdesk, and Zoho.
- **2015**: smart devices became our "first screen".
- **1997–2018**: the first social media platform, Six Degrees, was created in 1997 but it was the launch of eventual giant Twitter, in 2006 that found real growth, with 65 million tweets per day by 2011, a figure dwarfed by today's standards. In between, LinkedIn was officially launched in 2003, a year after Reid Hoffman founded the business in his living room, and MySpace – may it rest in peace – became the first social media platform to reach a million monthly users. And I haven't even mentioned Facebook! Overall, social media hit 3.8 billion users in 2018.

Today, companies design and maintain a range of customer channels, each incorporating multiple touchpoints, creating spiderweb of interconnected journey elements clustered around each customer.

Of course, the trajectory of technological development will only continue. If history has taught us anything, it is that the world has never looked like it does today, and it will never look like this again. We have since seen the rise and rise of AI, advanced automation, sentiment analysis (though beware some of the snake oil on this topic), and concepts like Web3.0. I have covered this evolution, albeit briefly, to illustrate that there are many developments in customer interaction throughout history, but despite the rise of the digital era, there hasn't been as much truly model-changing innovation this century. That's not to say we don't have new tech, but due in part to the persisting mindset, many projects have only yielded an "OEO":

New Technology + Old Organization = Old Expensive Organization

For all the new technology we have barely moved our thinking beyond the newspaper boy yelling "read all about it" on the street corner. Despite the advances of digital, so many companies are still just targeting, prodding, and ambushing customers, never pausing to wonder what they might need. At some point, we must mature past the pursuit of new customer channels for the sake of a digital adventure alone. For most, a management model has been the missing foundation to all the discussions about customer channels.

It has been in that environment that channels have proliferated and become siloes, disconnected from each other and unable to advance the measures of success that customer management should be advancing in business terms. Subsequently, the industry has, so far, failed to leverage the modern era to achieve the outcomes we would otherwise have realized. Returning channels to their rightful place, within the customer interaction pillar, they must:

- Operate in service of the customer.
- Inter-operate as if all are part of the one cohesive whole (the company).
- Collectively maintain a logical coherency from the customer perspective.
- Provide physical availability (sales) in the customer's context.

Okay, with all of that laid out for your consideration, the question becomes: how do we do all of that? Well, I'm glad you asked. Let's now talk about how we bring it all together.

PART C - CONDUCTING THE ORCHESTRA

Orchestration

So far we have advanced our customer management program by establishing and managing the identity of each customer individually, obtained and stitched across every available touchpoint. Then we have deployed intelligence to discern their individual intent and the jobs that they seek to achieve, session by session, journey by journey, and the interdependencies thereof. Next, we have begun to design, or re-design assets, channels, and touchpoints. We have done well. Now we must bring it all together (Figure 6.7).

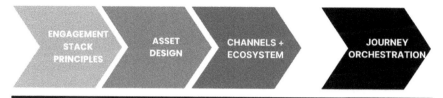

Figure 6.7 Interactions Progression: Stack to Assets to Channels to Orchestration

Mind the Gap

Before I explain the practicalities of customer journey orchestration, let's first discuss the reasons it is so critical and the additional problems it solves.

The premise of this book, I remind you, is that business lost its way and populist CX mythology emerged, in large part due to the rapid rise of technology and the absence of a management model tethering us to reality amid that storm. Well, all that technology and the increase of consumer choice, in a setting in which our ever-increasing connectedness was, ironically, causing us to feel even more time-poor, meant that society began to present some repeating patterns. The gap that emerged between those patterns and the approach of companies has been the defining failure of the populist movement (Figure 6.8).

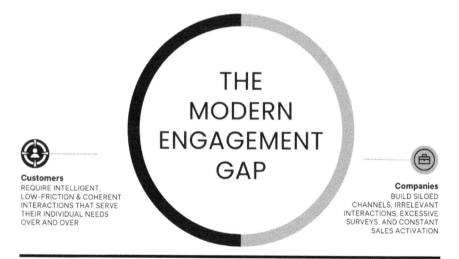

THE MODERN ENGAGEMENT GAP

Customers
REQUIRE INTELLIGENT, LOW-FRICTION & COHERENT INTERACTIONS THAT SERVE THEIR INDIVIDUAL NEEDS OVER AND OVER

Companies
BUILD SILOED CHANNELS, IRRELEVANT INTERACTIONS, EXCESSIVE SURVEYS, AND CONSTANT SALES ACTIVATION

Figure 6.8 The Modern Engagement Gap

As per the modern customer engagement gap, customers are targeted for sales and marketing activation, largely unregulated by customer context or service, and then fall victim to the misuse and over-use of surveys, again unregulated by customer context or service. Through it all, the customer's need remains unknown, as an aggressive corporate dementia is enacted across siloed and disconnected channels. The clutter builds up, destroying the path to mutual and sustainable value. Yet it is all avoidable.

Avoiding the Headless Body

Alex Mead is a well-respected and effective leader in the customer management field. As is common among such leaders, he has a pronounced bias to service; moreover, he is not afraid to share his frustrations about companies that let their customers down. The following is one of his public postings in 2023, and is a case in point as we consider the engagement gap:

> British Airways the 1990s called. They want their call centre back.
>
> I need to change a booking made just a few hours ago, but your app won't let me and you're "too busy to take my call".
>
> I've now tried calling six times in the last three hours and it's been the same each time …
>
> The same hideous generic IVR options (you should know I have a booking already) …
>
> The same "did you know you can do 'xyz' on our app or website to avoid change costs …" When in fact it's because neither your app or website work that I'm having to call you …
>
> Then after around 90 seconds you tell me "you are busier than usual" so can't answer my call right now … Then you disconnect me!! I don't even get the choice to wait …
>
> So, I don't want to call, but you force me to, and then you can't take my call. Just obscene …
>
> Your customer service / contact centre experience has been woeful for over a decade now and it's simply unacceptable … When we finally speak, I will just cancel the entire flight with your airline.

Consider this for a moment. The phone app and web assets were unable to determine or serve the customer's needs. The airline did not know why he was calling, despite his desperate attempts. And because there was no intelligent connection between the channels, the contact center that the company was directing Alex to use did not know why the company had done so (not that the company knew either). Subsequently, the IVR options were not curated to his need, and, to add insult to injury, the same lack of inter-channel intelligence resulted in the contact center trying to send him backward in his journey, to a point that had already failed him! His latent need for seamless and coherent interactions that met his requirements was met with siloed channels that did anything but, and he described the whole process as "obscene".

Obscene? Yes. Unusual? Sadly, no.

In truth, this is where customer management programs fail in a good many companies. The investment in channel and assets, as previously described, is present, but they operate in siloes. Moreover, the internal company structure and competing KPIs are simply not built to optimize the overall customer relationship. In the end, it is akin to headless chicken, thrashing about, no part of it aware or in sync with any other part. Not only is the return on the company's customer investments diminished, but the dysfunction is ultimately destructive. Companies with vast investments in technology, creative agencies, and a perceived or real mastery of distinct functions nevertheless find themselves in a world of diminishing returns, whilst their CX team celebrates benign measures.

Customering leaders must grasp the fundamental and inescapable reality that each touchpoint, application, channel, or connective journey is nothing more than a limb on the body of the company, and that no matter how much each of those limbs have been developed or internally prioritized, it does not function without a central nervous system and regulating "brain".

The goal of journey orchestration, then, is to build on the knowledge of individual identity and status, as well as upon that of individual intent, to provide the body with a head – indeed, to ensure it has a single "brain". This brain controls – or *orchestrates* – the body, ensuring that each limb, each digit, every muscle is co-ordinated and in balance with the whole body and is governed in relation to if, when, and how it responds to each customer, case by case, moment by moment. For illustrative purposes, this includes the spinal cord (the central structure) and nerves (sensing ability) that control much of what is thought, and felt, and what the body actually does as a consequence, including how it learns, re-learns, and reacts in an emergency. Ray Gerber, one of the pioneers of customer journey orchestration, has often talked about "autonomous orchestration",[60] which again conjures the idea of a living, dynamic being.

I hasten to note that all of this has been commercially available for a decade at the time of writing. It is not new or emerging and can present with no more complexity than common martech deployments. Journey orchestration enables a company to engage contextually at every turn, no matter how or where a customer chooses to interact. In this way, it mimics human to human interaction, applying context and judgment to both distinct and related interactions, conveyed through changes to body language, language, tone of voice, and so on.

Invisible Channels

As a rule of thumb, channels are best when they are invisible. As we touched on earlier, this is mastered when we abandon channel strategy in favor of a "channel-less" approach. Making them visible, or in focus, is to emphasize company over customer. What you will find is that customer assets, even great ones, are depowered when they operate in isolation. For instance, managers in charge of websites often have notional customer journey maps pinned to their wall, which start with the customer visiting the website. Well, if that is you, I have news for you: your customer's journey did not start there …

Of course, managers of contact centers have similar maps on their walls, which start when the line lights up in the center. Guess what? I have the same news. No matter whether we are talking about web, AI bot, assisted channel, store, sales assistant, service agent, partner, etc. – the customer journey is theirs, it is not owned by the company, and it's certainly not owned by the manager of a given "channel".

The need to focus on the entirety and nuance of the customer journey, and to consider each touchpoint for its value in that context rather than in isolation, was proven through research undertaken in 2016. Keeping in mind the explosion of channels was in full flight by then, this was timely work, and in recognizing the ongoing proliferation both since and to come, the results offer an important principle to take forward. The study in question was conducted by McKinsey[61] and underscores the point that isolated touchpoints or channels simply do not have the same power for good as comprehensive customer journey.

> [A]cross industries, performance on journeys is substantially more strongly correlated with customer satisfaction than performance on touchpoints – and performance on journeys is significantly more strongly correlated with business outcomes such as revenue, churn, and repeat purchase.

It is important, then, to discuss the primacy of journeys and the ingredients of orchestrating them: real-time decisioning, applied in a channel-less setting, and behaviorally oriented.

Service Bias Made Real

The product marketing departments of most orchestration vendors, like almost everyone connected to the CX movement, propose that the central value of their platforms is to better enable customer *experiences*. I submit that they are wrong: the underpinning value of orchestration is that the *service* imperative is made real.

Indeed, based on customer intent, it enables pre-emptive and proactive service, over and above the reactive service mode, and does so in real time. In contrast, most companies are only able to provide reactive service. Organizations with advanced orchestration can flip that on its head, courtesy of its unifying qualities. To make the point, let's use the telecommunication company example, where the home internet speed is operating at low levels and below reasonable customer expectations (Table 6.6).

Table 6.6 Levels of Service

Scenario	Service Mode	Company Actions
Customer runs speed test, gets poor result, and telephones the contact center.	Reactive	Company answers the phone, and/or company offers self-service options.
	Proactive	Company intervenes as soon as a poor speed test is completed (outbound).
	Pre-emptive	Company intervenes as soon as network performance issues are detected – before a speed test is conducted (outbound).

Notes:

1. While proactive and pre-emptive service are superior capabilities, all three are important and should operate together.
2. The ability to supercharge service capability via real-time orchestration is a central plank in delivering empathic and compassionate customer outcomes, and in leveraging the service response paradox, as explained earlier in this chapter.

Journeys are the Foundation

To best understand how we must orchestrate customer interactions, we must first properly understand the concept of the customer journey. It is a concept that is as misunderstood as it is popular, a problematic combination.

Customer journeys are a powerful way to express specific customer perspectives to those who are a long way from the operational front lines of a business, such as its board of directors, but ultimately, journeys are how customers express themselves regarding the jobs that they seek to complete. In recent history the concept of customer journey management has rightly become a mainstream function, but one accompanied by a widespread misstep – our ongoing use of the now redundant practice called "journey mapping".

To understand this, we need to head back to 2002 when it first became popular. Colin Shaw's[62] excellent work in the field, which he initially called "moment mapping", was ground-breaking at the time and he is largely credited for it becoming mainstream. Of course, it has evolved over time but remains largely based on a seemingly ever-green premise – that we can drive customers to desired outcomes, such as a purchase or advocacy. The true ambition of journey mapping was never really to *map* the customer's journey, but to design it, to influence it, to dictate it. When the great European explorers of the fourteenth and fifteenth centuries sailed down the coastlines of new lands, they charted what was there, not what they might have preferred to find. *This* is mapping. No dictation is involved.

To be fair, many organizations run studies to better understand customer pain points, their jobs to be done (albeit often this is selective in application), and then design interactions and their flows. That's the theory, anyway, and the thinking is right. It's certainly far superior to a great many companies that don't bother to do either. In practice, though, its outcomes are manifest in process management. This resembles more the marketing, inside-out, industrial work-flow, not a realistic customer one. While a process map works well for machinery or production lines, it does not work as an account of human behavior. Actual customer journeys are non-linear, subject to individual psychology, sociological and anthropological influences, the customer's intent, and the context of the moment. And, as I have already said, unlike processes, journeys are owned and managed by the customer – not the company.

Still, we must give credit to Shaw – in the context of the time in which his work was released, the process model worked very well and advanced customer management far beyond where it was. Equally, and regardless of execution, he successfully introduced the notion that customers are indeed on a journey, which is a critical principle and foundational to world-class customer manage-ment. But context is as always key, and you must remember that in the early 2000s the societal, technological, and customer landscape was very different (Figure 6.9).

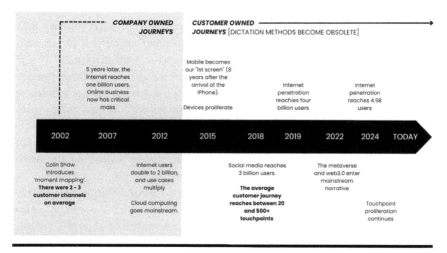

Figure 6.9 The History and Demise of Traditional Journey Mapping (Spinley, 2022)

So, what did this evolution mean for customer journeys?

Firstly, consumers now engage with brands in a truly channel-less way. Back in 2002 when journey mapping became popular, companies were managing no more than two or three channels, which largely operated in one direction: from brand to customer. Today a company can be managing literally hundreds or thousands of touchpoints, and many are now bi-directional in nature. Secondly, all this additional choice and connectivity has driven, at least in part, a mass evolution toward consumerism. We have become accidental narcissists, as Brian Solis would say, and customer expectations for seamless and frictionless interactions with our chosen brands have become universal; a new macro reality that spares no category. Whereas once companies could legitimately dictate a customer's path across a few largely one-way assets, such a task is now impossible.

- Customer journeys are diverse, sometimes independent but often interdependent, highly complex, inconsistent, and occurring in real-time across a multitude of touchpoints both physical and digital, sometimes simultaneously, and often on a series of whims.
- The customer journey is the customer's, not the company's. We are no longer in control, my friends – but we don't have to be to run highly effective customer operations.

Given this degree of customer complexity, the ability to master engagement based on live, individualized customer journeys is a key factor for success in customer operations today. Indeed, a study by Boston Consulting Group[63] demonstrates the transformational benefits of an all-of-journey approach, finding uplifts of 10–20% in revenue, 20–40% improvement in customer advocacy, and 15–25% reductions in cost to serve. Not only that, but the operational benefits of orienting operations around live custom journeys, which make orchestration an absolute imperative, are summarized in the study as:

> Companies can't build journeys discretely or in isolation; they need to reconfigure the way the organization and its people work and improve and track progress ... any company can coherently, consistently, and fully act on its belief that the customer is the centre of its universe ... [with] a customer-journey-at-scale transformation, even elephants can sprint.

Note the significant cost containment outcomes that are generated, largely due to scaling back notional customer "research" and yet obtaining more accurate data upon which to make investments, resulting in much less waste and significantly more accurate outcomes.

Again, it is important to draw a very clear line between what it means to be journey-led and simply conducting traditional journey mapping activities. Left-to-right process maps, static and linear in nature, are not representative of human behavior in the real world. The idea that they are is pure fiction, and to predicate absolute customer management on this belief is to doom it to failure.

This means that we must engage within the seemingly chaotic customer context, but that's okay, because we can! In one of life's ironies, the same march of technological advancement that created all that channel proliferation and customer choice, relegating classic journey mapping to the museum, is the same force that enables us to engage in new, richer, deeper, and more contextually relevant ways.

More Sales / Wait Times = Higher Friction

All this extra journey complexity is an opposing force to low friction, and therefore a challenge to the service layer. But in yet another irony, higher sales volume can create a new friction problem that requires careful management. While this is rarely understood amid the short-termism of sales and revenue orientation permeating the CX movement and digital teams, it is another problem that journey orchestration plays a central role in resolving.

Several studies have shown that just having to wait for service in a retail store, for example, can lead to consumer dissatisfaction.[64] This is even more critical where the service is required pre- and post the actual transaction (e.g., "I need to understand this about the product before I decide whether to buy it", or "I have bought this but now I have a problem"), or more widely across the journey.

We also know that in higher customer density settings (or any instance that creates a feeling of being crowded) customer perceptions – and therefore satisfaction – is negatively affected.[65] This has several implications. This first is missed by many. Those with stores, or other forms of in-person service such as roadside assistance or in-home installations, find that higher sales negatively affect customer satisfaction due to increased wait times and/or other forms of resultant friction. The second occurs in digital settings and takes the form of website lags, stock availability, or shipping delays resulting from high sales volume.

In some categories this can be difficult to manage, but thinking through how we might optimize our customer's choice of journey, to their benefit – often through acts of service – brings orchestration to the forefront of this issue.

Nudge

No doubt you have heard about nudge theory. It is a concept in a range of behavioral sciences that rose to prominence following the 2008 book *Nudge:*

Improving Decisions About Health, Wealth, and Happiness.[66]In essence, nudge theory proposes that through making changes to the "decision environment" we can influence the decision making and behaviors of the affected individuals. Nudge suggests that "adaptive designs" are able to change the choice architecture to which subjects are exposed, which is also one effect of orchestration.

For instance, if a company knows the individual and their specific intent at the time that they are visiting its store or website, for instance, it can augment their environment accordingly. This might mean the digital displays in the store present content for that specific individual, or that the sales assistant is alerted to a specific customer context; or that the colors, navigation prompts, messaging assets, or other features on the website are modified to their context. Dynamic routing of calls to the contact center and conversational prompts and priorities for human agents other examples.

By doing so, the concepts of nudge theory start to be made real in a very practical sense, germane to each individual customer. Naturally, this has application to sales conversion and in fact can be very powerful, because the company can subtly guide customers without subjecting them to an overt and potentially counterproductive activation. However, it has much wider application, as companies seek to embed a service bias and guide customers toward interactions that best meet their needs, for any manner of non-sales outcomes.

Choice Architecture

If you are aware of the "choice paradox" you may well be familiar with one of the defining works on the subject by psychologist Barry Schwartz. In his book *The Paradox of Choice—Why More Is Less,*[67] Schwartz analyzes the behavior of two different types of people, "maximizers" and "satisficers", and argues that eliminating consumer choices can greatly reduce anxiety (a form of friction) for customers. In short, too much choice can create paralysis and abandonment.

Schwartz references a study published in 2000 by psychologists Sheena Iyengar and Mark Lepper[68] in which shoppers at a food market were presented with 24 varieties of gourmet jam at a pop-up stand. Those who sampled them received a voucher for $1 off any jam of their choosing. On another day, shoppers at the same store were presented with a similar table but with only six varieties on display.

The large display attracted more interest than the small one. You may have intuitively guessed that, but now your intuition is going to let you down. Indeed, the trap so many marketers are seduced into, in their pursuit of frequency and reach, impressions, or, as many erroneously call it, "engagement", is the idea that volume wins. Just think of the mentality that tolerates, and rationalizes, systemic fraud within programmatic advertising. One might argue this is the same mindset. But it does not serve us well, because while more people stopped and looked at the big display, they were only 10% as likely to buy as people who saw the small display.

You see, when we overtly maximize choice, we risk minimizing actual engagement via heightened cognitive load (e.g., we make it too hard), and thus we reduce customers' motivation. Back in 2012, when the now defunct Thunderhead research team released its "Engagement 3.0" model, it explained:

> Engagement reflects a psychological and motivational state on the part of the customer.

If we kill or interact outside of the motivation, we kill, or never even achieve, engagement. So then, what's the implication of the choice paradox when companies offer an increasing number of channels and touchpoints, when they diversify their offerings, and when they adopt new distributions such the metaverse or Web3.0, or leverage emerging third-party ecosystems? Well, you might be surprised to hear this given what you've just read, but I say there is no reason not to do so – but you are playing with fire if you can't at the same time orchestrate the customer's journey, in their favor, dynamically reducing choice based on their context.

Remember the Hick-Hyman Law that we mentioned in the section about the services layer? Well, it aligns with the choice paradox, establishing that the time it takes to decide something increases with the number and complexity of choices. Thus, engagement is not about the number of your channels, touchpoints, assets, or offerings in totality, but about only the *relevant* channels and offerings – those picked by the customer (not the company) at the time of their choosing (not the company's) – being truly optimized such that the company is able, across any such combination, to hold the conversation the customer (again, not the company) wants to have. Remember: our mission is to help them to get done what they want to get done, quickly, however, wherever, and whenever they choose – no matter the volume of options that they might have to do so. To attain an attrition rate below the average, we must erect barriers to churn, and choice overload is one such barrier.

Summing up the Case

So, we have a channel and touch point explosion that has seen companies behave without coherency and become, as the analogy goes, *headless*. This proliferation has rendered traditional journey mapping obsolete; we have friction generated by virtue of our own success (e.g., sales create service delays) and the potential for adverse conditions from the unexpected failure of customer assets; we have potential customer paralysis because of choice overload; and we have an overriding need to shift into a service bias as part of the central mission of customering.

This is why orchestration is so essential. It is the antidote to the redundant journey dictation process, and a key enabling capability for customer orientation. When it comes to the overall customer interaction model and the subsequent brand health within the customer franchise, orchestration is the rubber hitting the road. It is the glue that regulates our multiple channel, touchpoint, and messaging assets, enabling constant service performance and, critically, customer relevance. As we do so, we allow trust to form naturally, the preferred customer propensities to be nurtured, and eventually our key metrics to flow in the right direction.

So, now that we understand its value, let's get under the hood …

Journey Orchestration in Practice

True customer journey orchestration combines three elements (Figure 6.10):

Figure 6.10 The Three Elements of Customer Journey Orchestration

To get started on orchestration, we must understand what powers it, and that, my friends, brings us to complex decisioning.

Complex decisioning, also known as real-time interaction management (RTIM), is the foundational capability – the engine, if you will – of customer journey orchestration. If a company is unable to deal with the complexity of multi-dimensional customer interactions, then it has no hope of orchestrating the overall journey. Complex decisioning goes far beyond the typical rules-based logic and automation. It operates in sequenced, iterative, and cyclic computation of intricate variables in rapid time, generating decisions and actions within 400 milliseconds as per the Doherty Threshold.

This was originally developed for the contact center, but its wider potential in a complex consumer world was obvious. I explained the graduation from RTIM to full orchestration at a Forrester event in 2021:

> Orchestration takes complex decisioning and applies it across every single asset, channel, and touch point. It is the orchestration of the entire customer journey in all its glorious complexity, no matter how they choose to construct it on any given day.[69]

While martech categories have made similar declarations, most have lacked the decisioning engine to make good on their claims, and, in the end, the adoption of those categories has been driven by comparatively simplistic marketing use cases (e.g., campaigns) rather than nuanced customer engagement ones. This is slowly improving, but readers should guard against accepting the use of terms like "orchestration" on face value. A sober assessment of actual capability is well advised.

In most (non-decisioning based) technologies, typical automation looks at a point in time action, taken by a customer, and triggers an action from the company. In other words, it relies on business rules: *if this, then that.*

An obvious example is cart abandonment. Many automation technologies will typically add a person who abandons shopping cart into a group to which they send a "re-marketing" message of some description, trying to get the customer back to complete their purchase. It is a model that has some success at the extreme end of the customer distribution, but it is woefully uninformed and inadequate for the majority of cases, as we will discuss in the next chapter (Figure 6.11):

Figure 6.11 Standard Automation

In contrast, complex decisioning draws on a multi-step, nuanced decision matrix and typically follows at least five stages. It starts with a comprehensive library of potential customer actions and messaging assets as previously discussed, which, I hasten add, very importantly includes the suppression of an action, a delay to the action, and even the cancellation of an action all together.

This *decisioning* is our brain. The company, in effect, can say anything it wants. It could gesture, or it could stay silent, and it chooses what to do – and how to do it – based on the variables of the data in the engine. We can design any interaction or message that we wish, and depending on the conditions, we can either use that interaction, use it in a nuanced way, partially use it, defer it, or not use it at all. In this way, complex decisioning is really a capability that mimics the human brain insofar as enabling context to inform judgment, on the fly. In traditional complex decisioning offerings, that process is often referred to as "next best action". When we advance to full orchestration, which considers all channels and the behavioral paradigm as well, many have graduated that term to "next best conversation" (NBC).

An "action" is, of course, one-way in nature; a "conversation", being two-way, is much more powerful and, again, mimics human interaction. When most people talk about "conversational commerce" they don't conceive of this level of sophistication, but this perhaps is the ultimate expression of that idea.

And so we start with a library of actions. These might be stored centrally, or distributed, or found in content management system (CMS) or digital experience platform (DXP) etc., and become available for decisioning to use in the moment. Now you have that concept in mind, let's break down the decisioning stages, and you will see just how more advanced it is than traditional automation tools.

For this section, I was delighted to collaborate with Henry Hernandez Reveron[70] at the Field Bell Institute and truly one of the foremost minds in marketing technology, architecture, and the use of digital capability. Here he explains the five stages of real-time decisioning (Figure 6.12):

Figure 6.12 The Five Stages of Real-time Decisioning

Actions and Action Sets

Actions are the tangible outcomes of the decisioning process, where the engine selects the most appropriate action based on customer data, context, and business rules. These actions are designed to enhance the customer journey in their favor and improve the likelihood of desired outcomes such as conversion, retention, or satisfaction.

Actions within CJO typically consist of several components that enable the decisioning mechanics:

■ **Content**: this includes the actual message, offer, or information that will be communicated to the customer. Content could vary based on the channel and the specific audience or customer cohort.

■ **Channel**: actions are delivered through various communication channels, such as email, SMS, push notifications, social media, or direct mail, as well as augmentation of web, cell, contact center, remote agents, or stores, et al. The choice of channel depends on factors such as the journey context, customer preferences, message urgency, and channel effectiveness.

■ **Timing**: the timing of actions is crucial for their effectiveness. Actions can be triggered in real-time based on customer interactions or scheduled to be delivered at specific times based on predictive analytics or predefined schedules.

- **Individualization**: individualization ensures that actions are relevant and tailored to each individual customer. This could include proactive service interventions or more traditional sales activation via tailored recommendations, offers, or messages based on customer preferences, CLV or churn propensity scores, cohort membership, or live behaviors.
- **Execution Rules**: execution rules define how and when actions should be executed. These rules may include conditions for eligibility, frequency capping, and sequencing to ensure that actions are delivered appropriately and in accordance with both customer orientation and business objectives.

Action sets are nothing more than a group of actions. More generally, CJO doesn't need the concept of an action set; however, advanced systems can utilize logical grouping of actions to further refine the decisioning engine and introduce sophisticated strategies based on tiers or layers where action sets provide an additional level of segregation within the universe of possibilities across company-to-customer interaction.

Static Exclusions

Static exclusions are predefined rules or criteria that prevent certain actions from being taken for specific customers or cohorts. These exclusions could be based on factors such as regulatory requirements, customer preferences (e.g., opting out of certain communications), or business rules.

Dynamic Exclusions

Dynamic exclusions are rules or criteria that are determined in real-time, based on the current context of the customer or the journey. These exclusions may consider factors such as recent interactions, behavior, transactional data, or environmental conditions. Dynamic exclusions help ensure that actions are relevant and timely for each individual customer, noting the Doherty Threshold.

Eligibility

Eligibility criteria determine which customers are eligible to receive specific actions or communications. These criteria may include demographic information, past and current behavior, transaction history, or predictive analytics. Eligibility rules help ensure that actions are provided only to the right audience and are likely to be effective.

Prioritization

Prioritization involves determining the order or sequence in which actions should be executed for eligible customers. Prioritization may be based on factors such as customer value, urgency, likelihood of conversion, or business goals and helps optimize resource allocation to maximize the impact of actions on customer outcomes.

During decisioning, these stages follow a sequence:

1. Action sets provide the pool of potential actions or communications that can be taken.
2. Static and dynamic exclusions ensure that actions are compliant, relevant, and timely by preventing irrelevant or unwanted communications.
3. Eligibility criteria determine which customers qualify for specific actions based on their characteristics and behavior.
4. Prioritization helps ensure that actions are executed in the most effective order, considering factors such as customer value and business objectives.

Once the final action is determined, a message composition is realized to deliver the content to the customer, and measurement, tracking, and analytics kick-off. Note that although we have described the stages of the decisioning process in a linear fashion, the reality is that, at scale, these stages are executed continuously, a constant stream of consciousness in a cycle of interactions, new consciousness, new interactions, and so on. The decisioning engine a vital and complex part of CJO.

***

Thank you, Henry.

All Channels and All Behaviors

To graduate to full customer journey orchestrating (CJO) let's now talk about what it means to orchestrate across channels – or, better yet, to be "channel-less" – and what it means to apply behavioral context. First, it is important to adopt a simple principle:

> *Channel aware, channel agnostic.*

As customers choose *when*, *where*, and *how* to engage, we must be able to respond as necessary to serve their need, no matter those elements. Thus, we must be both aware of their choices and agnostic to them, meaning that we do not impose our own internal values on their context. It is, after all, their journey, and our goal is to interact irrespective of their choices. Think about this way: we are about the customer themselves, not about the car they arrived in, or the seat they are sitting in.

The decisioning process takes into consideration the customer context at their touchpoint, as well as the overall journey context, all the existing knowledge about that individual, and all the real-time behaviors exhibited as the customer undertakes their journey.

Arbitration

The key to this is a concept called "arbitration". As you saw from the decisioning stages, the goal is to apply all that information and observance of the live customer, and to choose the best conversation to pursue with that customer, usually starting with the one that they have already initiated. To do so, an orchestration engine will typically associate all data, both static and dynamic, into a single customer profile to unify the customer insight. This makes it actionable.

A note: This does not mean that it must store that information itself. Instead, it may pull the relevant data from their "home" systems. For example, when observing a customer provide a membership number while on the website, it will associate that identifier to a system of record, such as the CRM. If found, the customer profile in the orchestration engine is augmented with access to the CRM data for that customer. But while it makes the association, it does not necessarily duplicate storage. It may only *reference* this data for the purposes of orchestration. I have made this point because of the persistent theme accepted by the industry, that all data must be centralized to be useful. This is valid architectural debate,[71] but for the purposes of orchestration access to the *right* data (not necessarily *all* data), and quickly, is far more important than where it is held.

From there, the orchestration engine ensures the correct conversation is occurring, customer by customer, from their very first interaction and all those that follow – from when they are anonymous through the stages of identification over various touchpoints, to the eventual state where they are fully known (verified), no matter the channel and touchpoints they present in. Leading platforms also use clever "half-life" decay algorithms that ensure the most recent customer intent and behavior is prioritized. We talked about "decay" in the section on capturing intent, and it makes sense to revisit that as part of arbitration, recognizing that:

- An interaction, or set of interactions, that occurred in the past may not be at all relevant to the interactions that are occurring today.
- Decay is a process, not a binary rule, and so the determination as to how prior events effect current ones require informed methods, though often these are out of the box and configurable.

As a very simple example from the company perspective, a customer may have had an application for a credit card denied three months ago, which will likely still be a material matter to the bank when arbitrating the promotion of a new home mortgage product, or in responding to their interest in the same. However, if that rejection was a year ago it is less relevant, and may – or may not – impact the choice of messaging to that individual.

In a more nuanced example, the customer who has just completed a speed test on their home internet, found very poor results, and then called the contact center should be routed immediately to an agent in the right department. Thus, the arbitration is not a message, but an augmented journey flow that is completely invisible to the customer. Better yet, the telecommunications company may choose to be proactive in their service to that individual without them having to call at all. Data from a system that shows that she is having issues, flows into the orchestration engine, which makes an immediate decision, or decisions, such as:

1. Send a text to the customer informing them that we are aware of the issue and are investigating.
2. Raise a ticket in the technical department to remediate the problem.
3. Trigger an action in the contact center CRM, complete with the relevant customer context, for an agent to make an outbound care call.
4. Suppress all sales promotions to this customer until their primary service issue is resolved.

Note that arbitration is not limited to the channel in which an initial interaction occurred, nor in the number or type of decisions that it can make immediately.

In the mid-term, however, how the company arbitrates that engagement will also consider the customer's detectable sentiment stemming from how the company addressed the issue. The time dimension is important. It informs the optimization of *ongoing* interactions across channels, and how they are modified based on the type of event, flow on events (conversations).

In advanced CJO platforms, that comes in the form of both out-of-the-box algorithms and configurable ones, as well as the ability to ingest models developed by a data science team if one exists.

Live Behavior Combined with Systems of Record

Orchestration is ultimately all about customer *context*, a concept that has been made to sound almost mystical in recent times but is in fact quite straightforward. Context is simply knowledge of an individual's situation – nothing more, nothing less. From a company standpoint, that knowledge is derived from two dimensions: the behavior of the person right in front of you, and your pre-existing knowledge of that person. Those two things combine to inform how you interact with that person at a given moment in time.

In other words, orchestration enables companies to mimic humanity. So, customer data and observable journey behavior make up the context, and companies can enhance this by understanding what device a customer uses, their location, and the touchpoint where interaction takes place. This is the first stage of enriching context.

Inferences

In the second stage of enriching context, advanced orchestration capability is also able to draw inferences about that context. For example, if Barry has made seven calls to the contact center in the last two days, it can be inferred that it is not an opportune time to promote new offerings to him. This type of context, in the moment, is often most important because it extends beyond determining the right conversation to have at the right time, and into scenarios where the company elects to withhold entire conversations all together. This is often called suppression and, to be frank, most companies are terrible at this, such is their bias toward sales and marketing activation, irrespective of customer context.

Governing Arbitration

While I have described orchestration as a kind of brain that makes real-time decisions on behalf of the business, customer by customer, that doesn't mean that the machines are taking over! The best orchestration platforms are configurable so that the parameters of engagement are governed within the context of the business itself. For instance, the company can rank the prioritization of conversations that occur at the last gate of the decisioning process, and, of course, it decides what type of assets exist in the library in the first place.

Equally, an orchestration engine should provide a range of out-of-the-box methods that allow the company to calibrate the balance between customer (outside-in) and business (inside-out) prioritizations, as well as enabling it to create its own custom prioritization methods within the tool itself.

CJO Unifies Other Technologies

Technologically, CJO is a very significant departure and graduation in maturity from the typical campaign or promotion-based messaging *at* the customer. This does not mean the death of typical marketing automation, which remains an important capability, but it certainly doesn't play the central role in more mature companies that it does in those that are less so. Those with more advanced customer operations have shifted from treating customers as "targets" to viewing customers as individuals – as we always have in physical settings – recognizing that they have unique and evolving needs.

I hasten to add that this is not a version of recent marketing "wokeness" (please excuse the term) as seen in the movement toward "purpose" enthusiastically proposed by those with little knowledge of brand management. Instead, it is a business value-based management approach, derived from the benefits of a bias toward service.

Considered properly, then, CJO is a unifying layer of capability that, in practical terms, combines automation, customer journey analytics, real-time decisioning, machine learning, and, of course, the favorite topic of those seeking to advance almost every field of management endeavor, artificial intelligence. It seeks to discern intent, visualize, analyze, and then *orchestrate* the right customer conversations and journeys, across and despite organizational siloes. In this sense it unifies not only the technology- and channel-borne assets and investments, but also the departmental structures, largely via the visualization process, enabling group-level prioritizations.

One company I consulted with used the concept of "Movie Tuesday", in which all the department heads – digital leaders, contact center managers, service management, overseeing executives, and more – attended a session once a month in which the customer journeys for the company were interrogated, live and on a massive screen – like being at the movies. As more insight emerged, hypotheses on different projects did as well, and each leader with some impact to the in-scope journey had a role to play. For the first time they were playing as one team, and the idea was to start inviting the CEO and members of the board so they could see for themselves the intelligence and work that was underlying the metrics presented quarterly.

But orchestration goes well beyond the ideas of journey analytics because it works in two directions: listening (discerning intent as previously discussed) and optimization.

Optimization, in this context, is an active, live, and *in situ* response to the customer. Equally, that response is likely to elicit another act from the customer themselves, which, in turn, will require the company to respond again. As we have covered, every response by the company must be delivered within 400 milliseconds, and so the horsepower of complex decisioning is critical to both ensuring the correct response and the fluidity of conversation needed to create engagement.

Finally, orchestration will also generate leads based on real-time customer behavior directly into a CRM or marketing automation tool, proving again, that great service increases sales.

Illustration of Target Architecture

If you are struggling with how orchestration might fit into your overall process model and other investments just remember that this is essentially the "brain", the central nervous system, of the company's engagement with their customers. This is not just true philosophically, but architecturally, as illustrated here (Figure 6.13).

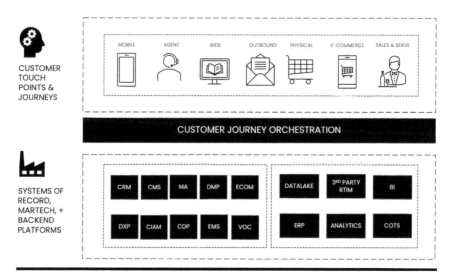

Figure 6.13 Customer Journey Orchestration as a Business Middleware (H. Hernandez Reveron, A. Spinley, 2024)

Notice how it functions as an intermediary between the company's systems or record, analytics, etc., its sales and marketing apparatus, and the channel and touchpoints with which the customers are interacting. This ensures that only one system of logic dominates all interactions, no matter the type, location, or touchpoint involved – and, equally, that customers are able to complete diverse journeys that traverse as many different forms as they wish without the company losing them, or the ability to maintain coherency and relevance throughout.

Finally, an orchestration capability should not be bi-directional only in terms of the customer interactions (conversations) that it enables; this also applies to the internal systems that it pulls data from. It should also be able to push newly enriched data *back* to these systems of record, including sales, leads, service cases, updates to customer contact details, their location, information on their devices, specific metadata, and so on.

This is important to grasp because the underlying principle here is that orchestration is great for the customer and, when executed well, even better for the company. Quite aside from the economics of enhanced customer engagement, the data generated is of the richest kind, and this can be piped directly back into company systems for analysis.

UK-based Marston's is the world's largest brewer of cask ale and I have chosen it for this case study[72] because, despite that, it is not a massive global conglomerate. It is all too easy to cite major corporations who use leading technologies, but my message here is that this is within the reach of "normal" businesses with "normal" budgets.

CASE STUDY: MARSTON'S

In 2016, Marston's began working with customer orchestration capability. As is quite typical of many companies, even those with lavish martech budgets, its engagement with customers was limited to non-contextual and transactional interactions.

The first thing that Marston's did was associate over 20,000 interacting customers with systems of record, and thus began the process of advancing its ability to identify its customers properly (the first pillar). It also began to capture the connected interactions of unidentified visiting customers as well, and, over time, began to stitch together customer identities, behaviors, and attributes (e.g. favorite beers, favorite pubs, who they drink with, are they young and single or do they have children in tow, and so on), across different channel and contextual settings.

This started to paint two pictures.

The first was that the nuanced interactions of individual customers began to expose their specific intent (the second pillar), and then in the aggregate, Marston's started to understand the major flows and patterns of its differing customer cohorts.

Now it was equipped go beyond simplistic trigger-based messaging, and instead interact (the third pillar) with customers, one by one, in real time, in an intelligent and coherent manner – all based on the context of each unique individual, their wants, needs, and their journey in whatever fashion or order, from email, the pub, Facebook, to the website, to delivery services.

As both the interactions and the data about the interactions improved, so too did the level of insight and contribution toward important company metrics. For instance, taking a journey-based approach, the company could detect the number of people that had not only responded to a paid advertisement taking them to the landing page of the website, but the subsequent journeys and deviations that ultimately impacted real conversion statistics.

At the time that this case study was first published, Marston's was reporting a six-fold increase in engagement with its customer communications, and in just over a year after the program began, it had advanced from the initial 20,000 customers it could match against systems of record to over 200,000 across properties including traditional pubs, hotels, and restaurants.

Turns out, the digital-to-physical divide is only real to those who choose to accept it.

***

As you can imagine, there is much more to the Marston's story, but it is one of immense success, born of operationalized customer-centricity over sales activation, and getting outsized sales benefits as a result. But they are not alone. Over the last decade or so, right around the world, you'll find leading companies applying the same capabilities for similarly aligned outcomes, in radically diverse fields. These reportedly include Pfizer, Liverpool Football Club, The Cleveland Cavaliers, The US PGA, Formula One, Telstra, Paddy Power, Page Group, AT&T, and ENBW.

Downstream Effects of Orchestration

Before we move on, we should sum the impacts of orchestration:

- Sustain psychological engagement.
- Limit journey abandonment.
- Diminish or remove customer friction.
- Make operational the critical bias to service.
- Resolve the choice paradox in touch point proliferation and offer diversification.

In today's context and scale, there is perhaps no more strategic capability for the restoration of customering's economic mission than journey orchestration. As a case in point, consider the below table from work I have done with a utilities company (which I am unable to name) (Table 6.7).

Table 6.7 Example Orchestration Outcomes

Benefit	Description	Value Points
NEW CONTRACTS Target: x% increase to annual growth rate	Contextual next best conversation (NBC) activation to anonymous customers pre- and post- trend line drop off points. Proactive monitoring and intervention on customer onboarding / contracting process.	• Board reporting. • Sales management. • Finance (revenue management). • Marketing (acquisition).
CONTRACTED TO RENEWAL Target: x% decrease in the annual customer churn rate, and y% increase in the annual uptake of sustainability offerings.	Proactive account management and interventions based on customer intent across the current contract life stages. Proactive renewal NBC nudges and intelligence served (just in time) to sales reps / call center / self-serve More contextual engagement to increase propensity of response on sustainability products.	• Board reporting. • Sales management. • Finance (revenue management). • Churn rates measured by customer management.
OPTIMIZATION OF MEDIA SPEND Target: x% increase in conversion on current spend level	Optimizing customer journey post the response (i.e., click through) to paid media (i.e., Google/social) for end game conversion rather than relying only the on the ad creative / offer. Better media integration and presentation based on more contemporaneous behavior(s).	• Marketing (advertising spend).
JOURNEY A/B TESTING Target: x% increase in conversion on current media spend and y% increase in conversion of in-channel promotion	Track journey variables on paid media conversion rates between unknown recognized, and verified customer cohorts, and by audience types. Track journey variables on paid media conversion rates between creatives, cohorts, or a combination. Track journey variables on in-channel promotions and offers to conversion between creatives, cohorts, or a combination.	• Marketing (advertising spend). • Marketing (promotion and offer conversion).
OPTIMIZATION OF SELF-SERVE x% reduction in Annual reduction in customer service call volumes and tickets, and y% reduction in unit cost to serve	Leveraging journey visualization within asset and channel design. Applying deflection activations within "my account" journey types. Optimization of NBC within existing self-service assets to improve performance and adoption.	• Finance (revenue). • Finance (profit).

(Continued)

Table 6.7 (Continued) Example Orchestration Outcomes

Benefit	Description	Value Points
CUSTOMER COMPLAINTS x% reduction in discrete complaints (any channel)	Preventive identification of journey friction points Continuous improvement / enrichment of NBC library Resolving service needs (intent) consistently and rapidly as a BAU characteristic	• Board reporting. • Customer complaints (where related to customer service) is an overall indicator for customer management.

As you can see, we have a range of stakeholders that benefit from a properly constructed orchestration capability – not least of whom are our friends in marketing, with improvement to their acquisition rates and in the cost to acquire through optimizing media spend. Equally, those with responsibility for overall revenue management are in play, and the roll up of board reporting come into focus as well.

Applying the First Three Pillars

Interactions is the piece of the puzzle everyone can see. It is the app, the website, the chatbot, the store sales assistant or service agent; it is the contact center and the messaging and all the other obvious activities. It is the tip of the iceberg that sits atop the waves.

But make no mistake, it is predicated entirely on the intelligence and capabilities that have allowed us to identify our customers, and to discern their intent, one by one for each customer, repeatedly.

Those who cannot – or, more accurately, *do* not – establish this capability in their customer operations will remain mired in transactional, low-value activities typical of the movement. And yet, it is also important to recognize that not all industries face the same challenges. The application of the management model, the level of investment made in it, must be calibrated to company context.

For instance, a diversified energy retailer must engage with customers in a much more nuanced way, across a range of job models and significantly more channels and touchpoints, than a pure-play e-commerce company. As such, I have summarized a high-level point of view for several industry verticals below. Please remember that this is (a) my opinion only, and (b) a generalized summary that requires review in each company setting (Figure 6.14).

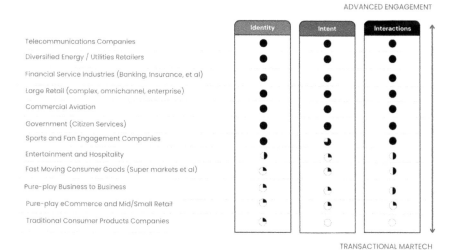

Figure 6.14 A PoV: The Applied Model by Industry

What I hope you have noticed is that those industries that reside at the top of the table require the application of markedly more sophisticated customer engagement theory, management discipline, and technology, applied within the management model. For those that are clearly only transactional entities, such as a pure-play e-commerce company, customers have a level of tolerance for – if not outright acceptance of – interactions that are in keeping with that type of entity.

That will mean that some brands can get away with constant sales activation like promotions, offers, upsell and cross-sell messaging, and other sales-based journey disruptions. But as the level of category customer nuance increases, brute force tactics are less and less tolerated. The mistake much of the customer management industry makes is to template its thinking, i.e., treat all industries the same. As such, we see short-termism and reductive mindsets dominate, and woefully inadequate practices applied to highly nuanced customer settings.

The role of the chief customer officer is to understand their industry dimensions alongside their specific company context and calibrate the model accordingly.

Notes

1. Paul Greenberg, *The Commonwealth of Self-Interest: Business Success Through Customer Engagement* (The 56 Group, 2019).
2. Bilal Ahmen et al., "The Impact of Customer Experience and Customer Engagement on Behavioral Intentions: Does Competitive Choices Matters?," *Frontiers in Psychology* 13 (2022): 864841; Roderick J. Brodie, Linda D. Hollebeek, Biljana Jurić and Ana Ilić, "Customer Engagement: Conceptual

Domain, Fundamental Propositions, and Implications for Research," *Journal of Service Research* 14 (2011): 252–271; Muhammad Zada et al., "Does Servant Leadership Control Psychological Distress in Crisis? Moderation and Mediation Mechanism," *Psychology Research & Behavior Management* 15 (2022): 607.

3. Jenny van Doorn et al., "Customer Engagement Behavior: Theoretical Foundations and Research Directions," *Journal of Service Research* 13 (2010): 253–266.

4. Linda D. Hollebeek et al., "Customer Engagement in Evolving Technological Environments: Synopsis and Guiding Propositions," *European Journal of Marketing* 53, no. 9 (2019): 2018–2023; see also Babk Taheri, Aliakbar Jafari and Kevin O'Gorman, "Keeping Your Audience: Presenting a Visitor Engagement Scale," *Tourism Management* 42 (2014): 321–329; Paul Harrigan, Uwana Evers, Morgan P. Miles and Tim Daly, "Customer Engagement and the Relationship Between Involvement, Engagement, Self-Brand Connection and Brand Usage Intent," *Journal of Business Research* 88 (2018): 388- 396.

5. Business Wire, "Research From Thunderhead.com Reveals Bold New Framework for Redefining Customer Engagement in the Digital Era," April 16, 2014. https://www.businesswire.com/news/home/20140416005192/en/Research-from -Thunderhead.com-Reveals-Bold-New-Framework-for-Redefining-Customer -Engagement-in-the-Digital-Era.

6. Neurological trust is more nuanced than this element alone, covered later in this chapter.

7. Mary Jo Bitner, "Servicescapes: The Impact of Physical Surroundings on Customers and Employees," *Journal of Marketing* 56, no. 2 (1992): 57–71.

8. B. Joseph Pine II and James H. Gilmore, *The Experience Economy* (Harvard Business Review Press, 1999).

9. Patricia Buckley and Rumki Majumdar, "The Services Powerhouse: Increasingly Vital to World Economic Growth," *Deloitte*, July 12, 2018. https://www2 .deloitte.com/us/en/insights/economy/issues-by-the-numbers/trade-in-services -economy-growth.html.

10. Customology, *The Unspoken Customer: 2023 Australian Customer Values Analysis* (2023). https://www.customology.com.au/the-unspoken-customer-download/.

11. Don Peppers and Martha Rogers, *Extreme Trust: Turning Proactive Honesty and Flawless Execution into Long-Term Profits* (Revised edn., Penguin, 2012).

12. Chatura Ranaweera and Jaideep Prabhu, "On The Relative Importance of Customer Satisfaction and Trust as Determinants of Customer Retention and Positive Word of Mouth," *Journal of Targeting, Measurement and Analysis for Marketing* 12, no. 1 (2003): 82–90.

13. United Nations Secretary-General, "Secretary-General's Address to the General Assembly" (2018). https://www.un.org/sg/en/content/sg/statement/2018-09 -25/secretary-generals-address-the-general-assembly-delivered-trilingual-scroll -further-down-for-all-english.

14. Katie Harbath and Collier Fernekes, "History of the Cambridge Analytica Controversy," *Bipartisan Policy Center*, March 16, 2023. https://bipartisanpolicy .org/blog/cambridge-analytica-controversy/.

15. Bernd Lahno, "Institutional Trust: A Less Demanding Form of Trust?," *Revista Latinoamericana de Estudios Avanzados* 15 (2001):19–58; Kaisa Henttonen and Kirsimarja Blomqvist, "Managing Distance in a Global Virtual Team: The Evolution of Trust Through Technology-Mediated Relational Communication," *Strategic Change* 14, No. 2 (2005): 107–119.

16. Kenneth J. Arrow, *The Limits of Organization* (W. W. Norton & Co., 1974). See also sociologist Niklas Luhmann, *Trust and Power* (John Wiley & Sons, 2018).
17. W. E. Douglas Creed and Raymond E. Miles (Eds.), *Trust in Organizations: A Conceptual Framework* (Sage Publications, 1996).
18. Kogut, B., & Zander, U. (1992). Knowledge of the firm, combinative capabilities, and the replication of technology. *Organization Science, 3*(3), 383–397.
19. Robert M. Grant, "Toward a Knowledge-Based Theory of the Firm," *Strategic Management Journal* 17 (1996): 109–22
20. Roderick M. Kramer, "Trust and Distrust in Organizations: Emerging Perspectives, Enduring Questions," *Annual Review of Psychology 50* (1999): 569–598.
21. Miia Kosonen, Kirsimarja Blomqvist and Riikka Ellonen, "Trust and Its Impersonal Nature," in *Encyclopedia of Networked and Virtual Organizations*, ed. Goran D. Putnik and Maria Manuela Cruz-Cunha (IGI Global, 2008), 1683–1690.
22. Roger C. Mayer, Hames H. Davis and F. David Schoorman, "An Integrative Model of Organizational Trust," *Academy of Management Review* 20, no. 3 (1995): 709–734.
23. Matthias Söllner et al., "Towards a Formative Measurement Model for Trust" (paper presentation, eTrust: Implications for the Individual, Enterprises and Society, 23rd Bled eConference, Bled, Slovenia, June 20–23, 2010).
24. Charles Duhigg, *The Power of Habit: Why We Do What We Do in Life and Business* (Random House, 2012).
25. Institute of Customer Service, *The UK Customer Satisfaction Index* (2023). https://www.instituteofcustomerservice.com/research-insight/ukcsi/
26. Chiefmartec, *Scott Brinker* [Blog page], https://chiefmartec.com/author/chiefmartec/.
27. Steven L. Vargo and Robert F. Lusch, "Evolving to a New Dominant Logic for Marketing," *Journal of Marketing* 68, no. 1 (2004): 1–17.
28. Quoted in Clayton M. Christensen and Michael E. Raynor, *The Innovator's Solution: Creating and Sustaining Successful Growth* (Harvard Business Review Press, 2003), ch. 3.
29. Craig Dowden, "Love is the Secret Sauce for Organizational Growth," *Psychology Today*, February 14, 2024. https://www.psychologytoday.com/au/blog/the-leaders-code/202402/when-business-is-love-love-is-the-foundation-behind-success.
30. Ida B. N. Udayana, Prayekti Prayekti and Eliya Ardyan, "Factors that Influence the Relationship between Customer Information Quality and Salesperson Performance," *Market-Tržište* 31, no. 2 (2019): 187–207.
31. See, for example, Eugene W. Anderson, Claes Fornell and Donald R. Lehmann, "Customer Satisfaction, Market Share, and Profitability: Findings from Sweden," *Journal of Marketing* 58, no. 3 (1994): 53–66; Eugene W. Anderson and Vikas Mittal, "Strengthening the Satisfaction-Profit Chain," *Journal of Service Research* 3, no. 2 (2000): 107–120; Valarie A. Zeithaml, Leonard L. Berry and A. Parasuraman, "The Behavioral Consequences of Service Quality," *Journal of Marketing* 60, no. 2 (1996): 31–46.
32. Ruth N. Bolton, "A Dynamic Model of the Duration of the Customer's Relationship with a Continuous Service Provider: The Role of Satisfaction," Marketing Science 17, no. 1 (1998): 45-65.

33. Klarna, *Klarna AI Assistant Handles Two-thirds of Customer Service Chats in Its First Month*, February 27, 2024. https://www.klarna.com/international/press /klarna-ai-assistant-handles-two-thirds-of-customer-service-chats-in-its-first -month/.

34. Paul J. Zak, "Why Inspiring Stories Make Us React: The Neuroscience of Narrative," *Cerebrum* 2 (2015).

35. Brendon Power of Telstra at Forrester CX, Sydney, 2022.

36. Daniel Kahneman and Amos Tversky, "Prospect Theory: An Analysis of Decision under Risk," *Econometrica* 47, no. 2 (1979):, 263.

37. Ulrich Schmidt and Horst Zank, "What is Loss Aversion?," *Journal of Risk and Uncertainty* 30, no. 2 (2005): 157–167.

38. Wenhua Wang et al., "Eliciting Psychological Ownership of Object by Marking Organizational Name: The Role of Belongingness," *Frontiers in Psychology* 12 (2021).

39. Cited in B. Joseph Pine II and James H. Gilmore, The Experience Economy: Competing for Customer Time, Attention, and Money (Harvard Business Review Press, 2020), p. 18.

40. Antonio R. Damásio, *Self Comes to Mind: Constructing the Conscious Brain* (Pantheon Books, 2010).

41. Ken A. Paller and Anthony D. Wagner, "Observing the Transformation of Experience into Memory," *Trends in Cognitive Sciences* 6, no. 2 (2002): 93–102.

42. Andrew C. Heusser, Paxton C. Fitzpatrick and Jeremy R. Manning, "Geometric Models Reveal Behavioural and Neural Signatures of Transforming Experiences into Memories," *Nature Human Behaviour* 5, no. 7 (2021): 905–919.

43. Chloe Steadman and Jack Coffin (Eds.), *Consuming Atmospheres: Designing, Experiencing, and Researching Atmospheres in Consumption Spaces* (Routledge, 2023).

44. WGBH History Unit. "Joe Wanamaker," *Who Made America?*, no date. https:// www.pbs.org/wgbh/theymadeamerica/whomade/wanamaker_hi.html.

45. The Editors of Encyclopaedia Britannica, "Sears," *Encyclopaedia Britannica Online*, December 7, 2022. https://www.britannica.com/topic/Sears-Roebuck -and-Company.

46. "The Popular Rise of Outlet Stores," *New Bedford Standard-Times*, 22 November 22, 2016. https://www.southcoasttoday.com/story/entertainment/books/2016/11 /20/the-popular-rise-outlet-stores/24495366007/.

47. Apple, "Apple Launches .Mac," *Apple Newsroom*, February 19, 2024. https:// www.apple.com/newsroom/2002/07/17Apple-Launches-Mac/.

48. Pine II and Gilmore, *The Experience Economy*.

49. Barbara L. Fredrickson and Daniel Kahneman, "Duration Neglect in Retrospective Evaluations of Affective Episodes," *Journal of Personality and Social Psychology* 65, no. 1 (1993): 45–55.

50. Zachary Zenko, Panteleimon Ekkekakis and Dan Ariely, "Can You Have Your Vigorous Exercise and Enjoy It Too? Ramping Intensity Down Increases Postexercise, Remembered, and Forecasted Pleasure," *Journal of Sport & Exercise Psychology* 38, no. 2 (2016): 149–159.

51. Lions, "RISE&FALL," *The Work*, no date, https://www.lovethework.com/work -awards/campaigns/risefall-238649.

52. Thomas Oakley-Newell, "7-Eleven to Limit Customer Savings on Fuel Price Lock Program," *C-Store*, February 1, 2024. https://www.c-store.com.au/7-eleven -to-limit-customer-savings-on-fuel-price-lock-program/.

53. Remedios Lucio, "7-Eleven's Fuel App Wins Canstar's Award," *Inside FMCG*, January 17, 2018. https://insidefmcg.com.au/2018/01/18/7-elevens-fuel-app-wins -canstars-award/.

54. Nick Babich, "Human Factor Principles in UX Design," *UX Magazine*, January 20, 2021. https://uxmag.com/articles/human-factor-principles-in-ux-design

55. Don Norman, *The Design of Everyday Things: Revised and Expanded Edition* (Constellation, 2013).

56. Derek Du Preez, "Salesforce's State of the Connected Customer Report – Expedite Your Digital Projects, but Don't Forget About Your Values," *Diginomica*, October 28, 2020. https://diginomica.com/salesforces-state -connected-customer-report-expedite-your-digital-projects-dont-forget-about -your

57. Statista, *Worldwide Digital Population 2024*. https://www.statista.com/statistics /617136/digital-population-worldwide/

58. Center for Mobile Communication Studies, *The Past, Present, and Future of Smartphone*, September 14, 2018. https://sites.bu.edu/cmcs/2018/09/14/the-past -present-and-future-of-smartphone/

59. "John Wanamaker's Grand Depot" [graphic]. Library Company of Philadelphia Digital Collections, no date. https://digital.librarycompany.org/islandora/object/ Islandora%3A60894

60. Thomas Wieberneit, "How to Orchestrate Customer Journeys in Real Time at Scale," *customerthink*, September 10, 2021. https://customerthink.com/how-to -orchestrate-customer-journeys-in-real-time-at-scale/

61. Ewan Duncan, Harald Fanderl, Nicolas Maechler and Kevin Neher, "Customer Experience: Creating Value Through Transforming Customer Journeys," *McKinsey & Company*, July 1, 2016. https://www.mckinsey.com/capabilities/ growth-marketing-and-sales/our-insights/customer-experience-creating-value -through-transforming-customer-journeys.

62. Colin Shaw and John Ivens, "The Physical Customer Experience," in *Building Great Customer Experiences* (Palgrave Macmillan, 2002), 15–40.

63. Bharat Poddar, Yogesh Mishra, and Anandapadmanabhan Ramabhadran, "Transform Customer Journeys at Scale – And Transform Your Business," *BCG*, November 8, 2019. https://www.bcg.com/publications/2019/transform-customer -journeys-scale-transform-business.

64. Dhruv Grewal, Julie Baker, Michael Levy, and Glenn B. Voss, "The Effects of Wait Expectations and Store Atmosphere Evaluations on Patronage Intentions in Service-Intensive Retail Stores," *Journal of Retailing* 79, no. 4 (2003): 259–268; Mark M. Davis and Janelle Heineke, "How Disconfirmation, Perception and Actual Waiting Times Impact Customer Satisfaction," *International Journal of Service Industry Management* 9, no. 1 (1998): 64–73; Karen L. Katz, Blaire M. Larson and Richard C. Larson, "Prescription for the Waiting in Line Blues: Entertain, Enlighten and Engage," *Sloan Management Review* 32 (1991): 44–53.

65. Sevgin A. Eroglu and Karen A. Machleit, "An Empirical Study of Retail Crowding Antecedents and Consequences," *Journal of Retailing* 66 (1990): 201–221.

66. "Nudge: Improving Decisions about Health, Wealth and Happiness By Richard H. Thaler Cass R. Sunstein" [Summary], *Edelweiss Mutual Fund*, no date. https://www.edelweissmf.com/Files/Insigths/booksummary/pdf/EdelweissMF _BookSummary_Nudge.pdf

67. Barry Schwartz, *The Paradox of Choice: Why More Is Less* (Harper Collins, 2003).

68. Sheena S. Iyengar and Mark R. Lepper, "When Choice Is Demotivating: Can One Desire Too Much of a Good Thing?," *Journal of Personality and Social Psychology* 79, no. 6 (2000): 995–1006.

69. "Customers Don't Care About Channels," Aaron Spinley at Forrester CX, Australia, 2022.

70. https://www.linkedin.com/in/hernandezhenry/

71. Inclusion Cloud, *Centralized Vs. Decentralized Data: Unveiling the Great Debate*, May 5, 2023. https://inclusioncloud.com/insights/blog/centralized-decentralized -data/.

72. "Thunderhead Meet Carston's at the Pub" [Case study], 2020. www.thunder-head.com

Chapter 7

Pillar 4

Measurement and Reporting

Understanding "Return"

As we contemplate the proper mission of customer management and its first three pillars – Identity, Intent, and Interactions – we now have the reference architecture needed to apply modes of measurement to outcomes, rather than to the measures unto themselves. Equally, it is very important to distinguish between the necessary investment in these pillars to deliver against the long-term economic missions of customering, versus short-term concepts like return on investment (ROI).

This may seem counter to a typical business case. It's not that return isn't important, but we must properly frame that before we measure it. ROI, in general, tends to inversely correlate with increases to profit, the second mission of customering, because it usually *diminishes as a company spends more, and increases as it spends less*, which tells us very little about actual return.

As an extension of another structural problem – the conflation of marketing with customering – we see marketing-related thinking in respect to ROI concepts contaminating measurement, not that ROI is without problems in that discipline either. In fact, Byron Sharp calls it a"stupid metric ... that can send you broke"[1] while Peter Field once labeled it "incredibly dangerous"[2] and back in 2004, London Business School marketing professor Tim Ambler wrote his seminal article, "ROI is Dead: Now Bury It".[3]

Alas, it remains common practice, in large part because marketers have often required the blessing of finance leaders to do their work, and folks that don't understand a field adequately will typically seek to frame it in their own terms, irrespective of suitability. Customering suffers the same dilemma, and for both, a strategically literate CFO is critical.

DOI: 10.4324/9781003513728-8

But even more damaging than generic ROI, a popular metric that has emerged in marketing circles is ROAS (return on advertising spend). Simply calculated, ROAS equals (revenue attributable to ads / cost of ads) × 100. For example, if you can attribute $40,000 in revenue from an ad campaign that cost $10,000, you have an ROAS of 4. Some scholars have said that this is a valid measure to judge physical availability efforts (near proximity promotion, etc.), but even in this use case, there is often a real problem determining an accurate attribution and incrementality. More broadly, though Tom Roach notes:

> Too great a focus on ROAS is leading to short-term thinking and under-investment, which in turn is stifling growth, and it has the potential to be far more damaging than ROI.[4]

I argue that when ROI and ROAS mindsets leak into customering – which should be an inherently longitudinal discipline where promotion is secondary – the damage is even more pronounced. Instead, we must measure the model's efficacy more strategically, and judiciously.

Option to Skip

Okay, so, this is going to get a little technical. The following pages prescribe the select measures to monitor the functioning of the model including service, experience, assets, and journey efficacy, as well as business tests:

- Effect on brand with customer cohorts.
- Churn rates and interdependence.
- Customer lifetime value.
- Customer lifespan (tenure).
- Customer profitability.
- Monetization of customers via referral.

And finally, we'll cover management and governance reporting.

It's highly important, but I understand that some may wish to treat this as a reference chapter, and if that is you, I won't be offended if you jump forward to Chapter 8.

Measurement Methods

Much of the work on this subject was done long before this book was even a twinkle in the eye of yours truly. Dr. V. Kumar is probably *the* pioneer when it comes to measuring the value of engagement. A globally recognized academic, his book *Profitable Customer Engagement: Concept Metrics and Strategies*[5] is an essential reference, and the period in which he released that book is important. Some theories that predate this era require updating validation, given recent evolutions of consumerism, society, and their relationship with technology.

At this point I am also going to recommend another book that I have previously mentioned, by my good friend Paul Greenberg. Among its many virtues, *The Commonwealth of Self Interest*[6] does a wonderful job of summarizing Kumar's work and, more broadly, is an essential reference for any budding CCO. If that's you, it should sit on your bookshelf alongside Dr Kumar's volume and, I hope, this one. While I draw on Paul's excellent summary, I will contribute select other approaches that are important to the measurement of this model.

As with any industrial management framework, a sound measurement strategy can be divided into two categories (Table 7.1):

Table 7.1 Model Tests

System Tests	Are my system components operating as intended?
Business (outcome) Tests	Ultimately, does the program meet conformance with target business outcomes, as defined in its mission[7].

When broken down further, our system tests will test for friction and effort, while we will seek to test the memorability of any target experiences delivered to in-scope customer cohorts; and, lastly, we look at particular asset utilization, e.g., websites, contact centers, phone apps, etc. Finally, to test the impact on overall business value, we will test churn, customer lifetime value, and for any monetization via customer influence.

System Tests – Friction

As established in the interactions pillar, a vast majority of interactions between companies and their customers are, in fact, services, and their primary characteristic is that they save time and are as easy to complete as possible. This is where we seek to be *frictionless*.

When we understand that friction triggers a high conscious state and increased cognitive load, we realize that we are talking about *effort*, and so that is also part of what we measure. Studies of effort[8] have largely been used to account for individual differences in intellectual performance and areas such as motivation and the availability of mental resources, and to explain the effects of stimuli or "stressors" such as noise, lack of sleep, time-on-task, and the like; but in the customer management context we are less concerned with comparable human performance, and more with the role of effort in behavioral outcomes.

For instance, if the dominant journey interactions for a customer who is exploring credit card options at Bank A are around 128 touchpoints and an average of nine minutes to make an application, there will be a higher propensity for success than at Bank B, which offers the same process across 223 touchpoints and 14 minutes. Accordingly, Bank A should see lower friction represented in its measurement than Bank B does. As a service characteristic, we must measure our ability to deliver ease of completion for customers.

All Behavioral Journeys

Casting your mind back to the section dealing with customer intent, you will recall that we have established that proper journey analytics provides the richest source of insight. It is observational – ethnographic – in nature and avoids the profound folly of asking people about their behavior.

The same principles, and instruments, also enable the testing of journey friction. For instance, leading tools offer:

- Most common paths across all touchpoints.
- Cross-channel interdependencies.
- Dominant paths as an aggregation.
- Most in-demand customer jobs.
- Dominant completion routes by customer job.
- Time to completion by customer jobs.
- Impact to time and completion by origin of journey.
- Drop-off points or journey-lag with jobs.
- Drop-off or lag within channels.
- Drop-off or lag at individual touchpoints.

As you can see, it allows companies to view aggregated customer activity (*actual behavior*) and customer jobs at the level of channels and individual touchpoints. The data generated is a particularly powerful source of determining two related dimensions:

1. The level of customer effort to complete their jobs.
2. The level of friction by journey, channel, and touchpoint.

Naturally, we are looking for these to be at as low as possible, noting that the former has a direct impact on the latter.

Customer Jobs

As already covered above, the efficacy of job completion is captured by the best journey analytics capabilities, but as a key indicator of service friction which allow us to weight and prioritize interventions, a core measurement focus must be the time and effort to complete specific customer jobs.

Again, please note that we are not talking about sales activations or sales conversion rates. These will occur downstream and because of a range of factors, including ease of journey. Of course, that is more in focus for pure-play e-commerce websites, and you will recall that we discussed the ratio of service to sales interactions by category as we closed the section on interactions. In the context of measurement, though, we must focus on service – being the jobs customers seek to complete – noting that in some categories this will naturally include sales conversions.

Most companies don't understand the distinction and default to measures that start and end with sales (e.g., ROAS). This is a classic example of inside-out thinking and is the antithesis of world-class customer management. Such short-termism is the reason for spam-like behavior in customer channels and is behind the decline in consumer trust globally.

Ironically, companies that frame value, and therefore their measurement and use case investments, in terms of the transactional dimension alone ultimately end up with lower customer lifetime value (i.e., they sell less!).

As an example of clear jobs that are not sales-based, consider the following:

- Check my bill.
- Charge my card.
- Make an application.
- Lodge a complaint.
- Find a branch.
- Test my Internet speed.
- Download an app.
- Update my details.
- Change my consent.
- Review my preferences.
- View my account.
- Ask a question.
- Report an issue.
- Make a return.
- Request a refund.
- Check a policy.
- Request a service.
- Cancel, or pause, a service.
- Find a product.
- Check availability or timing.
- Look up information.
- Locate corporate information.

The job of customering is to enable customers to complete theirs. Note, that these are only sub-jobs of a wider "episode". What I mean by that is that, together, these might serve a wider objective for the customer. For example, as a customer of an energy company, I might be moving to a new house. That is the actual job or episode – the sub-jobs that I need to complete might be: make an application, *and* update my details, *and* find a product, *and* request a service, *and* cancel or pause a service, *and* check availability or timing.

There is another aspect, and that is the fact that customers engage in multiple journeys and complete multiple jobs concurrently. For example, in addition to moving house I might also want to know more about sustainability products that the company can provide like smart meters and appliances, and I could be in the market to install solar panels on the roof of a new home.

Of course, smarter companies will look at how they can create optimized journeys that bundle up the jobs, to avoid the customer having to do each of them separately. In fact, they might create one touchpoint, from which the company takes over and completes the rest of the process so that customer must do as little as possible.

So, companies need to be able to optimize, and measure, at the various levels:

- Episodes, like move my house.
- Jobs, like update my details.
- All jobs, as described.

Based on measuring the friction present at all levels, the company can start to make improvement decisions. Some will regulate investment only to higher-friction areas based on a straight line relationship to conversion, or some other internal driver. Yet, customer sentiment is affected by the entirety of their stimuli with a brand, and allowing underperforming areas to continue because they don't more obviously correlate to internal values, is to ignore the customer context and damage its potential. As always, beware the inside-out mindset, the folly of short-term ROI, and the pitfalls of failing to calibrate the measurement system to long-term customer engagement – and risk. Beware, as well, those who would apply regression analysis devoid of this reality. More on that in Chapter 9.

We will soon talk about the business tests, which allow us to take a commercial view of the collective outcomes of our customer operations. When we are measuring friction, though, we must maintain an outside-in modus operandi. We must measure precisely what we deliver to our customers with no other lens other than *their* journeys, episodes, jobs, channels, touchpoints, and all of their interconnections.

Customer Effort Scores – But Not as We Know It

Having laid this foundation, it is important to acknowledge that this level of maturity in both management theory and technological capability is just not adopted in most organizations today. Instead, surveys rear their head again. Specifically, a CX department will use a customer effort score (CES) survey. A CES typically asks:

> *On a scale of 1 to 5, rate how easy [company/person] made it for you to [accomplish a task].*

The score is simply the percentage of respondents who "4 – agree" and "5 – strongly agree", and as you can see, it focuses on a specific task or interaction in the question.

While that can be argued to have value for specific episodes or jobs, it does not capture the level of insight truly needed. Nevertheless, it is used and used a lot, courtesy of the movement. The idea of sending a CES survey right after a service interaction to ask how much effort it took, as is recommended by its practitioners, is not totally without merit. The danger is that, in practice, it risks creating friction at the exact point (service) our model is seeking to avoid it, and often runs afoul of the peak-end rule. Not to mention that it adds to the global phenomenon of survey fatigue.

Having said all that, CES can be better incorporated as part of deep dive for prioritizing interventions where the constraints of an operating budget may not support resolution of all items that need improvement. In this instance, adding the perceived view of customers to aggregate journey data can be beneficial, and because you are using it in a more targeted way, you're far less likely to be annoying – or at least, you won't be as often.

There are three "gotchas", though, that you need to think about carefully.

Firstly, customers can be unforgiving, and as we discussed with self-reporting mechanisms, asking someone for a perspective means that they might just make one up! They may have never had a negative thought about the process they went through to move house because you have done a wonderful job bundling the sub-jobs and eradicating all possible friction, but now that you have asked them about it they might find a reason to be unhappy. Such is the human condition.

Secondly, and following from the first, when we ask someone what they think or what they want, we create a social contract. This is basic psychology. It means that they will now expect you to act on the advice that they believe they have given you. The movement will tell you that you can just "close the loop" with a simple acknowledgment and a thank you. Don't believe it. That's just not how human beings work (although it is important to always acknowledge feedback).

Thirdly, the impact of local culture on whether a response occurs also influences how it is provided and the tone, or language, used if it eventuates.

In summary, CES can be a useful tool when used in a highly targeted way to prioritize interventions, but it should not be used as the primary mechanism for measuring effort, or friction. That role must be filled by an advanced journey analytics capability. The latter's advantages over surveys are numerous and insurmountable, and it is no longer the year 2000. Our technological revolution has created all kinds of challenges, but it has delivered solutions too. Advanced journey analytics is one of those, and coupled with select and judicious use of CES, we can form a good picture.

Complaints Are Not a Measure

Many companies include the number of complaints as a key metric in dashboards presented to management. In my experience, firms need to be careful with this practice. In some instances, it can set up a mindset of tolerance for an "acceptable" level of unhappy customers, while in others it normalizes complaints in categories where there should not be any, or very limited instances. Others find that the single headline number obscures specific issues of materiality, the net impact on customers, and the real flow-on consequences.

At an event in 2022, I spoke to the "head of CX" at an airline that routinely seeks out customer feedback on its contact center. The volume of complaints was huge, truly frightening, but according to that executive it was "within the acceptable range for management", and no remediation was made to that channel despite the torrent of customer dissent. From the executive vantage point, performance had been so bad for so long that the dashboard hadn't moved, and so it was viewed as conforming to the KPI's goal of "zero degradation". You might laugh, but this is not that uncommon.

Complaints should be an exception at minor frequency, not a recurring theme of your customer program. If they are, park measurement efforts. Your system has failed and needs to be reconstituted for Identity, Intent, and Interactions as described.

Of course, complaints about products – outside of defect issues – often speak to a failure of market fit. While it falls to customer service teams to deal with the unhappy customer, they are only at the end of the line, and that data should be directed to the marketing department. This form of complaint is not a measure of the customer management program, although the individual customer context should form part of their adaptive profile for use for decisioning in their care.

Summary of Friction Measurement Methods

So then, a quick summary of methods available and their role (Table 7.2):

Table 7.2 Friction Measures

Test	Instrument	Benefit / Weakness	Frequency
Aggregate journeys	Journey analytics	Multi-dimensional, data is real-time, allows for data interrogation	Baseline, then after change, upon alert, and periodic as per the setting.
Sub-jobs Master jobs / episides All jobs			Baseline, then after change, and periodic.
Intervention			
Prioritization of initiatives from test outcomes	Journey analytics and Customer Effort Score	Rich interrogation of JA platform data, plus limited targeted customer perspective via CES. Supports business case for investment.	Only where there are competing interventions which require a business case.
	Regression analysis	Limited value as a corroboration. Weakness includes its pressumtion of linearity and constant variance, its reliance on self-reported data, and the act of isolating sentiment is imprecise.	Where there may be competing interventions.

System Tests – Memorability

As discussed earlier, experiences, while occupying the least number of interactions between company and customer, do have a disproportionate impact. This is somewhat of a double-edged sword. Most think of experience as a positive force, but it is just as powerful in the negative, and as a result of service failure most customer experiences today are just that, resulting in adverse feelings likely to generate negative memory.

We previously discussed other challenges for customer operations when it comes to designing for experience, including:

- Difficult, if not impossible, to sustain.
- Much more expensive for the company to deliver.

And so, in some settings it is an entirely valid strategy for a company to focus only on service-based interactions with its customers and leave experience to the brand management of the marketing department. The proviso here, of course, is that this only works where the marketing department does not presume to stage its activations in customer channels without understanding the impact on the customer mission, as is prone to occur in the absence of knowledgeable leadership across both domains.

But where companies have mastered their service layer, reflecting most of the interaction volume, it is entirely valid to explore the accelerative powers of experience. Certainly, in this case it is advisable, as it can have profound benefits for lifetime value and company profit.

There are two measurement layers to consider:

- Brand effect.
- Customer effect.

Brand Effect

As touched on briefly in Chapter 2, the management of brand is a dedicated and complex field within marketing. As part of positioning a company, it is concerned with concepts like distinctiveness and differentiation, both ocurring within memory.

As we know, memories are the basis of experience, and so the intersection is unescapable. If we design experiences for customers or specific cohorts of customers, we are ultimately adding to the memories that brand teams have created. It is arguable, then, that the impact of experiences created by the customer management team should be measured using the existing brand tracker tools of the marketing department, but that does not hold as much water as one might think, for several reasons.

- Firstly, the characteristics of your customer base, as a proportion of the total market, are not certain to be representative of the market. For example, Apple claimed a 24.7% share of the market for iPhone in the second quarter of 2023,[9] but its brand tracking will be concerned with the entirety of the market, which, for those who failed maths, leaves a whopping 75.3%. Remember, brand is a market-level function, not a customer one.
- Secondly, those who have become your customers may well have a different view and propensities to those that have not, *and* their attitude toward you is also colored by the fact that they have already chosen and used your offering, compared to those that have not.

So, the role of customer management is to ensure, firstly, that it does not diminish the brand positioning and memory structures that the company is striving to achieve, or to maintain, in the market. This may sound trivial but is not at all. It means mastering the service layer, and when I say "mastering", I really mean it. If a company can't do so, why would a customer believe their promises? Customer management leaders must be black belts in this field. That means serving the customer's agenda, first and foremost. In turn, this enables the greatest propensity for repeat custom in line with company market share. The relative few to have mastered this will preserve their company's brand in the minds of those who have engaged with it. From there, the stretch goal, if you like, is the creation of additional brand value ("brand upside") for specific cohorts using experiential tactics.

This takes us to the three levels of impact to the health of a brand within existing customers, that customering leaders must understand. Starting from the bottom and most common:

- **Brand Diminished**: as potential customers are attracted to a brand and begin to interact with the company, they encounter service failures. The promises of the brand are felt to be unfulfilled and the sentiment that the marketing team had labored to secure in the memory of that visitor is now compromised.
- **Brand Preserved**: this occurs when we master the services layer. Prospective and existing customers who visit our company can achieve what they sought to achieve. The interaction they chose may be entirely forgettable in of itself, but the customer need is fulfilled and there is no negative sentiment formed. While some may see this as a low-level aspiration, its execution is often much harder than lofty experiential tactics because it requires day-in day-out mastery of the customer operating model.
- **Brand Upside**: this is the rarefied air that so few occupy. Not only have they mastered the service layer, but they have also created target events that stimulate new positive memories, protecting and/or enhancing their custom (Figure 7.1).

All of this is important to understand because customer management is part of the wide anatomy of a business, and so its impacts – good and bad – are felt well beyond its department walls. None of this means that it has become marketing, nor does it mean that marketing runs customer management.

Note: the brand team is likely to include existing customers along with prospective, and a wide array of demographic (etc.) representation. That's fine. The customering team is focused only on customers, though a good collaboration between the two departments is always valuable.

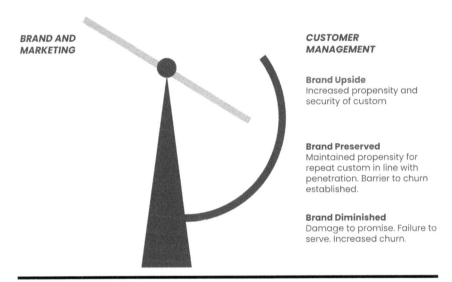

Figure 7.1 The Effect of Customer Management to Ongoing Company / Brand Value

Customer Effect

While brand tracking in the wider market is not the domain of customering, the uplift in customer sentiment because of the work of customer management absolutely is. Equally, it might be of interest to the marketing department, which is great, because it provides another vehicle for demonstrating the value of customering. Naturally, the customer management function requires measurement to obtain evidence of a "brand preserved" state in the customer cohort, and, if in scope, any "brand upside" resulting from a target experience activation. The instrument for this is the customer satisfaction (CSAT) method used as a comparative analysis tool, noting that satisfaction is a proxy for sentiment.

Pre- and Post- CSAT

As covered previously, "remembered satisfaction" will not report the same as "live satisfaction", but nevertheless the arguable strength of CSAT is that it was designed to test for sentiment, which is perfect for testing memorability of an experiential event at different points after the event itself. For those unfamiliar with the CSAT question and scoring process, it works like this:

How satisfied are you with the fireworks at the Gala Show?
Completely dissatisfied> 1 2 3 4 5 < Completely satisfied

Or:

> *I was satisfied with the house moving service.*
> *Strongly disagree> 1 2 3 4 5 <Strongly agree*

From there, the scoring calculation is as follows:

$$\frac{\text{Total number of \textbf{positive} responses (ratings of 4 or 5)}}{\text{Total number of responses}} \times 100$$

So, if 140 of 200 responses had a rating of 4 or 5, your score CSAT would be 70.

Keep in mind that we are establishing the customer's overall sentiment in relation to something *specific*. For instance, if we are an removalist company who helped a customer move house and surprised them with a handwritten note and housewarming gift (an experiential activation), then the last question (above) is about testing the favorable memorability of that customer, so it can be done quickly to gain an initial impression, or delayed, to test how strong that sentiment is at different time periods.

Having obtained that score, we can now compare it to the baseline. Of course, you must be careful to only test this among the cohort of customers that are affected, not the entire customer base (if there is a difference) (Table 7.3).

Table 7.3 Post-experience CSAT Comparative

Baseline CSAT	Experiential Activation	Baseline CSAT Among Effected Customers	Variance
58	House Moving	70	+12

Clearly, in this scenario the point-in-time uplift of 12 points to CSAT of the affected customer cohort, which may have been specifically targeted as a group that offers the most value through increasing their customer lifetime value (CLV), is a strong indication that the system within the management model is working as intended.

From there, the company can map the eventual customer CLV of affected customers and compare it to cohorts that were exposed to different activations or combinations. This last step is more of a business test, but I wanted to extend the use case for you here. There is also a flow-on effect, namely the referral or the influence of existing customers on prospective customers because of a particular experience, but this is a rare phenomenon and also a separate business test. We'll get to that shortly.

However, it is important to note three variables related to CSAT, both in setting the baseline and in subsequent comparable tests.

Firstly, we must acknowledge that the relationship between satisfaction and repeat custom (loyalty) is not always binary. Over the years, proponents of a direct correlation have included luminaries such as Peter Drucker and Theodore Levitt in the 1950s and 60s, and a range of significant others such as Philip Kotler with his "Marketing Concept" paper in 2000.[10] Yet, in a similar pattern to that of "usage drives attitudinal bias", it is also be true that where a customer is *already* loyal to a brand they will tend to report higher satisfaction, impacting typical satisfaction surveys. Indeed, in research unreleased at the time of writing (and so uncited), the question is posed:

> Is it the usage that is influencing the satisfaction score, or is it satisfaction that has influenced the usage?

In addition, the draft paper suggests that where a customer uses more than one alternative, the reported satisfaction of each is lower and that the scores of all decline the more alternatives that they use.

However, while this typically denotes satisfaction with a service generally, keep in mind that our goal here is to measure the memory effect of a target activation specifically – which offers a heightened mental and or emotional state (if it has worked).

There are two other dynamics at play:

- **Potential of Cultural Bias**: we know that people in "individualistic" countries lean more toward extreme self-reporting than those in "collectivistic" countries.[11] For example, an American is more likely describe a service as "amazing" or "horrible" than someone from Japan, where deep respect is a hallmark of society, and where middle-ground responses such as "fine" or "not satisfactory" are therefore more common.
- **Sample Representation**: customers who might naturally fit into "neutral" and "dissatisfied" categories are often less likely to respond to surveys, and so there can be an inherent weighting toward higher scores.

Even so, as a comparative analysis exercise of pre- and post-experience sentiment, I believe the practice holds.

Emotional Measurement

As established, experiences have a foundation of emotion and or feelings. Based on the proven links between heart rate and the brain, ground-breaking firm Immersion[12] has developed algorithms that offer reliable predictors of the neurochemicals in your brain by listening to your heart. This is the foundation of their tool "Lively". By sending out smart watches, rather than surveys, they gather data on the "emotional journey" undertaken by people in their normal environment, as they navigate the use of products and company interactions.

Applied to individuals during an experience, this measurement offers an exciting insight into its effect, from which their observed reactions and downstream behaviors can be compared, and correlations deduced. This use case is more likely for research in testing for new products (marketing), or new customer assets (customering), but can be used to observe everyday customer flows using sample cohorts.

System Tests – Asset Performance

In the interactions pillar we talked about asset design, and it is worth revisiting. We're talking about anything at all that touches a customer or is designed for their interaction – web pages, IVR, phone apps, customer communications, anything at all. Of course, the ultimate test of any asset is whether is it is adopted by customers and to what extent, but this isn't as binary as it sounds.

Different customers, use cases, journeys, and jobs place different loads on assets, so assessing utilization in isolation is just silly. As we have covered, when operating properly, assets (and channels) are just limbs on the same body and should never operate outside of the context of the whole. Nevertheless, the use of each is important to understand and we should note that customers interact with them in different ways and sequences, each having potential impacts on the other.

Asset Performance to Customer Journey (and Job)

This first test takes in the wider journey context: what role, or what effect, does the asset have regarding the overall journey from a customer perspective? To understand that we return to journey visualization capability that we discussed in Chapter 5 in relation to discerning customer intent.

These tools help us understand what customers are doing and how that changes in real time as result of a particular asset or channel. This is important, as it provides the net result of the asset in the context of the customer's job. I re-emphasize, the *customer's* job, noting that when *they* achieve *their* desired outcomes on a consistent basis, we see a correlated uplift in value exchange. Note that I have already covered the type of interrogations that this capability allows for. To refresh, jump back to the section on Intent.

Isolated Asset Performance

Despite the importance of the asset in context of overall customer outcomes, there is validity in testing the asset in and of itself. All measurements must be reflective of the customer ideal, not a transactional result of a company-led activity. For instance, if a company runs a campaign on paid Google ads, and interested recipients who click on that ad arrive on the landing page, the resulting traffic is not a measure of website effectiveness. Yet I have seen simple click-through rates interpreted in this way. What we need to be interested in is the customer-led outcomes, as met in the asset itself.

There are a range of methods to potentially apply, depending on the asset.

For example, one tech company purports to be able to test for user sentiment within their micro-browsing "signals". Its offering, it claims, translates various mouse-clicking patterns into psychological states. For instance, they cite detections such as "multi-clicking", "bird's nesting", and "scrolling", among others, as representative of stages of engagement. I have refrained from naming the company because it has been unable to provide me any scientific evidence of the correlations that it claims – and I have asked several times – nor have I found any independent supporting research to validate its claims or otherwise. There are several similar emergent capabilities, and while I am always interested in the advance of technologies that can serve to improve efficacy, this must be evidence-based. I encourage you to make sure that you have this mindset.

More obvious and proven system measures by channel or asset are for phone apps and contact centers. The former is usually an easier process, simply because if you know what you are doing phone app design is a very targeted process, resulting in a very targeted asset. I refer you back to the examples in the section on asset design, but, in short, most are designed for utility, like your banking app, membership app, or loyalty app. And so, most measurement focuses on pure utilization – the percentage of customers who have downloaded the app versus the percentage of those who actually use it against "baseline" frequency – and the impact of self-service on higher cost assisted channels.

Of course, in more sophisticated settings there may be different apps for different customer cohorts, or those with differing statuses, but in the end, the measurements for these assets are relatively straightforward, as are their correlations to measures such as customer lifetime value, churn propensities, and so on.

Contact centers are a little less obvious. Like every aspect of customer operations – and again, the premise for this book – there are no real standards, though there are rules of thumb upon which the global industry operates. Like all other channels, contact centers have been evolving. According to the *2023 Australian Contact Centre Best Practice Report*,[13] the contact center manager is accountable for:

- Emails (91%).
- Live chat (55%).
- SMS (45%).
- Written communication (44%).
- Social media (38%).
- Chatbots/intelligent assistants (26%).
- Video chat (6%).

So then, the measurement of the contact center, unlike phone apps, comprises the measurement of several channels within the "channel", and multiple mediums. Therefore, we can observe that managers tend to focus on operational outcomes, such as:

- Adherence.
- Absenteeism.
- Hold time.
- Forecast accuracy.
- Calls blocked.

In another report by the same organization, contact center managers were asked about what metrics were important to them. In order, their responses were:

- Customer feedback.
- Abandonment rate.
- Average speed of answer.
- Average handling time.
- First call resolution.
- Grade of service/service levels.
- After-call work.
- Sales/conversion.
- Shrinkage.

This broadly aligns with a "Top 10" list proposed by a leading voice in the sector, Justin Tippett,[14] which includes:

1. Grade of service (aka service levels).
2. Average speed of answer.
3. Abandonment rate.
4. Average handle time.
5. Shrinkage.
6. First call resolution.
7. Occupancy.

8. Cost per call (contact).
9. Attrition (turnover).
10. Call quality.

The thing I like about Justin's list is that it starts with customer-centric tests – grade of service, speed of answer, average handling – and includes first call resolution and call quality. Others, such as shrinkage, occupancy, and cost per call, are internally focused values that are entirely valid but must be balanced with, and secondary to, the values of the customers. There is also an industry model for the optimal "grade of service", called the Erlang Calculator,[15] that uses custom formulas based on standardized parameters to determine impact to contact center operations. For example:

■ If call volumes increase by 8%, how many additional agents will the business require to maintain service levels? And conversely,
■ Should average handling times decrease by 30 seconds, how many fewer agents would the business require?

There are many uses of the model, but it always strikes me that in such budget-constrained times very few attempt to optimize entire customer journeys such that assisted channels can be maintained and improved organically. For example, if the contact center can detect who the customer is and why they are making the call in the first place, it can:

■ Route them to the correct agent immediately.
■ Limit the identification process.
■ Reduces the time the customer has to be on the phone (improves serve level).
■ Lowers the cost to serve.

Indeed, so many of these measures are directly impacted by the intent and context of the customer. As a result, isolated measurements are complex and potentially problematic if you don't have the correct system in place to begin with. Look again at that list of priorities nominated by contact center managers. None of them are concerned with the role that they play in the customer's overall goal, or journey, or the context in which they arrive, nor with what might follow. This internally focused perspective is, of course, endemic in "channel strategy".

Asset Performance Test Model

Rather than prescribe systems tests, regardless of asset type, this should always be conducted in the customer's context and in keeping with the specific business. There are a range of valid channel tests that are good sources of data.

However, remembering that we are talking about *system tests* on the customer management model as having priority over any channel management model, the approach advocated is to apply the aggregate customer journeys that each asset is supposed to serve first, and use the results to inform targeted system tests of the asset second (Table 7.4):

Table 7.4 Asset Tests

Type	Function	Example
Inspection of Assets by Customer Journey and Job Completions	Identify performance of channels and assets within the customer JTBD framework across journeys	Journey analytics shows percentage of customers abandoning a web-based touch point in favor of calling the contact center, and variances by cohort.
Contextual Asset Performance Test	Revisit or re-define the success parameters of the web self-service asset to the customer context.	Test remediated asset by percentage and variances.
Specific Asset Performance Test	Predefined channel or asset specific tests, e.g. grade of service, abandonment.	Test remediated asset by percentage and variances.
Re-learn, re-test, and monitor.		

Business Tests – Churn Rate and Interdependence

The three components of the customer mission guide our business tests.

- Mission 1: contribution to market share.
- Mission 2: contribution to company profit and value.
- Mission 3: mitigation of commercial risk.

For all companies, the customer base is *the* most important asset and one of its biggest sources of risk. Of course, not all customer bases are made equal; they may have greater or lesser transience, variations in the distribution of income, differing vulnerability to external shocks, and so on. We have already discussed a range of laws from marketing science that show that typical market patterns affect these distributions as well, such as the proportion to which customer bases overlap between competitors, and the ratios between heavy and light buyers within categories.

It is a core function of customer management to optimize as many of these variables in the best interest of the business. The first task is to reduce the attrition of customers as much as possible, and so we return to the *Barrier to Churn Principle*, and the overriding objective to attain a rate of churn below the average. Everything we have discussed, from capturing identity to discerning intent though to managing interaction complexity, has all been in aid of this goal, and so now we move onto measuring how effective all these activities have been.

Before we get started, it is important to make clear that aspects of the marketing function will affect churn, irrespective of the customer management efforts. If the product turns out to be unfit for the customer's need, including when their need changes, or if the distribution of the product fails (physical availability), or if the price of the product changes and impacts custom – these are all examples of the tactical pillar of marketing. Combining good quality customer insight – see Intent – with statistical rates of churn, applied within cohorts, can assist in this diagnostic.

Baseline Calculation

To determine rate of churn, also called the rate of attrition, we take all active customers at the beginning of the reporting period, subtract the number of customers that have become inactive in that period, and then and divide that by the number active customers at the beginning of the reporting period.

$$\text{Customer churn rate} = \frac{\text{Active Customers at Beginning of Period – Active Customers at End of Period}}{\text{Active Customers at Beginning of Period}}$$

For example, if *Mothers and Daughters Pty Ltd* had 1,000 customers at the beginning of the month and only 900 customers at the end of the month, its customer churn rate would be 10% (1,000 – 900 / 1,000 = 10%).

Note: We do not include new customers that have been acquired in the period, as we are only looking for the number of customers "lost." New customers are a separate metric, and one that marketing, not customering, is concerned with. Those new customers will become part of the active customer count heading into the next reporting period.

While the goal of customer management, is to sustain a rate of churn below the average, it is more accurate to say a rate of churn below the average *in your industry*, and perhaps *in your region*, etc. You can find different sources of this information. For instance, Table 7.5 shows 2020 research by Exploding Topics:[16]

Table 7.5 Industry Churn Rates (USA)

Industry	Percentage Rate of Churn (US)
Financial services	25
Cable	25
General retail	24
Online retail	22
Telecommunications	21
Travel	18

Never underestimate what a reduction in church by even 2% can do for company profit and shareholder value.

The Reporting Period for Churn

Every category operates differently. I might buy groceries every week but only update my car every three to five years. That means I could theoretically "churn" from my local grocery store month to month, but this is harder to detect at the car dealership. Most categories aren't at either of those extremes, and their customer base will overlap with that of their competitors. For instance, I might buy my home electronics from three different online stores, and make the decision each time based on availability or price. None of those companies has created brand preference for me; they are effectively commoditized, but I am a customer of them all. How, then, do you define churn?

One of the means to get beyond these variances, which will play havoc with short-term numbers, is to apply a reporting period that makes sense for your business, most commonly using quarterly or annually cycles together with trend lines. Other business, such as the grocery store or subscription businesses, might use monthly cycles. Depending on the business you occupy, there is a literature available to provide this guidance.

Cohort Variance

It's also important to note that you will want to calculate churn by different customer cohorts. This can be instructive. For instance, there will be a different average industry churn rate for cell phone plan subscribers than for home internet subscribers, and that will be reflected in each telecommunications company. This means that the baseline is different, but can also indicate, depending on the variation of each, that one is doing a better job than the other. Simply measuring overall churn will deprive you of the ability to make those assessments.

More advanced companies that have mastered customer journey analytics and orchestration disciplines will surface transactional, behavioral, and interdependent characteristics leading up to churn events across any number of cohorts, determined by an almost unlimited number of variables. These firms are in the box seat not only to best understand churn, but also to intercept root causes that remain in the company's control, and to reduce churn below the average – most likely driving company profit as a result.

Revenue Calculation

Lastly, while I haven't included the calculation here, some firms like to calculate the direct revenue attrition, as distinct from the customer attrition. This enables a company to go straight to a short-term monetary assessment, within the reporting period, and to summarize all cohort churn rates to top-line revenue impact. We must be cautious with this, however, as it can lead to short-termism if the nature of the churn is not understood.

Other Measures not Included: ASCI, CM, and VES

There are three other measurements that you may have heard of, namely the American Customer Satisfaction Index[17] (ACSI), the Conversion Model (CM),[18] and the Value Enhancement Score[19] (VES). I haven't included them here, not because I don't think that they have value, but because I'm not convinced that they advance us beyond what we have achieved in the prior pages.

For completeness, the ACSI model assesses three elements that drive satisfaction: perceived quality, perceived value, and customer expectations. My argument is that it is the marketing department which ensures that the brand positioning, targeting (if applied), product and pricing strategy (etc.) are all market-oriented, and this will go some way to resolving the first two elements. Thus, it is not a pure customer management measure of effectiveness. I would also argue that merely meeting expectations, without experiential activation at occasional points in time, won't create the sentiment spikes need to offset normal industry churn patterns.

Similarly, the CM seeks to establish a consumer's level of commitment to a brand to make predictions about future loyalty. As the proponents of CM acknowledge, brand salience or mental availability is only one variable in retention, and, I would add, it is also a measure of marketing rather than customering.

Lastly, VES is a new scoring process, this time advocated by Gartner, purporting to measure customer loyalty, though I could find no scientifically founded evidence for this at the time of writing. Specifically, VES claims to assess a customer's ability to use the product or service, as well as the customer's confidence in the decision to purchase that item. It is calculated through a two-question survey where the customer is asked to rate their agreement with the following statements:

- After the interaction, I am able to achieve more with the product or service.
- After the interaction, my confidence in my decision to purchase the product or service is higher.

Given the closer association with customer context (jobs), VES certainly has a better basis than other systems that it proposes to replace. Still, it is important to remember that it suffers from the limitations of all self-reported data, especially when used to obtain behavioral insight, which is what VES claims to do.

Gartner's specific premise is that increasing a customer's "positive feelings" toward these specific factors expands the value that a customer derives (or more accurately: perceives to derive), which, according to Gartner's hypothesis, makes them more likely to:

- Renew their relationship with the company.
- Advocate on behalf of the company.
- Increase spending on the company's product.

Now, there is nothing inaccurate about the proposition that a person who feels strong positive feelings toward a brand will be *more* likely to manifest loyal behaviors, but, as we know, the subject is not so binary.

Specifically:

1. Emotional relevance to "commitment" is not universally correlated, e.g., no one is emotional about toothpaste.
2. The VES questions consider only interactions tied to the use of an offering, and to its purchase, excluding the service and experience layers of customer engagement which have significant effect on sentiment.
3. Unless pronounced in nature, a single interaction in isolation of the longitudinal company / customer context, is a limited input to long-term behavioral deductions.
4. The notion that customers become emotional advocates is at best exceptional, never normalized, and in most categories simply never occurs.
5. The ability to survey for trust – directionally similar to VES – has long been known to have reliability issues (see Chapter 9).

Bain's tripling down on NPS, despite its deficiencies (see Chapter 9), should be warning enough that consultancies may value the differentiation of an offering over the science. In the case of VES, it will be interesting to observe the outcome of the empirical studies that are sure to come, though I'm not sure how it can traverse the above issues. In the meantime, my advice is to await those studies patiently and heed the evidence, not the product marketing.

Business Tests – Customer Lifetime Value

We begin this section with the calculation of customer lifetime value (CLV):

> The sum of cumulated future cashflows, discounted using the weighted average cost of sales (WACC), of a customer over their entire lifetime with the company.

It is pertinent to note that customer loyalty is drawn from a combination of elements, inclusive of the level of market penetration that a brand already has. The law of double jeopardy states that the buyers of brands with less market share are slightly less loyal (in both buying patterns and attitudes), while the retention double jeopardy law states that brands with higher penetration lose fewer customers in proportion to their market share. It is also why benchmarking survey scores must be conducted carefully. The movement rarely understands these factors.

So, we have a degree of overlap with the effects of marketing and of customer management when it comes to loyalty outcomes, and ultimately both impact CLV. There is no research I am aware of into weightings between the two, but it is evident that market penetration can only be optimized when the service interactions that follow marketing campaigns are adequate, at least relatively so, such that customers are not at heightened risk of churn. Even then, frequency and value of customer interactions over time are, in many categories, attributable in large part to customer operations, and so CLV should be considered in this total context. There is no doubt that a company with a highly effective customer management regime outperforms those without one, all other variables being equal.

This was underpinned by a 2016 study by McKinsey & Company,[20] which is another corroboration that world-class customer management, resolved at scale, has very significant economic outcomes. It is noteworthy that the CLV measurement anticipates future revenue of the company, and so is forward-looking in nature, which is appropriate because the way we interact with customers today, quite obviously, impacts the propensities of their future behavior toward the company.

Applying the test to different customer audiences or cohorts also allows a company to consider how it might modify its interactions with differing groups, which is most powerful when a company is able to engage audiences dynamically (see Interactions).

The goal of course, regardless of approach, is to pay more attention to higher value customers, to increase the CLV of lower value customers (if appropriate / possible), or both. The various elements that can be include in the calculation, as recommended by Dr Kumar, include:[21]

- Average lifespan of a customer.
- Customer retention rate.
- Average profit margin per customer.
- Cashflow discount rate (estimate future value of cashflow).
- Average gross margin per customer over the lifespan.
- Period used for the calculation (often 52 weeks but should vary by category*).
- Costs of customer acquisition.
- Number of total customers.
- Number of customers acquired.
- Transactions per year of the customer (or other period as appropriate*).
- Average size of order (calculation differ by segment*).
- Total revenue for the year (or other period as appropriate*).
- Percentage of the cost of sales.
- Cost of sales.
- Marketing costs.
- Total costs.
- Gross profit total or average.
- Net present value.
- Net present value cumulative profit.

* These notes are additional to the original list

It's starting to look complicated, isn't it? Well, the overriding principle isn't complicated at all, and, ultimately, we are only seeking to establish the *relative* value of an individual customer or cohort. Sure, accuracy is important, and the more advanced the formula you apply the more likely you are to achieve that – but equally, the number of people in your organization who can understand it will diminish, which can be detrimental.

And so, we want accuracy sufficient to best inform the business that can be realized by increasing a CLV by x or y percent in isolation, and we want to balance that by being easily able to compare the performance of individual or groups relative to each other, over the same period of time. Most companies can achieve that balance by applying a relative simplified formula:

Customer lifetime value = customer value × average customer lifespan where the complete customer lifetime value formula is as follows (Figure 7.2):

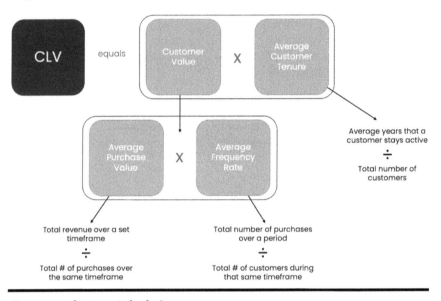

Figure 7.2 The CLV Calculation

While calculating CLV tells us how much revenue we're getting from each customer or cohort, it doesn't reveal how much profit the company makes from them. If we want to understand profit as part of CLV – and many executives do like to see this – you'll need to use gross margin. This is the percentage of total revenue that remains after subtracting the cost of goods sold (COGS). Alternatively, the next section provides a simple calculation for a customer profit analysis.

Determining Customer Tenure (or Lifespan)

Most companies have hard data around the tenure of custom, usually by cohort or those that originated in a market segment, while others make assumptions (they guess). Don't be the latter! If you don't have that data, there are a couple of ways to approach this.

First, use statistical patterns. For instance, if a retail bank has 100,000 fee-free pocket money accounts for under-ten-year-olds, they know historically what percentage will convert into student transaction accounts, and then full saving accounts, into personal loans, and eventually into mortgage holders, and onto other more advanced offerings that reflect mature age customers with more capital and assets. Each of these financial products has its own lifespan, and, as such, the conversion rates between them and their overall adoption rates provide a baseline total customer lifespan.

But this is still a broad-brush approach, applying all-of-industry trends that don't necessarily reflect an individual business; equally, it isn't very definitive or defensible. A far better approach is to calculate lifespan using internal data that should be relatively easy to obtain. The formula for that is:

Customer lifespan = 1 / Churn rate

The churn rate is simply the number of customers you had at the beginning of a period, minus the number of customers at the end of the same period, divided by the number of customers at the beginning.

Then we just divide the churn rate into 1.

So, for example, if McDonalds in New Zealand was to believe – and I have no knowledge that this is the case (I am literally making it up) – that in 2010 they had 2.8 million customers, but with the arrival of healthy preferences and more competition in that category they only had 2.5 million customers by the start of 2020, then their customer lifespan could be calculated as:

■ Churn rate: (2.8m – 2.5m) / 2.8m = 10.71%.
■ So, the average customer lifespan is 1 divided by 10.71% = 9.3 years.

However simplistic or advanced your calculation might be to capture the CLV of customers or their respective groups, it is one of the most important measurements of the industrial customer management model. Remember, while marketing invites members of the market to visit your company, customering has the job of hosting them. The better the host, the better the party, and the higher the propensity of guests to respond to future marketing, or to come back unprompted. CLV is the perhaps the ultimate measure of this success – or otherwise.

Business Tests – Customer Attributable Profit

In a company's income statement, there is no granularity provided in the calculation of its "Selling, General, and Administrative Expense" line (SG&A). The selling component is related to the direct and indirect costs of generating revenue, where "direct expenses" are those incurred at the exact point-of-sale for a product or service (e.g., transaction costs and commissions, etc.) while "indirect selling expenses" are incurred before and after the sale is made. This can also include the salaries, benefits, and wages for salespeople, travel, and accommodation expenses. Often, it doesn't include COGS or the marketing costs associated with acquiring the customer in the first place, but both represent valid cost.

Enter "Customer Profitability Analysis" (CPA).

While the marketing department assesses profitability by market segment or by product, CPA is a tool of customer management and, as the name suggests, it focuses on the profitability of customers, either individually or by cohort. In short, CPA compares the net income that customers generate over their lifetime (the CLV) with the total associated costs.

This can be calculated using different formulas, depending on how cost is allocated and treated, but they tend to yield similar results. As much as the precise numbers are important, it is perhaps more so that the approach is consistent, and what it reveals about the financial trendline that customers are exhibiting, relative to others and to the overall performance of the business.

The calculation is described as follows:

$$\text{Profitability per customer or Cohort} = \frac{\text{Customer Revenue} - \text{Average Customer Costs}}{\text{Number of (in-scope) Customers}}$$

If we assume that a business has an average revenue of $20,000 each year, across a specific group of 100 customers (Cohort A), resulting in $2,000,000 of revenue, while incurring average costs of $13,500 per customer, or $1,350,000 in total associated costs, we will use the following formula:

$$\text{Profitability of Cohort A} = \frac{2,000,000 - 1,350,000 \ (= 650,000)}{100 \ (= 6,500)}$$

Our total profitability for that cohort in the period is $650,000, and $6,500 per customer. As we trend that over time, we can measure the impact of customer operations on overall profit. Of course, our gross margin is calculated simply: (Revenue − Total cost) / Revenue.

Thus, 650,000 / 2,000,000 = 32.5%.

Considerations

Aside from the variables that the business may wish to ascribe with the cost calculation, there are several factors to keep in mind.

- World-class customer management does not treat existing known customers as if they are anonymous members of the market; therefore, direct attribution of revenue growth within existing buyers to external marketing is not appropriate by default.
- However, it is reasonable for some level of attribution in relation to long-term branding and promotions where incremental, especially in light buyers (where this is measured), but that is better accounted for in the cost line.

- When considering the revenue period, the longer the period the more indicative of a higher customer lifetime value by virtue of tenure. This means that the averaged or annually incurred costs should be extrapolated over the same period as the revenue line, but expenses such as customer acquisition cost (CAC) should be amortized across the period, rather than multiplied by it.
- When performing customer cost analysis, you must ensure that your data on customers' revenues and costs are reliable. It is difficult to perform CPA if you don't possess all necessary data or, as is common, you are thwarted by organizational siloes.
- CPA has been greatly advanced by the arrival of technologies that enable the rapid creation, visualization, and interrogation of customer cohorts on a behavioral basis, from which financial analysis can follow. Equally, its predictive analytics enable better forward estimates of individual customer and cohort values within those behavioral patterns. Moreover, the enhanced treatments that follow, whether through orchestration capabilities or other optimization initiatives, the resulting increase to customer engagement will invariably serve to improve the measured outcomes over time.

Business Tests – Increased Monetization of Customers via Referral

We have already touched on the role of well-designed customer experiences, which are predicated on creating memory, to advance the brand health of an organization within its customer base as distinct from the wider market. The measure of that activity that I advocated was a targeted use of CSAT, showing the score trend pre- and post- the experiential activation. In addition to testing the system effect of experiences, we can also recognize that a company that focuses entirely on its service layer can have a positive impact on customers by way of their relative encounters with competitive brands.

Companies are well advised to keep in mind that, as per the Duplication of Purchase Law, a brand's customer base actually overlaps with that of its competitors in proportion to their respective market shares, and so the popular ideas that CX-types love to warn us about, "brand switching", is somewhat reductive.

One of the implications of this law is that customers who overlap (i.e., are a customer of competing brands) are likely to make comparisons of how they are treated by each. This offers low-hanging fruit, by nature of the failure of most companies to ensure the lowest possible friction in the service channels.

It is a counter-intuitive and yet highly effective approach. I say counter-intuitive because it relies in the underperformance of the alternative, but on current evidence that is a bet I am almost always willing to make – and one that I have advised many companies to make also.

In a 100-yard sprint – or a marathon, which is probably a better analogy for customer management – you don't have to be the fastest over the distance if your fellow athletes keep falling down! Your job is to keep going, to stay upright, and to be reliable. Given the decline of customer service globally, that simple commitment will often pay dividends. Equally, you won't get to elevate your position through designed experiential activations if your service layer fails, and so this is imperative anyway – as we have already discussed.

There are two business tests to establish whether this is translating to hard numbers. The first, customer lifetime value, we have already covered. The second is a test of whether this has rendered referral revenue, which is monetary value outside of a customer's direct purchasing.

Measurement of Referral Values

A lot of companies, both B2C and B2B, place little if any emphasis on customer influence or referrals. Clearly, some categories are more ready-made for the use of formal programs than others, but there is strong evidence for the additive power of referral to company profit.

One study in 2010[22] found that the lifetime value of a referred customer was 15 times higher than a non-referred customer. It cited lower churn rates and, of course, a lower cost of sale, with higher journey conversion rates. The sample covered more than 10,000 customers over a 33 month period, finding that referred customers generated 25% higher profit margins over direct-revenue customers. This increase will not apply to all categories but, when combined with other studies that point in the same direction, the overriding message is compelling.

This should not be surprising. People will often trust their peers, more than they trust brands. The Edelman Group is probably the most recognized organization that studies and reports on the state of trust.[23] In 2003, its research saw a distinct change in what people reported as the sources that they rely on for truth. The move away from brands was underway and in its place was a new category:

"A person like me".

In other words, people trust other people who they feel that they can relate to, and so we saw the rise of influencer marketing. We've all seen the teenage, bikini-wearing health food evangelist on Instagram, but influencer programs have evolved significantly and they are now used by the largest B2B companies in the world. As a case in point, a friend of mine, Ursula Ringham, is the head of global influencer marketing at tech giant SAP and has filled similar roles at Apple.

One of the powerful attributes of influence is its potential to transform into qualified referral. This is an especially valuable source of contribution to market share calculations for many companies. For instance, in *The Commonwealth of Self Interest* Paul Greenberg writes about Dropbox's referral program:

> The referral program is directly embedded into the site almost anywhere you look. The incentive for referrals is more Dropbox real estate for both referrer and referee. In its first 18 months, there were more than 2.8 million direct referrals, and, as of 2016, 35% of all signups came from Dropbox's referral program.

So, if highly successful and yet radically diverse companies like SAP, Apple, and Dropbox understand the value of customer influence and referral, and invest accordingly, how do we measure for it?

Referral Management Costs

Well, to start with, we need our baseline – which is to say, we need to know what our referral program(s) cost us, relative to the cost of acquiring a new customer. Now, you know what I'm going to say: customer management leaders must NOT blur the lines and assume marketing functions. Acquisition really is the job of marketing, and so we don't want to do much more here other than to extract that value from them.

Of course, however that value is derived, it must be applied consistently, and here's a simplified way to do it. In general, you want a picture of *all* the relevant costs as one. You may include brand development costs, or, for ease, assume that applies universally and only include the relevant operational costs of running the referral program: technology, headcount (full-time equivalents, FTE), and, of course, the cost of any incentives applied to the referral.

Technology cost is relatively straightforward. If you have dedicated software then this is a cost; if not, then either apply an allocation of cost from existing systems, or don't. For the headcount measurement, just take the allocated FTE and multiply it by hourly costs for each person and total it. In larger organizations, there might be a dedicated team running referral, so just include the total department costs, but in smaller organizations this could be a part-time activity. For instance, if the function consumes 10 hours per month for a single person in the CRM team (for example), and that person costs you $50 per hour, you will estimate headcount cost to be $500 per month, and $6000 per annum.

In this case, let's pretend we are a large energy company with a small but dedicated referrals team that costs us $1,000,000 per annum, and we have allocated technology costs of $200,000.

Lastly, we'll need to know our cost of incentives. It's important to remember that these costs are only incurred as new business is closing. In other words, while the other costs (technology and headcount) are made as investments ahead of the curve, incentives are only paid after new customers are acquired. Still, they are a cost and need to be included in our program. Another thing to consider is that many companies don't use cash incentives for customers, and for very good reason. A 2004 University of Chicago study found that non-cash incentives were up to 24% more effective.[24] The Dropbox scenario is an excellent example. But if you use any form of incentive, you must calculate the cost.

Let's say that our energy company uses a very simple cash incentive, where every new customer referred by an existing one results in a credit of $500 to the referrer's account. That means if 1,000 new referrals are generated a year, the cost of incentives is $500,000, remembering that these unit costs are only incurred post-sale. So, assuming we hit our 1,000 customer target, our referral program will cost us $1,700,000 per annum.

A Basic ROI

Now, let's look at the upside end of the equation and get a view of the return on investment. We can apply a relatively straightforward approach, using the profit increase attributable to referred customers (25%) as proffered by the Wharton School, or any other increase percentage that you consider is appropriate to your business.

- First, calculate your average customer lifetime value, as already explained.
- Second, multiply your CLV metric by 1.25, as per the Wharton study, or apply your own multiplier. Yes, we have conflated revenue with profit here, and yes, you could certainly be a more accurate in your approach as part of determining your multiplier, but for ease of explaining this model we'll just use CLV. Thus, if our energy company has an average CLV of $17,640, your average referral customer is $22,050.
- Third, simply multiply this number by the total number of referrals you generate. If that is 1,000 per financial year as estimated in the cost model, your referral program provides an additional 22,050,000 PA.

Finally, divide this number by your referral costs:

- 22,050,000 / 1,700,000 = ROI of 12.9%

As a simplified approach, this calculation can be applied to both B2B and B2C businesses, but what if we want a more advanced model that serves those two distinct nuances? Again, we return to the master of measurement, Dr Kumar.

Customer Referral Value and Business Referral Value

Dr Kumar developed the measurement of customer referral value (CRV) for B2C companies, and its counterpart, the business referral value (BRV) measurement, for B2B companies. Again, both are a measure of "indirect" revenue.

The rationale for having two distinct formulas is that, per Kumar, the role of references in purchase is more prominent in B2B businesses. Equally, the same study by the Wharton School found that referred customers in a B2B setting not only spend more, as already discussed, but are 18% less likely to churn.

Now, there is an argument that the role of *influencers* is more prominent for consumer brands, and that *references* have more weight in B2B brands, and so it depends on your definition of "referral" but the BRV model, as distinct from its B2C sister, demonstrates that there are distinct characteristics of the two, necessitating differences in how they are measured.

CRV, for B2C companies, is defined as:

> The monetary value of a customer associated with the future profits given by each referred prospect, discounted to the present value (PV).

There are many examples of consumer companies that use referral programs. We used the fictitious example of an energy company in our first example, and, of course, we touched on SAP, Apple, and Dropbox earlier. As you can see from the below list, the range and type of elements for the calculation of CRV are much more advanced than our first example. They include:

- Number of years calculated into the future (projected customer lifetime).
- Number of customers who only join due to a referral.
- Gross margin, contributed by an individual customer who wouldn't have bought anything without the referral.
- Cost of the referral for a particular customer.
- Marketing costs needed for the particular customer's retention.
- Acquisition cost savings for the referral customer.
- Acquisition cost savings for customers who would have joined without the referral.
- The (time period) discount rate.

In contrast, BRV, for B2B companies, is defined as:

> The monetary value associated with the future profits as a result of the extent of a client's reference influencing a prospect to purchase.

In these businesses the calculation can be demanding, especially in factoring in potential third parties such as implementation or consulting partners, who each might claim either partial or total responsibility for the referral of, or influence over, the buying party.

The elements for its calculation are:

- Degree to which references generally impacted the purchase decision.
- Degree of influence that a specific reference had on the purchase decision.
- CLV of the buyer.
- Total number of converted prospects.
- Discount rate (in months).
- Time to purchase (the month a prospect became a client after the first month of observation).

Anyone who has worked in a complex B2B organization will instantly see the tensions that will arise in seeking to calculate a number of these elements. However, the complexity is present in the case for CRV as well. For this reason, I have decided not to dedicate pages of this book to playing out example calculations. There are just too many variables and it would require numerous side notes and caveats. Instead, my recommendation if the first example of reference program ROI is inadequate for your business is to get a copy of Dr Kumar's work. The takeaway here is that, subject to the type of business you are running, measuring referral values can be an important part of measuring your customer management program.

Summarizing Measurement

As you can tell by now, I do like a good table. They're a great way to capture a quick summary of a lot of content, by category, and after a long chapter looking at the measurement of the customer management model, let's close the section with another (Table 7.6):

Table 7.6 Summary of Tests

Type	Purpose	Method
System Tests	Are my system components operating as intended?	• Friction Test. • Memorability Test. • Asset and Channel Performance Test.
Business Tests	Ultimately, are the business outcomes being attained?	• Churn rate. • Customer Lifetime Value. • Customer Profitability. • Customer + Business Reference Value.

Be Careful with Benchmarking

Lastly, a note on benchmarking. This is one of the CX movements' favorite refrains. The notion of testing against a past or common state, as a trend or comparative, is appropriate. For instance, when we talked about system testing for memorability, we compared a baseline CSAT score with post an experiential activation. This is valid. But comparing a company's score with another company's, or indeed an industry's, is a more nuanced business.

It is well established that attitudes and beliefs reflect behavioral loyalty, and that consumers "know and say more" about brands that they use, and "think and say less" about brands that they don't. Therefore, larger brands always score higher on surveys that assess attitudes to brands because they have more users (who are slightly more loyal).[25] Yet most don't understand this and go about comparing their company to others in the category that aren't analogous in terms of size and market penetration.

Equally, sectors will often compare their scoring against other sector participants without understanding the extremely poor customer management practices inherent within it. While it may look good on the board papers, they mutually reaffirm each other and stay mired in mediocrity. And fields of customer management do the same thing. For instance, contact center managers like to cite industry benchmarks for a range of operational measures. The idea isn't terrible, but, again, isolated channels and isolated channel metrics is a limited lens.

In summary, use the benchmark, and beware the benchmark.

Company and Shareholder Reporting

Serious reporting of the customer franchise is, for the most part, inadequate. Even worse, a significant number of company leadership teams are fooled by vanity metrics.

Instead, the chief customer officer or equivalent should be concerned with the system tests that validate the effective working of the program's component parts so that they can maintain operational integrity over it, as well in ensuring that resourcing and human capital are both adequate to fulfill the objectives.

In contrast, when sharing with other senior management leaders and/or reporting to the full executive or board, they will want to be trending their churn rates and lifetime customer value statistics as inputs to the drivers of company profit, and there will be a range of ways they may wish to collaborate with the finance department. Before they do that, though, they'll need to educate these stakeholders on the pillars of the program, and the reasons for these two primary measures.

Yet there are legitimate questions about how the customer franchise must be reflected more broadly in company disclosures and valuations. It seems that, irrespective of setting (if most apparent in private equity-funded firms and full publicly listed entities), the relentless earning pressure and quarterly reporting requirements, pawed over by analysts and shareholders alike, drive companies down the path of short-termism. Instead of reporting on the business, the business is contorted to support the needs of the reporting. A focus emerges on near-term profit at the expense of customers through the reduction of quality, fee hikes, and service cost-cutting. In the medium to longer term, however, this erodes the value that customers can generate for the company, which becomes reciprocal, and so it is self-defeating. At best, attrition will return to the dreaded average, or, equally likely, to an above-average position.

In such circumstances, it is the impositions of the reporting regimes itself that must be governed. Otherwise, the tail will wag the dog, and eventually starve it.

As it stands, though, financial disclosure rules and corporate accounting practices place almost no emphasis on customer value, in an entrenched system that dates to the 1890s. The second problem is most pronounced in the USA, where the concept of shareholder primacy as originally rendered by Milton Friedman in the 1970s[26] has not evolved as it has in most other western jurisdictions. Instead of a directors' fiduciary responsibility being to the company entity itself, directors in the USA are mainly concerned with shareholder perspectives, which inherently promotes self-interest and increased short-termism – and activism. There has been an alternative model proffered, the "age of customer capitalism",[27] which sought to align customer and shareholder value, but it hasn't been appreciated by shareholders and so the reporting regimes maintain their nineteenth century roots.

The accounting profession has debated these types of issues for a long time, and bodies like the International Accounting Standards Board have increasingly sought to introduce reporting on intangible assets such as, apparently, customer value, although detractors question the reliability of valuation methods and, as always, the cost on business to comply. Nevertheless, more companies are starting to inject customer metrics into their annual reports, perhaps reflective of more contemporary business thinking. Writing in the *Harvard Business Review*, Bain and Company's Rob Markey reported that companies such as

> Costco, AMC Entertainment Holdings, Humana, and American Express, increasingly report various types of customer value metrics. Most telecommunications companies – including Verizon, AT&T, and T-Mobile – do as well.[28]

Ratios

Of course, at investor or shareholder level, it is reasonable to present both marketing outcomes and customering outcomes in the same section of the report. Marketing will focus on penetration in keeping with its mission, and so reporting is likely to highlight new customer counts, brand metrics, and potentially the measured effect of a major campaign or seasonal initiatives. In contrast, customer reporting should focus on the revenue security (risk and control) and profit attribution due to the robust management of the customer resource, as an input to share price if relevant.

Having said that, it is important to remember that external stakeholders have much to review and consider in company disclosures, and so it is a valid pursuit between a CCO, CMO, and CFO to explore ways to report high-level corresponding metrics that consider both the market and the customer franchise. One approach is that of ratios, such as those used in financial reports for liquidity, operating efficiency, financing, and profitability. An obvious example is the "current" ratio, the ratio between the current assets and current liabilities, on the balance sheet as shorthand to indicate liquidity.

An example of a ratio that draws on both a marketing metric and a customer one is the CLV:CAC ratio. As you already know, customer lifetime value (CLV) is a customer management measurement. What we haven't covered in detail is a common marketing measure called customer acquisition cost (CAC).

$$\text{Market to Customer Value Conversion} = \frac{\text{Customer Lifetime Value}}{\text{Customer Acquisition Cost}}$$

This ratio is an indicator of the health of both functions as seen through the lens of overall market to customer performance. Different companies will determine different parameters that the ratio should meet. For instance, subscription business models rely on multi-year customer support to underpin their annuity revenue stream. I am told that a ratio of 3:1 is quite typical, although these businesses differ greatly. Keep in mind, though, that this does not denote profit as it doesn't include all your operating costs. According to a study by KBCM Technology Group,[29] the average time it takes for new customers to become profitable is 2.4 years, which makes that 3.1 ratio look a little skinny – but consider the seismic economic benefit if the customering team uplifts CLV, and resolves a 4:1 or even a 5:1 ratio …

It is also important to remember that CAC is essentially an average at a point in time, and that as a company's market penetration and efficiencies increase, the average cost attributable to each customer should reduce. Therefore, what is an acceptable ratio will vary by a range of factors, not least of which is share and, potentially, the stage of business maturity.

Another model that applies the ratio concept is that of customer-based corporate valuation (CBCV) which advocates for using unit economics and diagnostic values to concepts like loyalty. You should note that this model is from Bain and Company and the approach to loyalty management is based on its historical advocacy of NPS, a measure that is now disproven, but the concept is directionally sound. It is based on four interdependent calculations, the very first of which is "the customer acquisition model, which forecasts the inflow of new customers", (marketing), and goes onto modeling the customer retention and purchase frequently (customering).

Despite the discussions about ratio's my preference is to report CLV, lifespan, and customer profitability (and their trends) as both performance metrics and financial controls, specific to the customer management function, leaving marketing to identify its line items separately rather than cojoined. This can help alleviate the conflation of the two at a governance level, and ensure their oversight – and funding – is in accord with their distinct missions.

Notes

1. ITB Community, "Why Marketers Should Be Wary of 'High ROIs'," *ITB*, June 16, 2022. https://www.itb-community.com/articles/why-marketers-should-be-wary-of-high-rois/.
2. Charlotte Rogers, "Why Chasing ROI Could Kill Your Business," *Marketing Week*, November 26, 2019. https://www.marketingweek.com/dangers-marketers-chasing-roi/.
3. Tim Ambler, "ROI Is Dead: Now Bury It," *World Advertising Research Center*, September 2004. https://www.warc.com/fulltext/Admap/79369.htm.
4. Tom Roach, "Beware of ROAS, ROI's Dangerous Digital Twin," *Marketing Week*, October 12, 2022. https://www.marketingweek.com/tom-roach-roas-roi-dangerous-digital-twin/.
5. V. Kumar, *Profitable Customer Engagement: Concept, Metrics and Strategies* (Sage Publications, 2013).
6. Paul Greenberg, *The Commonwealth of Self-Interest: Business Success Through Customer Engagement* (The 56 Group, 2019).

7. To recap, see "Defining the Economic Mission" in Chapter 3.
8. G. Mulder, "The Concept and Measurement of Mental Effort," in *Energetics and Human Information Processing*, ed. G. R. J. Hockey, A. W. K., Gaillard and M. G. H. Coles (Springer, 1986), 175–198.
9. Statista, *Market Share of Apple iPhone Smartphone Sales Worldwide 2007–2023*, January 23, 2024. https://www.statista.com/statistics/216459/global-market -share-of-apple-iphone/
10. Philip Kotler, *Marketing Management: Millennium Edition* (Prentice Hall, 2000), Ch. 4.
11. Chuansheng Chen, Shin-ying Lee and Harold W. Stevenson, "Response Style and Cross-Cultural Comparisons of Rating Scales among East Asian and North American Students," *Psychological Science* 6, no. 3 (1995): 170–175.
12. www.getimmersin.com.
13. Australian Customer Experience Professional Association, *2023 Australian Contact Centre Industry Best Practice Report* (ACXPA, 2023). https://acxpa.com .au/2023-australian-contact-centre-industry-best-practice-report/.
14. Justin Tippett, "10 Most Popular Call Centre Metrics, KPIs & Benchmarks," *Australian Customer Experience Professionals Association*, December 5, 2023. https://acxpa.com.au/popular-call-centre-metrics/.
15. Robyn Coppell, "Erlang Calculators Explained," *Call Centre Helper*, March 29, 2017 (last modified March 18, 2024). https://www.callcentrehelper.com/what-is -an-erlang-calculator-100496.htm.
16. Josh Howarth, "Average Customer Retention by Industry (2024)," *Exploding Topics*, December 5, 2023. https://explodingtopics.com/blog/customer-retention -rates.
17. The American Customer Satisfaction Index, *The American Customer Satisfaction Index (ACSI) - National Cross-Industry Measure of Customer Satisfaction* (2024). https://theacsi.org/.
18. Trevor Richards, "Using the Conversion Model to Optimize Customer Retention," *Managing Service Quality* 6, no. 4 (1996): 48–52.
19. Devin Poole, "A Better Way for Service to Predict Future Customer Loyalty," *Gartner*, November 18, 2020. https://www.gartner.com/smarterwithgartner/a -better-way-for-service-to-predict-future-customer-loyalty.
20. Ewan Duncan, Harald Fanderl, Nicolas Maechler, and Kevin Neher, "Customer Experience: Creating Value Through Transforming Customer Journeys," *McKinsey & Company*, July 1, 2016. https://www.mckinsey.com/capabilities/ growth-marketing-and-sales/our-insights/customer-experience-creating-value -through-transforming-customer-journeys.
21. From Greenberg, *The Commonwealth of Self-Interest*.
22. Philipp Schmitt, Bernd Skiera, and Christophe Van Den Bulte, "Referral Programs and Customer Value," *Journal of Marketing* 75, no. 1 (2011): 46–59.
23. Edelman Trust Barometer (no date). https://www.edelman.com/trust/trust -barometer.
24. Scott Jeffrey, "The Benefits of Tangible Non-Monetary Incentives," *Engagement Strategies Media*, 2004. https://www.enterpriseengagement.org/articles/content /8288816/the-benefits-of-tangible-nonmonetary-incentives/.
25. Byron Sharp, *How Brands Grow: What Marketers Don't Know* (Oxford University Press, 2010).

26. Milton Friedman, "A Friedman Doctrine – The Social Responsibility of Business Is to Increase Its Profits," *The New York Times*, September 13, 1970. https://www.nytimes.com/1970/09/13/archives/a-friedman-doctrine-the-social-responsibility-of-business-is-to.html.

27. Steve Denning, "The Triumph of Customer Capitalism," *Forbes*, January 10, 2020. https://www.forbes.com/sites/stevedenning/2020/01/10/the-triumph-of-customer-capitalism/?sh=7aee11b24fb7.

28. Rob Markey, "Are You Undervaluing Your Customers?," *Harvard Business Review*, January–February 2020. https://hbr.org/2020/01/are-you-undervaluing-your-customers.

29. Myya Daigle, "2020 SaaS Survey Results- COVID Edition!," *For Entrepreneurs*, no date. https://www.forentrepreneurs.com/2020-saas-survey/.

Chapter 8

Managing the Collision

Now that we have reviewed the formal marketing and customering management process models, noting their distinctions, we are able to look critically at the relevant points of intersection and how to best manage them.

You may have heard the term "customer marketing". This is a descriptor of both valid and invalid activities, but beyond the practical delineations it stems from the mindset that cruels effective customer management: the idea that customering is merely an act of marketing (selling).

It is not. In fact, *within* the customer franchise, the reverse is true.

In practice this means that providing customers with promotions and other forms of incentivization is appropriate only to the extent of the customer's context. Customers are not anonymous members of a segment. They are known individuals and, irrespective of the degree to which that has been truly established, expect to be treated accordingly. So sales activities are secondary in function; they are the follower, never the leader, in the equation, and yet, as we have discussed, a strong service bias toward customers increases their propensity for purchase. Of course, this requires an educated execution model as described in the preceding chapters, something neither the populist movement nor the typical use cases of mainstream martech have an intellectual or commercial interest in, or the patience for. Thus, the shortcuts to rampant and blunt force sales activations reign, as does customer trauma, evidenced by the work of regulators to protect our customers – from us.

In contrast, this chapter will address how we manage the collision properly. The common objective of customer management and marketing is to improve of the ratio of light, moderate, and heavy buyers. This is, in essence, where the fields collide. Having considered the management attributes of both fields, it's worth summarizing their distinctions, which is a good time to reflect on the Bowtie model (Figure 8.1).

DOI: 10.4324/9781003513728-9

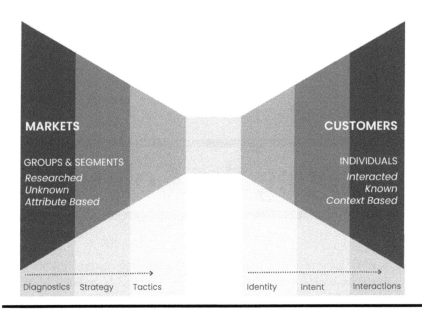

Figure 8.1 Marketing to Customering Bowtie Model (A. Spinley, 2022)

I was recently asked for a comparative business definition of the two process models. It is a daunting prospect to succinctly capture the essence of two complicated fields, in comparison to one another, but I think the following is accurate, and should now ring familiar:

> The marketing mission seeks growth via the acquisition of new customers, marked by a rate above the average; while the customering mission aids marginally in the increase of market share, it improves company profit materially by optimising customer value over the long term, marked by an attrition rate below the average. Marketing is an inherently inside-out procurement model targeting mass; customering is an outside-in service model attending individuals.[1]

Taking it down a level, we might summarize the distinctions as (Table 8.1).

Problems arise because the grayed box (customer revenue) is typically all a marketer is concerned about, and without understanding the impact on the customer franchise holistically, nor the long-term economics, they may become the proverbial bull in a china shop.

Table 8.1 Marketing and Customering Focus Points

Marketing ...	*Customering ...*
Increases new revenue.	Increases current revenue and profit.
Increases market penetration a lot.	Increases market penetration a little.
Aims for an acquisition rate above the average.	Aims for a churn rate below the average.
Targets large groups of people (markets and segments) at once.	Serves individuals, one by one.
Relies on research of unknown groups.	Relies on discerning the intent of known people.
Applies general and "personalized" mass communications.	Applies individualized interactions.
Establishes brand at the market level.	Protects or advances brand at the customer level.
Utilizes programmatic and triggered activation.	Utilizes nuance, behavioral, and longitudinal context.

The Unintended Consequence of the Marketing Funnel

Back in Chapter 2, we talked about the marketing funnel, and you may recall that I used a four-stage model to explain its role in setting objectives, which I include here again (Figure 8.2):

80% Aware   58% Consider   29% Preference   21% Purchase

Figure 8.2 A Basic Marketing Funnel

You might also recall that I am cautious about funnels that include later stages such as "re-purchase" or "loyalty", especially because while it *is* important to know the conversion rate between first purchase and repeat transactions, this is rarely the sole responsibility of marketing. At issue is that their inclusion is often problematic due the incorrect assumptions and behaviors it can drive.

And you might recall that I believe that this misconception, along with a wave of technologies that are built on its faulty premise, are responsible for the global collapse of customer service. Companies, instead of mastering a properly conceived management model for customer engagement, lean into the hard-sell mindset of constant promotions, offers, sales messaging, etc. at almost every turn and, as I have I said, paradoxically, have eroded the propensity of customers to realize their maximum potential lifetime value.

While it is harder for companies to move a brand from awareness to consideration than to conversion (purchase), many marketing operations teams who traverse – and often trample – the customer franchise are not known for their strategic awareness, and trigger-happy digital sales tactics reign. This focus on the end of the funnel, without truly understanding it, has two major implications. The first is the questionable application of marketing resources; the second is lack of competence both to discern the difference between the market and customers, and then to apply relative treatments. So, the funnel is a great place to begin this chapter, and I'll start by offering an alternative (Figure 8.3).

Figure 8.3 Marketing to Customering Funnel

First, we have colored the "purchase" box differently (white) to denote the dual role of the two functions. This is not always the case, but it is usually so. Second, we now have a later stage to denote "loyalty" conversion, but, unlike most funnels, we have not assumed that function to be delivered by marketing. The gray boxes are indeed all about the market, while the black box is delineated for existing customers (notwithstanding the consistent background role of brand). If companies simply applied this color coding and distinction, it would prompt more appropriate operational conversations.

The typical assumption that marketing tactics alone should apply here is often catastrophic, causing the collapse of trust and a reduction of purchase propensity. Yet there is a valid functional intersection. The theory of "physical availability" – the ease of access to brand interaction and purchase – is an important element of marketing. Traditionally, this simply meant that a store was close to you, though there are more nuanced examples. For instance, frictionless payment incorporated via a customer phone app (e.g., Uber) also serves this principle, albeit nuanced to the needs and journey context of the individual customer.

This is, of course, a customer channel, not a marketing one, and so you can see the intersection in action. However, it is also at this point that firms, wielding martech, get it so wrong via "personalization".

The Limits of Personalization

Personalization has its place as a capability within the communications function of marketing's tactical pillar, but its most common applications are not an effective capability within customer management. To start with, personalization is very badly named, because it was never about the actual *person*. It exists to serve the marketing mission by way of a sales tactic. For instance, by adding a person's name to an email, rather than simply addressing it "Dear Consumer," it was reported that open rates improved by 28% due to the familiarity effect. This has a reasonable basis in psychology, and it worked. But then things got silly.

A sweeping and commonly accepted narrative emerged that personalization is important because customers "love it when we treated them like a human being", which is partially true – although as explained, that was never the goal of actual personalization efforts. If you don't believe me, just begin a casual conversation with anyone you like in the CX community or with a technology vendor about the benefits of personalization, and you will hear little else other than "acquisition" and "conversion" and so on. Their language gives it away.

No, it was never about the actual customer. It was always about the business growth objective – it was *marketing*. Another dynamic that personalization spawned, in the digital sense, is companies' propensity to overcommunicate. Equally, their communications are limited to little more than sales activation such as email promotions, web banners, SMS messaging and the like, which are high-frequency in nature. And yet we know from research[2] that there is a direct correlation between customer contact frequency and the tenure of the overall relationship, to the strength of that relationship. Of course, to state the obvious, enhanced relationship strength is manifest in greater customer retention rates[3] and, eventually, in higher sales, profits, and even market share.[4]

The same research found that duration "moderates the effect of frequency". In other words, for shorter-duration relationships, such as those experienced by light buyers of a category or by customers in making an infrequent purchase (e.g., buying a new car), contact frequency *enhances* that strength of relationship, but it has no effect at all on customers who are part of longer-duration relationships. Such distinctions are not something that personalization junkies tend to understand, having no genuine regard for customer context.

Now, before you assume that means spamming practices are fine for the low-frequency buying categories, note that customers who have a longer "relationship" with a company tend to perceive that to be a stronger relationship. So, when we bombard them with unsolicited communications and promotions, we create conditions that disincentivize their longer-term engagement. In short, we undermine our own commercial performance.

A Marketing Hack

Returning to the idea that customers *love* it when we treat them like a human being, this is only partially true because, frankly, customers do not go around *loving* companies. No matter how wonderful we think our product or brand may be, people have way better things to love and think about. The whole notion of turning brands into religions and customers into disciples is total nonsense, but industry people tend to get carried away.

Consider an unnamed ad executive who ran an experiment in which he browsed his most frequented websites, first in untargeted mode with browser history and cookies cleared and location tracking disabled, and then in targeted mode with everything turned back on – allowing himself to be sold. He compared the two and claimed that being targeted by ads made him feel

> as though I am falling into a warm bath of relevance and recognition.

This is a great reminder that we must begin any conversation about personalization by understanding that it is a sales and marketing hack and that this underscores that customer proximity has nothing to do with it. As with anything, the underlying mindset determines the execution, and in the case of the intersection between marketing and customer management, the common execution of personalization seeks to "trigger" messaging *at* customers. It is not geared to intent, or any deep understanding of customer context. Rather, it is a model that rationalizes and provides pseudo-justification for rampant sales activations, over and over and over.

Perhaps the most obvious example is "cart abandonment". The usual narrative is based on a scenario in which a person has navigated to a shopping cart but has left the website without completing the transaction. Immediately, marketing automation kicks in. It adds that person to what martech vendors erroneously call a "segment"[5] and if the company has contact details it sends a messaging intervention, typically an email or SMS.

The message itself usually falls into one of two categories:

- ■ "Hey Steve, don't forget to complete your purchase" (or similar verbiage).
- ■ "If you complete your cart today, Steve, we'll give you an extra 10% off!"

Companies might use the first one where the products in the cart were unable to be discounted any further. Either way, the process map looks like this (Figure 8.4).

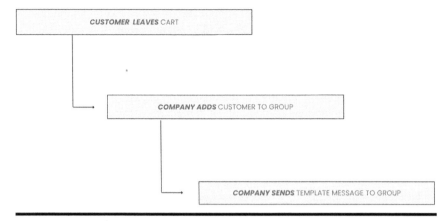

Figure 8.4 Cart Abandonment Trigger Automation

The generally accepted attitude is that this is a *personalized* and targeted interaction because the message was (a) triggered based on a customer action, and (b) used their first name, etc. But it runs into a bunch of problems. Consider the following:

- What if Steve abandoned the website session but completed the transaction on his mobile app?
- What if Steve called the contact center to complain about the price of shipping – which is why he left the cart?
- What if Steve had landed on the website from a price comparison aggregator, indicating that his most likely reason for leaving was price?
- What if Steve was standing in the store in front of the product when he checked online, suggesting that he was comparing the online price or availability, or whether he should just have it delivered?

In any of these situations, do you think that the template message would have been welcomed by the customer? And, given the completely incoherent choice of message, what is the net effect to that customer's perception of the company? Sending a confused broadcast marketing message to an existing customer is significantly more damaging to that person, to their relational duration and trust, than it would be if they were not a customer at all. This is why we must master the intersection of these two areas.

While this example again proves that most personalization is never about the actual person, there's another problem to emerge with the cart abandonment use case. With so many companies choosing to try and tempt people back by using a discount, they have effectively trained their customers to abandon the cart! Savvy individuals will do so on purpose, await the lower price offer, and complete the purchase then. In the process, the company has increased its cost of sale and reduced its per unit margin, and its overall profit.

This stems from the practices of many martech teams, which are almost totally incentivised on revenue, resulting in near-constant price promotion. Not only does this distract from serving customer needs, but it undermines the brand through increasing price sensitivity. Great customering ensures a sound pricing policy in customer interactions, ideally inherited from the marketing department as we discussed in chapter 2. This is another key point of intersection.

Of course, cart abandonment is just one example. Martech vendors and many others sell the concept of personalization in various forms, almost always based on triggered events. But in truth, "triggering" is a seriously limited approach in isolation because it relies on a remote data point. A trigger lacks the substantive context that is only surfaced through the entirety of a customer journey, as evidenced using our good friend Steve as an example. And so, at a tactical level, it has many holes; even more problematically, it can have a detrimental effect to the long-term health of the customer franchise. Countless studies have shown that people simply do not enjoy companies that are in constant sales mode.

In fact, there is some indication that targeted sales messaging (and advertising) is perceived as untrustworthy by its recipients. Rory Sutherland, of Ogilvy, once said:

> Indiscriminate advertising is more trustworthy than targeted advertising.[6]

It is a position derived from the principle of "messaging" versus "signaling". Messaging involves being able to deliver a message rapidly to an audience because brand trust is established. Signaling, however, occurs when the recipient has no established trust in the sender. Sending a message to someone about coming back to a shopping cart after they have completed it or are busy complaining about shipping costs, for example, is not supportive of brand trust.

Applying this principle was Don Marti, an ex-strategist at Mozilla. He had a live model – and perhaps still does – that uses "norm-enforcers", those who punish brands they don't trust to tell the truth, to test signal effectiveness.[7] It's very clever. What the model shows, consistently, is that what recipients regard as "honest" signalers tend toward long-range, non-targeted communication. Those regarded as "dishonest" apply highly targeted advertising and messaging. It is precisely because it *is* targeted that it is less trustworthy. It's an example of how big data concepts can come unstuck very quickly when applied without a nuanced understanding. Irrespective, we find that there are two main messaging models that are common today:

- Traditional (broadcast approach).
- Personalized.

The latter has become one of the industry's favorite terms, and a sacred cow for vendors, consultants, and practitioners alike. Many regard it as the frontier and very definition of "best practice". However, there is a third, significantly more sophisticated model, which is only possible where companies have established properly constituted customer management as advocated throughout this book.

Individualization, is not a messaging model at all. As you read in Chapter 6, it starts, ends, and evolves through customer context, and is oriented to the loftier state of engagement. However, this would be somewhat naive if it didn't incorporate the legitimate function of sales, and so relies on the principle of *Customer-Governed Application of Marketing Communications.*

Customer-governed Application of Marketing Communications

When colliding two fields of management, it is always most fruitful when each is well established and mature. In customering, those qualities are historically absent; the four pillars management model provides the missing procedural integrity, enabling us to properly consider value. The intersection must be governed by three principles:

- There is a business imperative to convert new customers into repeat customers as part of the economics of sustained market penetration, meaning marketing communication is critically important.
- Any new customer has transitioned from an anonymous member of a market or segment to a known individual, meaning the servicing of their needs as surfaced through their intent is key to unlocking their ongoing custom and enhanced profit.
- The nature of all interactions with existing customers, including marketing communications, is subject first and foremost to the context of the customer, followed by the company.

In reflecting on these principles, the reference model is summarized in a classic Venn diagram. The below figure captures the point at which the inside-out sales philosophies of marketing collide with the outside-in individual service philosophies of customering. This introduces the concept of *Customer-GGoverned Application of Marketing Communications* (CGAMC) (Figure 8.5).

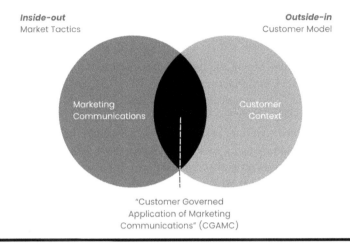

Figure 8.5 **Customer-Governed Application of Marketing Communications within Individualization**

CGAMC requires that for all existing customers as distinct from non-customers, their specific behavioral context and intent is *primary* over transactional data attributes. This means that marketing communication is modified, suspended, or canceled all together, based on the unique context of the customer that would have been the subject of the communication.

Examples of CGAMC

A telecommunications company has a cohort of customers that they have labeled "Group A". This group meets two data attribute criteria: They are (a) Apple iPhone users, and (b) they are in the final year of their mobile plan (Table 8.2).

Comparing Models

Of course, it is important to remember that CGAMC is predicated on the notion that there must be promotional communication in the first place. That is its starting point. Its origins are therefore marketing ones, and so the customer is still not entirely central, but the relationship has two parties, and both are entitled to their perspective (Table 8.3).

As you can see, the jump from personalization (low-level maturity) to individualization (advanced maturity) is a big one, without an intermediate step. But this does not suggest that it is too difficult. Instead, it demonstrates that personalization is grossly overstated in effect, and that organizations can achieve significant advances relatively quickly.

Table 8.2 Example of CGAMC

Marketing Communication to Customer Group A	Customer Context	CGAMC
Offer on the latest iPhone as part of early mobile plan renewal	Is two months behind in their bill and has visited the deferred payment plans page.	Suppress promotion. Instead, arrange outreach via contact center to see if we can help customer in financial distress.
	Customer internet is down, or speed is poor.	Suppress promotion. Activate ticket to resolve and advise customer. Only when service issue is resolved, release promotion.
	Customer is searching latest Samsung phones.	Add to Group B (Samsung users) or Group C (users of both) and send revised offer(s).
	Customer has just made complaint via the contact center.	Suppress promotion. Activate ticket to resolve and advise customer. Only when service issue is resolved, release promotion. Release may be deferred for a period defined by nature of complaint and or outcome.
	Customer is standing in the store right now!	Supress promotion. Activate next best action of conversation via the sales assistant, in support of their primary need. Maintain suppression or release promotion via the sales assistant given channel proximity.
	Customer is on the offer sign-up page.	Suppress offer.
	Customer has had more than six communications in the last three weeks.	Suppress offer. This customer exceeds the saturation point. Throttle the communication by releasing the offer in two weeks' time.
	The customer has clicked on a sponsored ad (e.g., Google search) for the promotion, viewed the webpage and plan options, called the contact center to ask about billing cycles, and is now standing in the store.	Suppress offer until store visit complete. Modify and withhold message based on updated customer context.
	No relevant activity.	Send offer in the batch.

Table 8.3 Summary of Interaction Models

Model	Characteristic and Maturity	Outcomes
Traditional Broadcast Marketing Communication	Mass market approach to individuals. **Entry level maturity**	Irrelevant messages are constant. High cost of promotions. Lowers campaign conversion rate. Price tactics may compromise profit. Ironically mirrored in programmatic advertising – despite its claims Brand diminished. Reductive to CLV
Personalized Marketing Communication This is the dominant model today. Most companies apply marketing automaton capability to this end	Mass market mindset tempered by triggered sales messaging. Attributes are confused with context. **Low Level of Maturity**	Irrelevant messages are common. Variable improvement to cost of promotions. Usual uplift to short-term conversion rate. Can diminish customer sentiment. Price tactics common, compromising profit. Brand diminished in most cases (long term) = Impact to CLV is category-dependent
Individualization (applied Customer-Governed Application of Marketing Communications)	Individual approach to marketing goals. Context trumps Attributes. **Advanced Level of Maturity**	Lowest possible cost of promotion. Increased conversion rates. Better data for campaign statistics. Protects customer sentiment. Qualities that preserve brand. Additive to CLV

Practices by Category

While the above table provides a comparative summary, this must be applied in context of the operating environment, and it is not only the company's context that is in play here but also the norms expected within their customers.

Let's use the two ends of the continuum to illustrate this point.

The Transactional Extreme

At the most transactional extreme, we have pure-play e-commerce aggregators. Obvious businesses that fall into this category are Amazon in the USA. and Alibaba in China. There are smaller but equally well-known companies operating regionally or across different parts of the globe, such as Etsy, StockX, and companies like Groupon, Catch, or Kogan. Aside from aggregators, we also have global trading sites like eBay or geo-specific companies such as New Zealand's Trademe, along with sector-focused e-commerce businesses such as travel and bookings websites, again with a range of big players in each region, headlined by the likes of Airbnb.

It is important to understand that these are companies that people go to expecting an entirely transactional set of interactions. They are quite literally hoping for a promotion to come their way! They are there to search, browse, and to buy – and so people are fine with suggestions and offers in that setting, if they are reasonable. Consequently, personalization sales and marketing tactics, throughout the entire customer interaction, are contextually appropriate. There are, of course, exceptions, such as when someone is seeking to update account details, payment information, delivery preferences, etc., but those exceptions are few and easy to ringfence. This is the transactional extreme, which most businesses simply do not occupy, so beware the populist folly of comparing your company to the likes of Amazon …

The Complex Extreme

Let's use an energy retailer as an example of a company at the other end of the continuum. The energy and utilities sector (power, gas, and water) has been heavily disrupted by a range of factors. As it battles de-regulation that constrains the performance of its traditional business model, the rise of competition from third-party service providers and aggregators has seen many in the retail end of the sector diversify their offering. At first, this meant forays into distribution (the overhead and underground lines that deliver the power), sustainable products, and the smart grid and home devices. The latter two served to create new forms of customer interaction, but this was the tip of the iceberg.

Over time, many energy retailers became aggregators. Today, when you visit your energy company, you may find that you can subscribe to internet services, mobile subscriptions, and television streaming services such as Netflix, as well as a whole range of financial products. New revenue streams, born of entry into new consumer categories, also had the effect of complicating customer journeys. Multiple service billings, overlapping cycles, the implication of late payment or distressed customers in one line bleeding to the others, the risk of a degraded customer perception resulting from product or customer service failures impacting the CLV of individuals, the referral business implications, and so forth and so on, are all profound.

In addition, these businesses are not single-trick behemoths with all their chips placed on the web channel. They can typically manifest multiple web assets, phone apps of various types, smart devices, consumer appliances, contact centers, corporate retail stores, information centers, and/or partner retailers.

However, many power and utility companies are regularly at the bottom of customer satisfaction polls, clearly indicating that most have not mastered this complexity and that their common personalization-based communications just do not serve the heavily nuanced customer setting. And they're not alone. At the same time as energy retailers started to compete in the finance, internet, and entertainment subscription markets, so too have telecommunications companies diversified their operations in exactly the same ways. It is quite possible that we are moving away from dedicated utility providers, and toward consumer brands that offer them all. Indeed, the most complex consumer business are arguably not the Amazons of the world. They are banks, automotive, airlines and airports, insurance companies, diversified consumer companies such as professional sports and stadiums, and yes, energy and telecommunications retailers.

Consider the continuum from deeply transactional businesses at one end to deeply nuanced consumer businesses at the other. Your company will fit

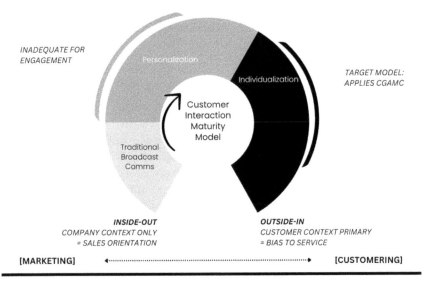

Figure 8.6 The Customer Interaction Maturity Model

somewhere on the spectrum, and your interaction model must reflect that position. For most, individualization should be the target model, applying CGAMC to optimize the marketing within the customer franchise, maximized by the inherent bias to service and customer context of true customering (Figure 8.6).

Notes

1. "A Comparable Definition: Marketing v Customering" (A. Spinley, 2022).
2. Tracey S. Dagger, Peter J. Danaher, and Brian J. Gibbs, "How Often versus How Long," *Journal of Service Research* 11, no. 4 (2008): 371–388.
3. Kevin P. Gwinner, Dwayne D. Gremler, and Mary Jo Bitner, "Relational Benefits in Services Industries: The Consumer's Perspective," *Journal of the Academy of Marketing Science* 26, no. 2 (1998): 101–114.
4. Lawrence A. Crosby, Kenneth R. Evans, and Deborah Cowles, "Relationship Quality in Services Selling: An Interpersonal Influence Perspective," *Journal of Marketing* 54, no. 3 (1990): 68–81; Robert M. Morgan and Shelby D. Hunt, "The Commitment-Trust Theory of Relationship Marketing," *Journal of Marketing* 58, no. 3 (1994): 20–38.
5. See Chapter 9, "Never Segment Customers."
6. Unbound, "Unbound London 2018: Behavioural Economics, Innovation and Beyond with Rory Sutherland," YouTube Video, 1:13, August 18, 2018. https://www.youtube.com/watch?v=PWiB5H18aug.
7. Don Marti, "Simulating a Market with Honest and Deceptive Advertisers," *Don Marti* (Blog), June 11, 2018. https://blog.zgp.org/simulating-a-market-with-honest-and-deceptive-advertisers/.

Chapter 9

Correcting the Record

Congratulations! You've now read this book. I hope that throughout that process, you may be realizing that all those noisy folks behind much of the popular CX rhetoric are wrong about a good many things – and you'd be right. I'm often asked to explain various myths of the industry, and why they are either ineffective or damaging, and so this final chapter is dedicated to that subject.

In the main body of the book, I've already dealt with why most of the populist movement is largely illiterate in experience, despite its constant use of the word; why traditional journey mapping, despite widespread use, is outdated; and why survey use to understand behavior, and therefore intent, is deficient in the extreme. But there is so much more, so, let's correct the record.

Never Segment Customers

As we covered in the diagnostics pillar of marketing, "segmentation" is a defined, market-level activity, and for a range of reasons it is not appropriate to use the term, or its concepts, in customer management. The reason that many people do, of course, is that they have inherited it as jargon, without thinking too much about it. Many would argue it's just a term they use, and that it is a non-issue. But if we want to be professionals, language matters, and when we have more discipline in this regard we are less prone to misadventure.

William Stanton, noted author of marketing textbooks,[1] said:

> Market segmentation is the process of dividing the total market for a good or service into several segments. Each of which tends to be homogeneous in all significant aspects with others within the segment, and heterogeneous from those in other segments.

DOI: 10.4324/9781003513728-10

Notice those words: "total market". This is not a customer franchise concept. The management process to refine each segment of a market to the degree of homogeneity within and heterogeneity to others, is through proper market diagnostics across a range of dimensions – demographic, firmographic, socioeconomic, etc. – and then technical segmentation practices. In contrast, every customer is an individual, and their representative value to the business over time relies heavily on this individualism, which invokes very different dimensions manifest across identification, intent, and interactions.

One deals with large groups of people, potentially many millions, while the other deals with each person, one by one.

Nevertheless, there are always groups of customers that are delineated by commonalities, and these can be extensive. For instance, common behaviors, common products that they have bought, all customers with a CLV over or below a certain threshold, all customers that use a common journey flow, all customers that haven't paid their bill, all customers with a preference of yellow, and even customers that fall into a combination of groups, e.g. all customers that like receiving their invoice via email and have an active account and have a low CLV … and so on and so forth. But these cohorts, or audiences, are dynamic, their populations forever altering. They are not static, nor researched, nor assigned by the company.

Marketing does not require this granularity. Segmentation is more than enough to serve its mission – and some don't even do that. In fact, it would be reductive, damaging even, to replicate the detail and dynamism of customer cohorts in the marketing mission. Segments, in contrast, are heavily researched because as part of the positioning process they contribute to the long-term performance of the company as it relates to market penetration, in pursuit of acquisition above the average. The idea that a segment is formed simply because people abandon a shopping cart, for example, is an ignorant and harmful over-simplification.

Equally, it doesn't work! The individual context – e.g., understanding *why* Jan abandoned the cart – is far more important in order to know what to do next. That nuanced process of engagement based on individualization has absolutely nothing to do with market segmentation. Moreover, a person can only be a member of one market segment. If they fall into more than one, the segmentation process has failed. This is a core tenet of that discipline.

By juxtaposition, and as described in chapter 5 (Intent), companies can query journey data with myriad variables, and a customer can fall into multiple cohorts or audiences – almost without limitation. This is critically important to the granularity that customer operations require, and that marketing operations do not.

It is important that the meaning of segmentation, as a technical term of marketing, is not diminished by an uneducated CX movement, or, for that matter, uneducated marketers or digital teams. It is equally important that customer management leaders apply terms, consistently, that are relevant to their mission. Segmentation is not one of them.

Not a Brand Differentiator

One of the favorite refrains of the CX movement is that it is a critical source of differentiation, and to be fair, it was Gartner who in 2018 reported that of the respondents to their survey, "81% say they expect to be competing mostly or completely on the basis of CX".[2] However, competing, or differentiating, at the market level is not the function of customer management, and Gartner's respondents are, respectfully, ill-informed.

Differentiation is part of the brand positioning process within market strategy. It is often recognized as the little brother of another concept, distinctiveness, as the two principal levers in establishing salience, being the target memories in the minds of target consumers. The marketing management and creative process, and these terms, are domiciled within that field. Like segmentation, they are not available to be re-imagined by those who don't understand them to begin with. So, let's explore what differentiation is, and why it is not generally an outcome of customer management.

Uniqueness versus Relativity

The earliest work in differentiation, in the 1940s, introduced the concept of the unique selling proposition (USP) which evolved into the more commonly accepted term: the unique value proposition (UVP). This was conducted by renowned television advertising pioneer Rosser Reeves, recounted in his later book,[3] but this has been gradually debunked, or at least, significantly modified.

So, what is the problem with the good old-fashioned USP? Well, it starts with the very first word: "unique". It is almost impossible to be truly *unique*, for two reasons.

To begin with, most products or services serve a need that exists somewhere in the market. Consequently, all alternatives tend to start from that same place, and so trying to be deliberately unique is often only possible by compromising the core value that a market might want. Of course, the way a company forms brand or product positioning may provide a little creative wriggle room, but that's usually to do with distinctiveness rather than differentiation, and if the best positioning is based on market need, it doesn't give you much leeway.

Secondly, you really can't control all the external factors. Even if you achieve some magical uniqueness today, that could change tomorrow. A competitor might copy you or arrive at the same kind of positioning, either because they have similarly well-constructed market research or perhaps just coincidentally. The fact is, you don't control all the variables.

So, because uniqueness is almost impossible, and certainly unreliably sustainable, this leaves us with *relativity*.

In other words, you don't need to be unique at all: you just need to be *different* (root word of differentiation), and that difference is *relative* only to the alternatives. For instance, I am thinner and taller than my cousin. He has Cook Island heritage and probably weighs a good thirty pounds more than me, despite not being as tall. Now, if we are the only two options available, and the market for our services is the NFL, they're probably going to pick him. But if the market is the NBA, they are probably going to pick me. I am not light, but he is less light. He is not heavy, but I am less heavy. He is not short either, but I am less short. It is our difference, relative to each other in context of the market, not our uniqueness, that contributes to the end result.

Market Level

Notice we are still talking about market-level activities here, not customer-level activities. The idea that Company A will have more customers than Company B if its customer service is superior only works if all the other potential variables are equal, and if all people in that market are customers of both, because otherwise how would they compare?

Of course, they are not customers of all alternative brands, and so are unable to make wholesale differential determinations, even if they wanted to. Thus, the oversimplistic claim that CX provides brand differentiation does not hold water.

Expanding on Relativity

However, there is limited application, noting specific dynamics, where customering does provide competitive values alongside mental and physical availability, etc., because while it does not operate at market level, it can still have a favorable impact on light buyers. We know through the Duplication of Purchase Law, that a brand's customer base overlaps with that of its competitors in line with respective market share, so the reductive warnings about "brand switching" are not so black and white, or universal across categories.

Nike's market share in "sports inspired footwear" was around 27% in 2015.[4] Applying the Pareto 60:20 marketing law, this means that approximately 21% of the total market who are Nike customers are light buyers who also use competing brands. Given this overlap, it does create the opportunity for a light buyer to compare their treatments at the hands of the alternative companies, though this usually requires a trigger point – such as frustration – to prompt the effort. This is what many confuse for "differentiation", which falls flat when we discover that there really are no data that show any pattern of this as a universal driver of market share, despite popular claims to the contrary.

Now, Nike itself, as a mass consumer brand with limited direct contact with its customers, is not the ideal case study to talk about the customer management, but for most customer-facing brands these numbers reinforce the need for world-class customering.

Understanding the angles is important. Individually, if a person has interacted with the service channels of both Company A and Company B, they might form a preference for Company A based on perceived superiority of service, tempered by the fact that preference is rarely based on one dimension. For instance, if Company B is still 10% cheaper in a category with price sensitivity – and assuming the Company A's brand position has not offset that sensitivity – then they may still select Company B despite its inferior customer service.

Note that we have only added two variables: price sensitivity and brand power. There are more, but the point is made. Also note that the equation changes the moment that the individual does. Another person may be comparing Company A with Company C, not Company B. Relativity is not uniform; it depends on the individual context of each customer, and so their decisions may be different, or the same, for different reasons.

Equally, differentiation can have distinctive attributes at different stages of the marketing funnel, and in the case of customer management, those attributes occur in the consideration, purchase, post-sale, and re-purchase stages, along with service stages throughout their lifecycle. In this context, you can absolutely argue that customer management *might* have some impact on competitive advantage assuming there are conscious decisions being made (and often there isn't) but you can't be definitive.

In conclusion, to secure the customer asset and advance company profit we are better off focusing on the Barrier to Churn Principle to maintain company brand, and experiential activations to enhance it, *both occurring within the customer franchise*. While these can play a role in the competitive battleground for light buyers, they do not do so in isolation, and even so, that portion of the customer base is usually a small sample of the overall market. Thus, the claim that CX is a driver of brand differentiation is false.

In truth, this is another example of the confusion between marketing and customering.

Accept that NPS Doesn't Work

It is common to find Fred Reichheld's Net Promoter Score (NPS) in use across customer management departments the world over. Indeed, it is the most common and widely used metric and has been sold to company boards as a principal performance measure. Equally, CX departments often use NPS as a tool for extracting additional budget, or to quasi-justify their work, and likewise among teams that deploy customer-facing assets or channels.

Originally proposed by Reichheld as "the one number you need to grow",[5] NPS was almost immediately popular with managers and reached two-thirds of Fortune 1000 firms.[6] Not only did it take, but it stuck, although the fact that it has endured likely has a lot to do with the advent and dominance of populism described in the early chapters of this book. Contributing to its ongoing use, Bain and Company – where Reichheld is a Fellow – has doubled down, treating NPS as brand code central to the firm's own positioning and differentiation.

Yet, right from the start, NPS was spurned by academia.

The critiques were many, beginning with methodological issues with the original NPS study. For example, this assessed past but not future sales growth rates by simple correlations with static NPS levels, measured at only one point in time. Empirical studies aiming to replicate Reichheld's results have generally failed to do so, and have instead found that generally NPS has no impact on sales[7] or growth.[8]

Many companies see their NPS score go up while their customer retention rates decline. Or they equate NPS to acquisition rates in isolation, and even as that improves the profitability of the business may be stagnant or in decline. Doesn't sound like the only number we all need, does it? Yet the movement hasn't blinked.

Many send an NPS survey to a customer right after they have completed an interaction, their rationale being that it will capture the immediate sentiment generated. They miss the critical point, though, that no interaction occurs in isolation and no sentiment is driven by an isolated event, unless it is impossibly wonderful or utterly horrendous. It considers neither human behavior itself, nor the primacy of journeys.

Of course, any metric can by gamed. For example, when Tarryn and I purchased a new car, the salesperson told us that their personal income depends on getting a minimum 5 out of 5 on the satisfaction survey. I chatted to him afterwards about it and he told me that the practice of telling customers this was not only standard, it was mandated by branch managers who also required high scores to earn their bonusses. A few years ago, a large bank was fined several billion dollars because the metric it used to reward employees was "new accounts opened", which resulted in the opening of accounts that customers didn't want, or even know about.[9] The Banking Royal Commission in Australia also surfaced all kinds of deeply unethical behavior[10] that I would bet was a result of cultural issues, at the heart of which are people gaming incentives. Indeed, there are countless examples like this. Culture sure does eat strategy for breakfast.[11]

There is a saying that if you can't measure it, you can't manage it, but a far better saying may be that if you don't know how to manage it in the first place, you won't know how best to measure it. That's certainly a truth that we need to adopt as we embark on transitioning away from populism and toward a credible, evidence-based, and disciplined management of the customer asset.

The NPS question with which you may be familiar is inherently oriented toward existing customers, who are the only ones able to provide an answer:

How likely is it that you would recommend [Organization X] to a friend or colleague?

Respondents give a rating between 0 (not at all likely) and 10 (extremely likely); depending on their response, they fall into one of three categories to establish a NPS score.

To calculate your company's overall NPS, work out the total number of respondents who replied, the total number who gave you a 9 or 10 (promoters), and the total number who gave you a 0 to 6 (detractors). Finally, subtract the percentage of detractors from the percentage of promoters. Based on this, the company's NPS will be a number from –100 to +100, a higher score being more desirable.

When you consider the actual question, you can see why so many companies use it as a transaction-based customer loyalty metric, and why it has become a darling of the survey vendors and their largely subservient CX movement. For instance, testing sentiment at each touchpoint is a classic vendor sales tactic designed to increase their license revenue, and companies everywhere obsequiously play along. In other circles, NPS is widely taught as a tool of marketing even though, as you will see, its use for this has also been widely debunked by marketing scientists. Nevertheless, major companies like Best Buy, Delta Airlines, Apple, and GE all use NPS for this purpose,[12] as do countless others around the world (Table 9.1).

Table 9.1 NPS Respondent Categories

9 or 10	Promoter
7 or 8	Passives
0 to 6	Detractors

Score Volatility

The issues with NPS start with its scoring. The "net" part of NPS, where low scores are subtracted from high scores, means across such a wide scale that the net score is very volatile. You can have several firms that have the exact same mean average score of, for example, 8, but depending on the precise distribution of individual scores across the sample, you can get wildly different scores.

Furthermore, even slight variations in that distribution can make for very different NPS outcomes, which makes trend analysis something of a lucky dip.

If your score goes up and everyone celebrates, it might just mean you had an ever so slightly different distribution to the previous period; next time the same slight variation the other way could send it crashing down, leaving the relevant team or manager to scramble for an explanation.

This may explain why some firms who once published their NPS score in annual reports have gone rather quiet on the subject, and why those that used it as part of executive compensation no longer do so. Scoring issues aside, the specific claims of NPS are threefold:

- It is correlated to growth (market share).
- It is a predictor of sales.
- It is a measure of loyalty.

Not an Indication of Growth …

To start with, there is no resolved evidence for the growth argument. That's not to say that you won't come across companies with wonderful growth rates, high NPS scores, and an assumed correlation. But it is the order of the association that undermines the correlation. Very high-growth companies are often riding a high degree of favorable market sentiment. Remember when Uber came along, and how many saw it as a symbol of a new digital-enabled social movement? Well, it wouldn't surprise if they had amazing NPS scores at the time, right? In other words, a high NPS score is often reflective of growth, not the other way around.

In fact, Professor John Dawes has done extensive work on this subject,[13] drawing upon longitudinal data for NPS and revenue to find that:

- Future growth isn't enhanced through a better NPS.
- NPS does not serve as an indicator of future revenue growth.

Secondly, the whole premise of the NPS idea is that growth is substantially impacted by existing customers, but, as we have discussed previously, this not the case. Existing customers can play a contributory role in virtue of mitigating the churn rate, but this aspect by far the junior partner in comparison to new customer acquisition. The second part of the same argument is that customers impact market responsiveness to the brand through "advocacy", as is inherent in the term "promoter". Again, this is possible in some settings, but it is by far the junior partner in comparison to the mental and physical availability attributes of the brand itself.

I should also note that while someone may be a promoter, as per the NPS process, the likelihood that they would recommend your product or service is much lower. CXers who take these terms literally, are, to be frank, delusional. As we discussed in the previous chapter, people have far better things to love; they also have far better things to talk about. Actual recommendation, where it occurs, relies on a range of factors such as cultural and market norms, and situational context, which makes someone's "promoter" NPS status irrelevant in real life.

On the flip side of the coin, the good news is that those who are deemed to be "detractors" are also just as unlikely to bad mouth the business. That is usually reserved for when companies really screw a service interaction up. Sadly, though, there are plenty of examples of that!

... Nor a Predictor of Sales or a Measure of Loyalty

You may well be asking, if a low churn rate can assist in overall market share, what about using NPS to measure loyalty and, as a seemingly logical extension of that, what about using it as a sales predictor?

Well, there really is no evidence in support of either. A 2021 study[14] investigated NPS as a predictor of sales growth (Reichheld's original idea) and revealed what many had long suspected: there is no sustained evidence to support the claim that changes in NPS have predictive value when forecasting sales.

There are potential exceptions where a range of conditions are met – for example, where purchase events occur in the very close proximity to the origination of the sentiment. There are a range of other conditions that would need to be present, however, and a consumer psychologist could write a hefty paper on it. For general application it simply does not serve as sales predictor. I'm sure many marketing leaders would argue that it is a low-value endeavor anyway, compared to a focus on executing core marketing strategy.

But the primary finding of the abovementioned study was that:

> NPS should be used as a measure of brand health and not as a customer loyalty metric.

Two things to point out here. First, it is only brand health *among customers*, who are, after all, where the sample comes from. In many instances, customers are not necessarily representative of the whole market or archetypal of others who have chosen not to purchase. Second, as many will quite reasonably ask, wouldn't great brand health among customers translate directly to loyalty? Are we not talking about the same thing? But as reasonable as the question is, the answer is no. Brand health does not translate to loyalty per se. Other conditions – the barrer to churn principle, social contracts, transaction costs, structural incentives, etc. – are necessary to the equation.

As we have already touched on, customers are rarely exclusive. The Duplication of Purchase Law has established that a brand's customer base overlaps with that of its competitors, in proportion to respective market share. What that means is that, very often, your customer is already buying from a competitor.

Or, put another, more provocative way, consumers are "promiscuous" and enjoy a casual but consistent relationship with you. Therefore, there is a difference between loyalty and exclusivity. The former does not require the latter, but may still provide a desirable customer lifetime value. The trick is to increase the proportion of time they spend with you, over the alternatives, and over time.

Before you rush to counter that NPS might still measure repeat custom (loyalty), irrespective of exclusivity, let me agree that this is a definite … maybe. I can't give you a hard yes because (a) the volatility of the scoring makes it an unreliable source of trend data, and (b) this is measured more effectively with hard data.

So, to recap, NPS has a volatile scoring process, is not an effective indicator of growth, nor a predictor of sales, nor a reliable measure of loyalty – and yet over 70% of Fortune 1000 companies use it for precisely those purposes! The real success story of NPS is its adoption, not its function.

Don't be fooled by agenda-based "research" from vested interests, vague correlations, and misappropriated technical concepts. The evidence is in, we must move on from NPS.

Break the Survey Fever

The use of surveys is entirely valid, but their extraordinary misuse and over-use has been nothing short of toxic to the proper customer mission.

In Chapter 5, when we talked about the need to discern customer intent and to obtain behavioral insight, I presented a range of established validity issues with the nature of self-reported data. And yet, the populist movement continues to over-index on survey software, and many of its practitioners regard the administration of feedback and insight as *the* definitive function of their vocation, a stark contradiction between the evidence and the industry. It is worth exploring this subject a little further than in the earlier chapters.

Initially an educational research tool, survey software began targeting corporates in the mid-2000s. However, conversion was relatively slow, challenged primarily by the omnipotence of Microsoft Excel.[15] Constrained corporate budgets naturally prioritized mission-critical technologies that the humble survey could not compete with, and in response the category's strategy has been something of a shell game.

In a masterful positioning, it first reduced and then proliferated the idea of a "voice of customer" (VOC)[16] – an inherently marketing concept – accessible only through customer surveys. It then disseminated the outlandish notion that, unlike any other field of business, feedback is foundational to practice. Its messaging played on loss aversion and derision, with organizations that sought their customers' opinion at every turn lauded as "CX leaders" while those that did not were deplorable "laggards". The wide adoption of the now debunked NPS system in Fortune 500 companies helped entrench the narrative.

Of course, the headline proposition has been that we must obtain "insight" to truly understand customers, a reductive half-truth that, on the evidence, doesn't support the use of surveys as prescribed. Moreover as discussed in Chapter 5, self-reported data is fraught with issues that are well known outside the movement, if not within it. Most obviously, it generates what are called "response biases", which according to Paulhus[17] involve

> a systematic tendency to respond to a range of questionnaire items
> on some basis other than the specific item content (i.e., what the
> items were designed to measure).

For instance, Fiske and Taylor[18] write that people are prone to "self-enhancement" and seek to "maintain positivity about the self", inherently at the cost of reality. In fact, it is routine for responses to misrepresent how respondents actually think or behave ("socially desirable responding".[19] Other known issues include "acquiescent responding", where respondents "agree" without considering the question's intent, and "extreme responding", where they give extreme ratings on scales.[20]

Even more systemically, self-reporting practices assume that people "have access to the psychological property that the researcher wishes to measure" and "are willing to report that property".[21] However, as established in Chapter 5, we really do not possess the level of self-awareness as to why we do the things we do that self-reporting measures take for granted.[22] In summary,

> self-reports are a fallible source of data, and minor changes in
> question wording, question format, or question context can result
> in major changes in the obtained results.[23]

There is a lot more to this subject, including theory on remedies to improve the performance of the vehicle. I covered some in Chapter 5, but such remedies can be complex, have limited applications, and require the expertise of accomplished social scientists not typically found in a CX department. Suffice it to say, while the pursuit of rapidly actionable customer intelligence is legitimate, surveys as the primary method of its attainment are not.

To combat these inconvenient facts, an increasing tactic of the category has been to dazzle the movement with statistical analysis, distracting it from the underlying data quality issues. But as the industry followed this perceived increase in managerial rigor and reporting, it failed to recognize that:

1. Much if the data generated was of poor quality, if not false.
2. Most of the statistical analysis use cases yield little or no new knowledge.
3. There are limited actionable applications that affect customer engagement.
4. This was actively increasing customer friction.

Finally, to maintain the illusion, the category has sought to re-brand itself. Today, very few people in the industry will tell you that they send and analyse surveys. Instead, their business card will invariably read, "experience management professional". Of course, this is another clever invention of product marketing, not a field of professional practice as its thin veneer would have us believe. To start with, human experience, and memory, is neurologically impossible to manage (see Chapter 5). Put another way, "experience management" is a scientific contradiction in terms. Imagine, then, the brashness of its next invention, the "XM Scientist", to reinforce the original fable.

In the end, this rebranding, coupled with misapprehensions related to "VOC", "insight", and self-reporting, has taken advantage of an industry bereft of more scientific bearings, with the results reflecting Solow's Paradox – more investment, lower productivity.

Apply Caution to Statistical Models

Statistical models are used everywhere and with good reason. Case in point, the journey analytics capability described in Chapter 5 relies on Markov chain analysis[24] and Bayesian logic[25] – but they have also been used to mischievously justify the over-use of surveys.

For instance, correlation analysis aims to establish whether a pair of variables are related, without proving causation. It presents a statistical relationship between an independent variable and a dependent variable by detecting patterns within datasets. For example, the manager of a contact center may explore the relationship between average hold time (the independent variable) and the CSAT score (the dependent variable) to ascertain whether the time a customer spends on hold is related to their score.

Invariably, such analysis finds a correlation, notwithstanding that a customer's sentiment may be impacted by other factors at the time of measurement. Additional variables derail many correlation tests, however, and in real life there can be many such "confounding variables".

But let's say the correlation is correct. What exactly has that manager learned?

In common law, the *stare decisis* doctrine obligates courts to follow historical cases when making a ruling on a similar case, thus preserving precedent. Similarly, a "scientific fact", a true datum, is established and verified via repeated and careful observation of the pattern or measurement, and thereafter becomes a reference for future practice. It is *argumentum a fortiori* (meaning "argument from the stronger reason"), which draws on the confidence of established position to affirm a second, implicit proposition.

In other words, that contact manager should have already known that hold times are a source of friction (an existing position)! They should know that contact centers are part of the service layer where friction is definitely negative (another existing position), and thus, it has an adverse impact on the mission of customer management (the second and obvious proposition). We see all kinds of correlation analysis in use today, and it is my suspicion that it exists in this volume because companies have been sold on the practice by those who profit from the extraneous use of surveys.

Regression analysis is also popular. The rationale is that it helps a business focus on improving what matters most to customers. Building on correlation analysis by using coefficients and p-values, it is a statistical measure of "the proportion of the variance in a dependent variable, that is explained by the independent variable(s)".[26]

One example given in a recent publication recounted how a hotel wanted to understand the drivers of customer satisfaction related to their guest check-in process. They asked customers for typical 1 to 5 satisfaction scores for:

- Check-in speed.
- Bellhop support.
- Ease of finding check-in desk.
- Employee friendliness.

The results suggested the hotel should focus on one area – training for frontline staff – over other aspects that appeared to be less important to customers. But again, it misses the key point, which is that all the above elements are components of the service layer, are incorporated in terms of customer psychology, and that each is essential to the service journey. In other words, effective customering requires that they be treated as integrated, rather than isolated. Of course statistical analysis is a legitimate field, but in this vocation it is often used as creative demand generation for survey software.

The Feedback Fallacy

In my career, I have observed meetings in which customer teams based their entire agenda on "feedback" (survey data). This is not uncommon. Around the world, the movement views this as the foundation of almost everything that occurs thereafter. You may you have come across diagrams like Figure 9.1:

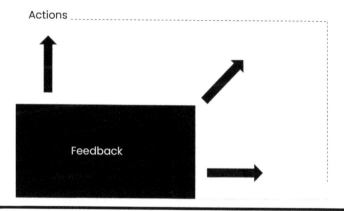

Figure 9.1 The Feedback Fallacy (Image Source: Unnamed Consulting Company)

This was presented to clients by an advisory firm that claims to base its CX services on marketing science. In its presentation, it made the fundamental mistake of conflating marketing and customering, and then erroneously applied the concept of research in a way more appropriate to the diagnostics pillar of marketing. Equally, I might add, little of what was presented in that session had any basis in marketing science either – but that's another story.

What is important to understand is that while feedback is useful in some respects, it is not *foundational* to customer management.

Rather, the foundation of any field of practice is relevant expertise. I labored this point when discussing the arrival of the scientific era and the formation of professions. If a person or team does not know how to do the job in the first place, there is little point in querying customers. One company I've worked with advocates asking customers how they want website pages to be designed, in total ignorance of the navigation design standards that have existed for many years. It's a bit like asking users how many metal prongs should be on a power adapter, ignoring electrical manufacturing standards. There are so many examples of this kind of absurd survey use as "feedback".

Of course, market research is valid for marketing in the same way that UX research, ethnographic and otherwise, is very important to product design. But research does not tell a marketer how to be a marketer, or a designer what the navigation standards are, or a development team how to design, or how to code.

And that's the difference.

Delight Is not Sustainable

Many in the customer management vocation labor under the idea that we must constantly "delight the customer". They are crushed under the weight of expectation and, ultimately, disappointment, and needlessly so. Delight is neither sustainable in the human condition, nor by the company.

If you've ever been to a local fair and tried to lob a ball down the throat of a swiveling clown, you may have noticed his mouth wide open as he stares off with that far-away unseeing look. His demeanor is all happiness and joy, as much as an inanimate object can exude it, his outrageously jubilant features only slightly tainted by the odd chip in his paintwork. The battle scars of a long existence being hauled around fairs all over the countryside, only for strangers to throw things at his face, are slowly catching up with him. But he smiles on.

Of course, if you ever met a real person walking around with a similarly vacant yet enchanted look fixed to their face, mouth wide open in some kind of bizarre ecstasy that no one else understands, you would – quite naturally – cross the road at the earliest opportunity. The premise that we can sustain our customers in the neurological state of delight, like these fairground clowns, is a silly one. Human beings live in highs, lows, mountains, valleys, and somewhere on the plains the rest of the time, and our interactions with companies really don't occupy any real significance in our busy lives. We just want to get done what we want to get done.

It is also important to remember that in any business we are constrained. We do not live in a land of limitless budgets and resources, and we are also inhibited by law, by time, by the labor market, by the mindset of people, by industry regulation, by macroeconomics, by market dynamics – on and on it goes. Thus, it is just not possible to deliver expensive experiential activations all the time. What you can do is provide foundational outcomes through a bias to service, and then, occasionally, find a way to create a target moment of delight, which might make an impression precisely because it is an *exception*, not the norm.

One of my favorite examples of an experiential activation is from Coca-Cola, called "Invisible People".[27] The initiative honored the workers who built Singapore's city infrastructure, many of whom were away from their families for long periods of time. Coca-Cola partnered with the Singapore Kindness Movement, which coordinated thousands of school children to write "thank you" messages to these unsung heroes and took a Polaroid snap of them with their notes. These were tied to cans of Coke and delivered to the workers using drones (how cool!), totally surprising and delighting them. And warming the hearts of all Singaporeans as well.

Now, that's delight! But … That's a marketing activation, not a customer management one. Nevertheless, the point here is that Coca-Cola couldn't do this every day, and even if they could, once it is expected then it is no longer novel and, therefore, no longer delightful. The prerequisite for delight is always surprise.

Short version: delight is not sustainable in your customers' psychology (unless they're a wooden clown), nor for your budget, and can't be foundational to your customer program.

Reject Agenda-based Research

Another favorite pastime of the movement is agenda-based research. Time and again, the industry generates "research" claims that should trigger immediate suspicion. As we discussed already, populism is not weighed down by critical thought, and it does not often discern when an agenda is at play.

In July 2023, Barclays Corporate Banking released a report titled *What's in Store in Retail*,[28] which claimed that 70% of consumers believe sustainability is a determinant in where they choose to shop. Make no mistake, I am deeply concerned about global warming and our collective response, or lack thereof, but I was immediately skeptical.

As a survey of 600 senior retailers and 2,000 British consumers, it was a weighty sample – but, as is often the case, the questions seem to be designed for a target result. In this case, consumers were asked to say which of six environmental, social, and governance (ESG) factors presented to them were material to their decisions about where they choose to shop. In court, that's called "leading the witness". It's a bit like asking toddlers if they want a peach, apple, or banana and then, despite never offering them alternatives such as potato chips, reporting that 70% of toddlers prefer to eat a banana for their afternoon snack, or that 100% of toddlers want fruit. That's precisely what this type of supposed research does.

In Chapter 2, where we discussed the diagnostics pillar of marketing, you may recall that a key principle of market research is to first use qualitative data to identify the variables and only then move to quantitative surveys to measure the outcomes. Agenda-based research typically skips qual – which it replaces with its own biased value system – and goes straight to quant.

In Barclays case, that was sustainability. The findings are compromised from the get-go, all in support of a pre-defined, company-desired proposition. Marketing professor Mark Ritson wrote about Barclays report in his column for *Marketing Week*:[29]

> The results portray UK shoppers as remarkably attuned to all the various ESG issues. Two-thirds of the population are driven to shop at locations because of all these factors. Several of them – treatment of staff, treatment of suppliers – represent a driving factor for three-quarters of British shoppers. Wow!
>
> The results do seem a little at odds with the reality of high street shopping. If the fair treatment of staff is such a driver for purchase how come Amazon "we time your piss breaks" UK Ltd is one of the most popular retailers in the country? If supplier treatment is also top of the list, how come Tesco – "we squeeze suppliers to keep prices down" – is so huge? And if support for

local communities is so incredibly strong why does US private equity-owned Morrisons do so well? Based on this data, shouldn't most British shoppers be avoiding all these top 10 retailers and shopping at the Co-op and Oxfam instead?

In fact, Ritson provided a contrast using research from Kantar[30] of over 100,000 people, based on actual purchases and analysis of respondent verbatim comments instead of pre-supplied notional themes. This found that environmental issues were only mentioned by 4%, ethical issues by 6%, and sourcing by 1%. Barclays other sustainability factors didn't rate. Consider, as well, that for both marketing and customering – but especially for customering, which is dominated by the specific and nuanced wants and needs of individual people – the other major problem is that we really can't use surveys to unearth behavioral intent, as I have explained earlier in the book. Again, that Margaret Mead quote:

> What people think they do, what they say they do, and what they actually do, are entirely different things.

Another recent example comes from a software company, which released a study in 2023 into the state of trust among consumers. Sounds great, except for the fact that it was based on asking people to self-report. I have dealt with the (un)reliability of self-reporting extensively in this book, and this continues in the measurement of trust. In fact, the literature here is vast, from the earliest investigations in 2000[31] through to Sofianos[32] at the close of 2021, who cited 86 related studies. There are simply so many issues – from divergent personality traits to question language to contextual settings etc. – that there can be no endorsement of the practice. As Sofianos summarizes,

> biases and interpretation limitations make self-reported trust measures unreliable.

Of course, the software vendors' agenda was plain. The study served as a contrived and uber-simplistic premise that companies should "listen" to customers to ensure trust – undisguised sales code for "send more surveys".

As you can see, agenda-based research is so called because it is exactly that, and it's rife in the movement. Many such works of fiction ask us to believe that consumers are aware of industry topics and, not only that, that they have opinions about them! We are asked to accept that as people go about their busy lives they think about brands, channels, chatbots, loyalty programs, the cloud, experiences, and of course, their own patterns of consumption behavior and decision making. Not only are we asked to accept that nonsense, but we are asked to pretend that this is a definitive source of credible data, on equal or superior footing to empirical research and behavioral observation.

To close, I offer a sample of actual claims that are either totally and utterly incorrect, exhibit a complete lack of understanding of the topic they have supposedly researched, are just way too generic to be even remotely credible (or all the above). Others are so ridiculous as to be humorous. The companies involved shall remain unidentified for their own benefit but see if you can spot the likely methodology problem, and/or the obvious agenda.

- 96% (of respondents) say that customer experience is a key differentiator.
- 77% of consumers say inefficient customer experiences detract from their quality of life.
- 70% of consumers are more likely to recommend a brand with a good loyalty program.
- 77% of consumers say they are likely to stay with a brand that has a loyalty program.
- Two-thirds of companies compete on customer experience.
- 75% of customer experience management executives gave customer experience a top score for being incredibly important to business.
- 77% of consumers view brands more favorably if they seek out and apply customer feedback.
- 80% of customers say they are more likely to do business with a company if it offers personalized experiences.
- 75% perceive that modern engagement capabilities will enhance their experience.
- 76% will use a company that can minimize menu selections and get them to the right individual quickly.
- 68% felt modern engagement capabilities expanded their options for interacting with brands, helping make engagements contextual.

Forget about "EX"

One of the many popular refrains of the movement is "employee experience", or EX. Of course, the notion that a happy, positive, and safe culture in customer-intensive departments such as a contact center will almost certainly yield positive customer outcomes is not in dispute. Equally, there is no doubt that if a firm has a high number of customer complaints that correlate to poor employee satisfaction scores in the relevant departments, this may suggest a root cause issue. Or it may not. Either way, it's a valid point of inspection and naturally, where there are indicators that customer outcomes are compromised by employee-related issues, there is work to do.

Nevertheless, that does not suddenly make the entire company culture the responsibility of those who are supposed to be concerned with the management of customers, and who likely do not inhabit the executive and board levels where such issues are decided. While it is certainly true that the environment employees operate in affects customer service, it does not do so in isolation:

- Does the environment in which employees operate affect financial management?
- Does it affect procurement teams?
- Does it affect marketing operations?

The answer to all of the above, and every other field of business, is yes. Employees are, after all, human beings. They are the products of their environment, affected by anthropological and sociological forces that impact their sentiment toward the workplace together with the performance of technical skills, the inter-relationships that they have within the organization, its systems, and people.

Causal Layered Analysis (CLA)[33] is a method used in the practice of foresight (futurology), at the intersection of social science and the strategy discipline. I was privileged to study it under its inventor, world-renowned futurist Professor Sohail Inayatullah. In simple terms, it seeks to understand why things are, by identifying the three levels that impact how we perceive reality and make decisions.

- **The litany:** things as they are.
- **The system:** the way of organizing that creates the litany.
- **Worldviews:** the view / perceptions of those that create the system.
- **Metaphors and myths:** the underlying personal factors (e.g., psychology) and sense of identity that inform our individual worldviews.

As you can see, while we think of corporate organizations as inhuman inanimate objects designed to create value, they are in fact very reflective of the human beings within them, especially in the more senior ranks, but also in the collective population that ultimately encodes its cultures (there is never just one).

Indeed, culture is a direct result of the operating model and the environmental tone. The very best corporate leaders understand this. It has almost nothing to do with company slogans, virtue-signaling, or foosball machines in the cafeteria. For example, companies in certain categories often exhibit a hardcore sales orientation that runs the risk of fostering a spreadsheet-wielding, over-forecasted, micro-management style entirely contradictory to the work–life balance and mental health posters that adorn the company's hallways.

The operating construct, comprising the behaviors of leaders and the most repeated and practiced processes – not the posters – signal what the company really values, and, in turn, how staff believe they must behave, be perceived to behave, and how they feel about that. But this is true no matter the field of business. So, then, why is it that CXers, almost to the exclusion of other parts of businesses that are equally affected, take their eye off their most important ball, to claim internal employee experience within their remit?

Well, this is another symptom of the well-established impact of populism and overbearing software companies upon the movement. This is why, at almost every CX conference you can attend, two central ideas are sown:

a) EX is critical to CX.
b) CX practitioners should lead the way.

Soon enough consultants joined the chorus (for obvious commercial reasons), and the mantra took hold. But while customer management has a valid interest in affected employees as related to its core mission, it would be better to focus on its own backyard before assuming a corporate mantle it will never legitimately bear. This is yet another noisy misdirection, in place of a laser focus, where it counts.

Notes

1. Edward Russell, *The Fundamentals of Marketing* (Bloomsbury Publishing, 2010).
2. Chris Pemberton, "Key Findings from the Customer Experience Survey," *Gartner*, March 16, 2018. https://www.gartner.com/en/marketing/insights/articles/key-findings-from-the-gartner-customer-experience-survey.
3. Rosser Reeves, *Reality in Advertising* (Macgibbon & Kee, 1961).
4. Statista, *Forecast of Nike's Global Market Share in Athletic Footwear 2011–2025*, Statista, 2024. https://www.statista.com/statistics/216821/forecast-for-nikes-global-market-share-in-athletic-footwear-until-2017/.
5. Frederick F. Reichheld, "The One Number You Need to Grow," *Harvard Business Review* 81, no. 12 (2004): 46–54.
6. Jennifer Kaplan, "The Inventor of Customer Satisfaction Surveys is Sick of Them, Too," *Bloomberg.com*, May 4, 2016. https://www.bloomberg.com/news/articles/2016-05-04/tasty-taco-helpful-hygienist-are-all-those-surveys-of-any-use.
7. Neil A. Morgan and Lope Leotte Rego, "The Value of Different Customer Satisfaction and Loyalty Metrics in Predicting Business Performance," *Marketing Science* 25, No. 5 (2006): 426–439.
8. Timothy L. Keiningham, Bruce Cooil, Tor Wallen Andreassen, and Lerzan Aksoy, "A Longitudinal Examination of Net Promoter and Firm Revenue Growth," *Journal of Marketing* 71, no. 3 (2007): 39–51.
9. Brian Tayan, "The Wells Fargo Cross-Selling Scandal," *The Harvard Law School Forum on Corporate Governance*, February 6, 2019. https://corpgov.law.harvard.edu/2019/02/06/the-wells-fargo-cross-selling-scandal-2/.

10. Royal Commission into Misconduct in the Banking, Superannuation and Financial Services Industry, *Final Report*, (February 4, 2019. https://www.royal-commission.gov.au/banking/final-report.

11. Often attributed to Peter Drucker but in fact of uncertain origin.

12. Khadeeja Safdar and Into Pacheco, "The Dubious Management Fad Sweeping Corporate America," *Wall Street Journal*, May 15, 2019. https://www.wsj.com/articles/the-dubious-management-fad-sweeping-corporate-america-11557932084; Steve Denning, "The Basics of Leadership Storytelling," *Forbes*, November 9, 2011. https://www.forbes.com/sites/stevedenning/2011/11/09/the-basics-of-leadership-storytelling/?sh=89265434a7d5; Sunil Gupta and Valarie Zeithaml, "Customer Metrics and Their Impact on Financial Performance," *Marketing Science* 25, no. 6 (2006): 718–739.

13. John G. Dawes, "Net Promoter and Revenue Growth: An Examination across Three Industries," *Australasian Marketing Journal* 32, no. 1 (2022): 144135822211320.

14. Sven Baehre, Michele O'Dwyer, Lisa O'Malley, and Nick Lee, "The Use of Net Promoter Score (NPS) to Predict Sales Growth: Insights from an Empirical Investigation," *Journal of the Academy of Marketing Science* 50, no. 1 (2021): 67–84.

15. Pierre-Nicolas Schwab, "Excel Dominates the Business World... And That's Not About to Change," *Market Research Consulting*, April 16, 2021. https://www.intotheminds.com/blog/en/excel-dominates-the-business-world-and-thats-not-about-to-change/.

16. Abbie Griffin and John R. Hauser, "The Voice of the Customer," *Marketing Science* 12, no. 1 (1993): 1–27.

17. Delroy L. Paulhus, "Measurement and Control of Response Bias," in *Measures of Personality and Social Psychological Attitudes, Vol 1: Measures of Social Psychological Attitudes*, ed. John P. Robinson, Phillip R. Shaver, and Lawrence S. Wrightsman (Elsevier eBooks, 1991), 17–59.

18. Susan T. Fiske and Shelley E. Taylor, *Social Cognition* (2nd edn., McGraw-Hill, 1991).

19. Ibid.

20. Delroy L. Paulhus and Simine Vazire, "The Self-Report Method," in *Handbook of Research Methods in Personality Psychology*, ed. Richard W. Robins, R. Chris Fraley, and Robert F. Krueger (The Guilford Press, 2007), 224–239.

21. Charles M. Judd and Gary H. McClelland, "Measurement," in *The Handbook of Social Psychology*, ed. Daniel T. Gilbert, Susan T. Fiske, and Gardner Lindzey (4th edn., McGraw-Hill, 1998),180–232.

22. Jerome Kagan, "The Meanings of Personality Predicates," *American Psychologist* 43, no. 8 (1988): 614–620.

23. Norbert Schwarz, "Self-Reports: How the Questions Shape the Answers," *American Psychologist* 54, no. 2 (1999): 93–105.

24. Meelan Chamling, Biswajit Bera, and Sudipa Sarkar, "Geospatial Environmental Modeling of Forest Declining Trend in Eastern Himalayan Biodiversity Hotspot Region," in *Forest Resources Resilience and Conflicts*, ed. Pravat Kumar Shit et al. (Elsevier, 2021), 417–433.

25. K. A. Andersen and J. N. Hooker, "Bayesian Logic," *Decision Support Systems* 11, no.2 (1994): 191–210.

26. Sebastian Taylor, "R-Squared," *Corporate Finance Institute*, November 22, 2023, https://corporatefinanceinstitute.com/resources/data-science/r-squared/.

27. Joss Davidge, "Coca-Cola's Happiness from the Skies" [blog post], *The Marketing Society*, no date. https://www.marketingsociety.com/the-library/coca-cola%E2 %80%99s-happiness-skies.

28. Barclays, *What's in Store for Retail? Exploring the Drivers of Change across the UK Retail Sector* (Barclays Corporate, 2022. https://www.barclayscorporate.com/ content/dam/barclayscorporate-com/documents/insights/Industry-expertise-22/ whats-in-store-for-retail.pdf.

29. Mark Ritson, "Badly Designed Surveys Don't Promote Sustainability, They Harm It," *Marketing Week*, November 1, 2023. https://www.marketingweek .com/ritson-badly-designed-surveys/.

30. Kantar, *Global Issues Barometer*, no date. https://www.kantar.com/campaigns/ global-issues-barometer.

31. Edward L. Glaeser, David I. Laibson, José A. Scheinkman, and Christine L. Soutter, "Measuring Trust," *The Quarterly Journal of Economics* 115, no. 3 (2000): 811–846.

32. Andis Sofianos, "Self-Reported and Revealed Trust: Experimental Evidence," *Journal of Economic Psychology* 88 (2022): 102451.

33. Sohail Inayatullah, "Causal Layered Analysis," *Futures* 30, no. 8 (1998): 815–829.

Epilogue

Closing the Loop

It is time for a collective maturation of this vocation, so that it may one day take its place as a genuine profession complete with codified management process, disciplinary language, a legitimate educational infrastructure, and a well-regulated barrier to entry.

As the next wave of technological advances falls upon us, established professions have an opportunity to advance their mission and their models and scan the horizon. They can ride the wave of opportunities that comes from another area of my work, that of *platformed innovation*. That's for another time, but the message is clear: to truly grasp the opportunities of our time, and those of our tomorrows, we must first establish a codified management baseline.

And so, there is much work to do.

The context at which we have arrived – an era of populism in place of legitimate customer management – is in many ways understandable. While industrial execution has been sadly wanting, there is no argument that directionally, at least, the goal of increasing the focus of companies on their customers has been correct.

The struggle to calibrate proper customer management to the digital era, is perhaps akin to a toddler learning to walk. Stumbles are inevitable. But that analogy does not fully hold when you consider that the foundations of customer service long predate the digital era. So, why the decay of core customer service values in recent years?

The scientific revolution – which marked the emergence of "modern science", when developments in mathematics, physics, astronomy, biology, and chemistry transformed the views of society about nature – is widely held to have commenced with the Copernican Revolution from 1543 and to have culminated in the "grand synthesis" of Isaac Newton's 1687 *Principia*.[1] In macro-historical terms, we are not long into that revolution. Our long engrained human traits of storytelling, campfire fables, passing tales among ourselves, and of superstitions

DOI: 10.4324/9781003513728-11

still underpin a penchant for lazy intuition over evidence where guardrails – like those found in the bona fide professions – are absent.

As the digital waves of opportunity washed over the world from the turn of the current century, the functioning of customer service turned again to these stories, and, frankly, to myths.

Certainly, the rise of digital was the wind beneath the wings of populist CX as the arena moved along at unprecedented pace. Of course, it was not alone. Close cousin, the marketing vocation, even with decades of established academic rigor, has also been tossed around by populism like a dinghy in a storm. But those wounds are self-inflicted, because despite all its managerial and academic infrastructure, marketing has continued to resist erecting a barrier to entry into its ranks. And so, it is a vocation of extremes. On one hand, it boasts a formally qualified cohort and academic leadership, and its first scientific "laws" were established in the 1990s, advancing what should be an established profession. On the other hand, there is a cult of personalities and masses of patently untrained, yet opinionated, practitioners. It is, indeed, a wide gamut.

But the CX movement does not enjoy such a distribution. There is no gamut, no real curve. Far too much of its majority live on a diet of blatant folklore that only thrives due to the cult-like deportment of its most vocal. They fall prey to that well-intentioned but largely ignorant penchant for intuition and stories, a kind of woke-ism, or flat-earther group think.

Of course, it was never willful. A vacuum will always be filled, and the absence of an industrial management model was a cavernous and unfortunate one. In its place, the digital era saw a tidal wave of newly funded software start-ups chasing the financial market's latest bubble, and in no time at all, the ether was filled with buzzwords and sales slogans, echo chambers, and communities – the modern campfire.

Software use cases masquerading as management theory and "best practice", many without an iota of evidence, invaded with such force that an entire industry was conquered. Excited junior and middle managers seeking to take on the shiny new era of "CX" were quickly indoctrinated. As companies doubled down, they elevated responsibility for the oversight of customers to the executive table, in seats that were too often occupied by generalists, and soon they too were consumed by the same vortex. Then the next wave of young, enthusiastic people in the early stages of their careers began to learn their trade from those described above. The layers built. With no governing model, we lost sight of the mission and, in less than a decade, had entrenched practices devoid of proper value.

Yet the cause of the effect is also instructive. The issues produced by the absence of an industrialized management model can be solved by the presence of one.

The four pillars model of customering sets out a management framework to restore the core tenets of customer service in a contemporary setting. It seeks to weed out the various misdirections by contrasting them with disciplines occupying linear constructions of value that can be validated through evidence, and tested for effect. I grant you, this probably isn't as sexy as the hype surrounding the populist movement, but I promise you, it's far more effective – and offers a vastly more meaningful career.

Yet, even with the adoption of such a model, customer management will not become a genuine profession until it enshrines all four key elements of established professions: industrial practice, disciplinary language, aligned education, and a barrier to entry (Figure 10.1).

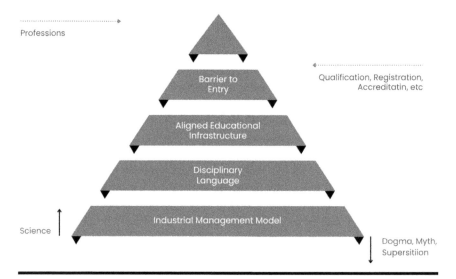

Figure 10.1 The Hallmarks of Professions (Spinley, 2024)

This model offers a basis for the first two layers and, perhaps, a foundation of the next two. The need for an academic infrastructure imparting consistent and sober management theory around the world simply cannot be overstated – and is the driving force behind the Field Bell Institute. Then, and only then, will the industry have an opportunity to enshrine a barrier to entry, ensuring that only those qualified to lead customer operations do so. Friends, we are a long way from closing that loop, but I submit, we must do so.

Over to you …

END

Note

1. The Editors of Encyclopaedia Britannica, "Principia," *Encyclopaedia Brittanica Online*, last updated March 15, 2024. https://www.britannica.com/topic/Principia.

About the Author

Aarron Spinley is a Fellow at the Field Bell Institute (www.fieldbell.org), recognized as a foremost mind the realm of customer science and noted for his signature approach: measuring the intersection of established management method, complex economics, and scientific precedent to confirm and systemize, or disrupt, for effect.

As a writer or commentator, Aarron has featured in leading publications including Forbes, ZDNet, MyCustomer, CMO, Mumbrella, and Mi3 Media, and has appeared on five continents as a sought-after keynote speaker. He is an alumnus of global brand-name consulting and technology firms, and a member of the world's largest company directorship organization, the Australian Institute of Company Directors. Aarron works with brands, executives, and event partners around the world. More information: www.spinley.co

Index

Page numbers in bold indicate tables, while page numbers in italics indicate figures